Parenting
Is Persuasive Influence

Beth Brown

Kelsey ~
May God bless you
richly!
Beth Brown

Publishing Designs, Inc.
Huntsville, Alabama

Publishing Designs, Inc.
P.O. Box 3241
Huntsville, Alabama 35810

All scripture quotations, unless otherwise indicated, are taken from the New American Standard Bible. "Scripture quotations taken from the New American Standard Bible®, Copyright © 1960, 1962, 1963, 1968, 1971, 1972, 1973, 1975, 1977, 1995 by The Lockman Foundation. Used by permission." (www.Lockman.org)

Printed in the United States

Library of Congress Cataloging-in-Publication Data

Brown, Beth, 1957-
  Parenting is rocket science / Beth Brown.
      p. cm.
  Includes bibliographical references and index.
  ISBN 0-929540-09-3 (alk. paper)
  1. Parenting—Religious aspects—Christianity. 2. Child rearing—Religious aspects—Christianity. I. Title.
  BV4529.B696 2006
  248.8'45—dc22
                          2006000734

Dedication

This book is lovingly dedicated to some of the most special people in my world. To my precious parents, Sherman and Vivienne Garner, thank you for giving me the best you had to give. Thank you for modeling consistent devotion to God and teaching me the joy of service in the Kingdom. Thank you for giving me a strong appreciation for the generations of faithful Christians that have strengthened our family. When God picked out my parents, I'm glad He chose you!

To my wonderful in-laws, Herman and Lois Brown. Thank you for all you have taught me through the years. Thank you most of all for the phenomenal job you did wiring my wonderful husband, Eldon. You did a marvelous job preparing him to be the godly husband and father that our home needed.

To my dear husband, Eldon. Thank you for being so committed to being the husband I needed and the daddy that our girls needed. Being a wife and a mother has been a joy and a privilege because of your love and leadership.

To our precious daughters, Amy and Barbara. Wiring your rockets has been the best adventure a parent could ask for. When we look back at the parenting years, we can smile at the love, joy, and laughter you brought to our home. Daddy and I are incredibly proud of the godly ladies you have become. We look forward to watching you become wives and mothers some day. Take the best from what we have given you and use it in your new homes. Be wise enough to recognize our mistakes and choose better patterns for your own homes. May God bless you richly as you fly with the Kingdom Fleet and as you prepare to wire your own rockets. You will be wonderful wives and mothers.

To Bill and Fredde Path and family, thanks for letting me be part of your lives during a very special year. Thank you for all you taught me and for letting me be part of your family. Your godly influence will always be a part of my life.

To Pam O'Neal, thanks for your love and friendship. Thank you for the wisdom you have shared with me through the years. You are always a blessing to me.

Special thanks to Lynn McDaniel Giddens, Ray Boynton, Lamar Pennick, and Steve Raab for being willing to read portions of this book and for making very valuable suggestions.

To all the young parents who have allowed me to have their children in my Bible classes. I've learned a lot about parenting from watching you. I have great hope for the next generation because of some of the wonderful things I see happening in your homes.

To all the elders and their wives who have modeled for us the best way to do "family." Thank you for your example, your love, and your leadership. You have been a blessing to our family and we are grateful.

To all of the parents who have allowed us to keep their children through the years, and to all the little ones who have been in our home. Thank you for the love, the laughter, the sweet conversations, and the adventures along the way. You have enriched our lives and we will always love you for it.

Beth Brown
January 2006

Contents

Introduction

New Baby Syndrome

Kevin stood quietly by the window enjoying the sunrise. In his arms he held the most precious creature he had ever seen. Little Katie was only one month old, and already she had her daddy wrapped securely around her little finger. Andrea, Katie's mom, was enjoying a chance to sleep a little longer before time to nurse this little girl with the amazing appetite.

Their first month with this sweet baby had been a roller coaster of emotions. Kevin and Andrea loved children and knew they wanted to have at least two of their own. They felt prepared for parenthood until the moment in the delivery room when the nurse laid that red, wrinkled, adorable angel in Kevin's arms so she could help the doctor finish caring for Andrea. Kevin was holding a tiny baby for the first time. The ones he had handled before were bigger and a lot more durable. He was glad a nurse was close by.

The first week at home was fine. Andrea's mom and dad had flown in from Texas to help out until Andrea felt able to take over. With two very experienced parents and two rookies willing and eager to learn, caring for one small baby wasn't too difficult. The 4-to-1 ratio gave Kevin and Andrea a real edge. Andrea's mom seemed to sense what Katie needed and handled her very comfortably. Andrea's dad loved babies, and he thoroughly enjoyed holding the newest addition to their family. Katie was never more content than when she was snuggled up with her grandpa. Andrea had often gone to sleep that first week to the comforting sounds of her daddy quietly singing a restless Katie back to sleep as he walked the living room floor.

As soon as Kevin and Andrea bade farewell to Andrea's parents, a sense of panic came over them. What if something happened with Katie that they didn't know how to handle? Andrea had always been very stable emotionally, but since Katie's birth, she cried spontaneously and without provocation. Kevin had been patient and understanding, but Andrea's new emotional displays worried him. He wondered how long it would be before his easy-going wife was back on an even keel, emotionally. He had to go back to work next week and he wasn't sure Andrea was physically or emotionally ready to be alone with a baby all day.

Now that Kevin and Andrea were on their own with Katie, life became much more complex. They were determined to excel in parenting, but feelings of insecurity often overwhelmed them. They didn't always know what to do when Katie cried. How could they know what that new bundle of life was trying to communicate? They hadn't learned yet which kind of crying meant she was hungry, which one meant she was in desperate need of a new diaper, and which one meant she was cold or lonely or bored. They were often frustrated because they felt they should be doing a much better job of parenting.

Many young parents have experienced what Kevin and Andrea were feeling. Parenting, for many folks, is something they felt prepared for until the moment they were "thrown into the deep end of the pool" and forced to survive this new career.

One reason for the roller coaster of emotions is that most of us have spent quite a bit of time preparing for our careers. Parenting is a unique career, and like Kevin and Andrea, most of us didn't have a lot of training before being handed that cute little bundle of energy. Even those who have had a lot of experience with children, and those who have read books to prepare for parenting can feel as if they are drowning while adjusting to this new career. Being "on call" twenty-four hours a day, seven days a week can be overwhelming as well as exhausting. Add to that the fact that the precious little one doesn't speak adult language. Babies come equipped with a marvelous assortment of grunts, grimaces, and fascinating facial expressions; but they are not on the same page, linguistically, with their poor, sleep-deprived parents. As a bonus, just so parents don't oversleep, babies are equipped with an earsplitting wail that is sure to make frazzled nerve endings run for cover.

When Kevin and Andrea gave Katie her first bath after Grandma left, they noticed that something was missing. There wasn't a label from the Manufacturer stamped on that child with an 800 number to call or a web site to access when technical difficulties were encountered. They would have been a lot more secure if that kind of technical assistance had been available.

Now you know the reason for the book you are reading: to provide some technical assistance for the job at hand. Don't think for a minute, however, that this book will replace the most important book in your library, the Bible. This book is intended to pull important concepts from God's Word and help you apply those ideas to the job God has given you.

The Analogy	
Launch Pad	A Christian home
Rocket	A precious child, created in the image of God
Chief Engineers	The parents to whom God has entrusted one of His special creations. Their assignment is to spend eighteen to twenty years "wiring" the rocket so it is fit for the Kingdom Fleet.
Assistant Engineers	Those who help wire the rocket: teachers, baby sitters, daycare workers, scout leaders, coaches, friends.
Launch Date	When the child will leave home to become an independent adult.
Mission Specialist	God, the Creator of Heaven and Earth, the Designer of each of the rockets that we must wire.
Kingdom Fleet	The body of Christ; the church the Lord established.
Wiring Diagrams or Schematics	The pattern used to wire the rocket.
Devil's Diagram	Satan's counterfeit wisdom that proposes to sabotage the rocket.
Master's Schematics	Complete written wiring and testing instructions as recorded in the Word of God.
Warnings	Special instructions from the Mission Specialist to help us avoid technical difficulties.

Our world is filled with all kinds of books for "dummies." Parenting isn't a job for dummies. Many of the skills parents need to develop are learned and refined "on the job." The goal of this book is to help parents look at themselves, not as dummies, but as competent, capable rocket scientists who can do the job that has been given to them. Because it is easier to accomplish a task when one has a clear mental image of the assignment, we are going to explore the analogy that *Parenting Is Rocket Science.*

Where Do We Start?

Via the launch pad, parents will return one of two things to the Father: a wise and capable servant of the Lord or a foolish, immature, incompetent nincompoop. Many parents have an unclear view of the job assignment. They either fail to recognize the goal for this mission, or they are so busy trying to survive the day-to-day challenges of parenting that they have lost sight of the goal. Parents who are operating from the Devil's Diagram will succeed in rearing foolish, immature, and worldly children who are unfit for the Kingdom Fleet.

Many parents act more like frogs than engineers. They hop from diagram to diagram in total confusion. The wiring in the rockets entrusted to them is very sloppy and doesn't work well. They ignore warnings and struggle with technical difficulties.

Parents who are really focused on the goal and are operating from the Master's Schematics are training faithful, capable servants who will be ready for their launch date and will be properly prepared for the Kingdom Fleet.

If you find yourself and your family in the wrong area and want to get back to the launch site, don't give up. The Creator we serve is a Mission Specialist when it comes to fresh starts.

Talk to the Creator and ask forgiveness for losing site of the launch date. Ask for help in tearing out the wiring you have messed up and for help in wiring correctly. Pray daily and ask the Creator to lay straight paths in front of you and help fix the loose wiring you have left behind. If your children have already been launched and aren't flying well, ask the Lord to help you show them how to get their wiring redone.

The Bible provides guidance and strength for your task by providing the Master's Schematics for the job at hand.

Master's Schematics

» "Whenever he speaks a lie, he speaks from his own nature; for he is a liar, and the father of lies" (John 8:44).

» "His divine power has granted to us everything pertaining to life and godliness, through the true knowledge of Him who called us by His own glory and excellence" (2 Peter 1:3).

» "Be diligent to present yourself approved to God as a workman who does not need to be ashamed, handling accurately the word of truth" (2 Timothy 2:15).

» "Have nothing to do with worldly fables fit only for old women. On the other hand, discipline yourself for the purpose of godliness" (1 Timothy 4:7).

» "See to it that no one takes you captive through philosophy and empty deception, according to the tradition of men, according to the elementary principles of the world, rather than according to Christ" (Colossians 2:8).

Drill for Skills

Making Connections

_____ Launch Pad	a. child
_____ Rocket	b. those who assist in wiring
_____ Chief Engineers	c. God
_____ Assistant Engineers	d. the Church of Christ
_____ Launch Date	e. worldly wisdom
_____ Mission Specialist	f. Word of God
_____ Kingdom Fleet	g. Christian home
_____ Devil's Diagram	h. parents
_____ Master's Schematics	i. date when child leaves home.

Troubleshooting

1. Why do new parents sometimes feel overwhelmed?

2. How much preparation did you have for the job of parenting?

3. As a new parent, what did you find most difficult?

4. What have you learned "on the job" that you wish you had known ahead of time?

5. What is the most important job that parents have to accomplish?

6. Why should parents have the launch date firmly in mind?

7. How can an engineer train himself to recognize the Devil's Diagram just by listening?

8. How can a busy engineer become more familiar with the Master's Schematics?

Section

1

Rocket
Science
101

1

Parenting with Confidence

One of the most important things a Chief Engineer must learn is how to act with confidence, even when humiliation, fear, or frustration has completely stymied the few confident feelings that were available.

Retrieving "Pulpiteer" Benjamin

Joan and Paul have been married for five years. Joan taught school until Benjamin was born two years ago. Now they have three-week-old Bonnie and she is adorable. Today, Joan is looking forward to going to worship with her family for the first time since Bonnie's arrival. She can't wait to hear all the "ooh's" and "aah's" as people see Bonnie for the first time. Just as they are walking out the door, Paul's pager goes off. He must go to work but hopes to meet the family at church shortly. Paul hurries to help get the little ones into their car seats and makes sure Joan has what she needs.

Joan loves the little congregation where they worship. They have a new building and are making do with folding chairs until they can afford to buy pews. As Joan comes in carrying Bonnie and the diaper bag in one hand, she is holding on to a bouncy Benjamin with the other one. She had hoped to sit near the back in case she had to go out with the baby. As she looks around, she realizes the only seats available are up front. As she's getting settled, she hears a few little giggles coming from the people sitting near her. She looks up from unwrapping Bonnie's blanket to discover that Benjamin is no longer sitting beside her. He is on the stage where the preacher and song leader are getting ready to begin the worship services.

Joan is aware that every eye in the building is trained on her little family and the drama that is unfolding. She is very embarrassed but she has to handle this. She quietly motions for Benjamin to come to her. He shakes his little head and stands his ground. Joan snaps her fingers and says sternly, "Benjamin Allen Smith, you come here!" Benjamin stomps his little foot and says, "Not gonna!"

Thankfully, the cradle roll teacher, Mrs. Hopkins, is seated behind Joan. She puts her hand on Joan's shoulder and whispers, "Let me have the baby."

> **Joan is aware that every eye in the building is trained on her little family and the drama that is unfolding. She is very embarrassed but she has to handle this.**

In front of the entire congregation, Joan goes up to retrieve Benjamin, who decides to make a dash for freedom. He gets almost all the way to the other side of the stage before his mom can grab him. Down the aisle they go with every eye trained on them. Joan wouldn't mind if the earth broke open to swallow both of them.

However, there is more embarrassment to come before it's over. It's too cold to take Benjamin outside to spank him, so Joan has to make do with the ladies' restroom. Joan knows that ceramic tile amplifies sound, and she is sure that every ear in the congregation is tuned in to what is happening in the restroom.

However, with Benjamin under control, Joan picks him up and carries him all the way back down the aisle. As she sits down on the metal folding chair, Benjamin's shoe accidentally hits the chair with a loud "clang," and a song book falls to the floor. Joan slinks down in her chair, physically and emotionally drained. She tries in vain to concentrate on the worship instead of on her humiliation.

Embarrassment over incidents like this one is normal. However, Joan can rest assured that she did the right thing. She acted with confidence and did what was best for her child, regardless of her own feelings. Almost any experienced engineer would sympathize with Joan. Most of us have "been there, done that." One benefit to having children is that they do improve one's humility.

The Source of Confidence

One of the most important services a Chief Engineer can provide for the rockets in his charge is to be a confident parent. Engineers who recognize that the skills they are using were given to them by the Creator will look to Him for guidance and instruction. That "God-confidence" as opposed to "self-confidence" will provide strength and wisdom for each day's wiring projects. When parents are confident, a child is more secure and emotionally stable. Confident parents encounter fewer technical difficulties when they are wiring their rockets.

For a person who was reared in a strong Christian home with a mom and dad who loved each other, who rarely fought, and who were good parents, parenting will be easier than for those who come from single-parent homes or from very dysfunctional families. One goal of this book is to enable parents to be capable, competent role models for their children in order to rear the next generation of the Lord's disciples for life in His service.

Parenting Flashback

Let's consider the home in the last few generations to get a feel for how parenting has changed since our grandparents were children. During the Depression years, there wasn't a lot of nurturing in most families. People worked from "can see to can't see." There wasn't a lot of time for extra nurturing because people were too busy trying to survive. Discipline was strict and harsh, with little time for long arguments and explanations. A child who did not obey quickly had an unpleasant encounter with a razor strop or a hickory switch.

Many of the children who were reared during the Depression became parents who wanted to give their children everything they never had. They wanted their children to feel loved. They felt the discipline they received was too harsh, so they reared their children in a more permissive environment.

During World War II, our nation was in a crisis mode. Many of the women had to work in the factories while the men were defending the country. After the war, when men were once again available for the work force, some women gladly went back home. Others continued to pursue careers. They bought into the idea that a woman can have a good career and that her husband and children can benefit from her improved self-esteem and from the extras her paycheck could provide.

During the early 1950s, there were pretty standard rules about child rearing. Many moms were still at home. If a mother worked, it was often as a secretary, nurse, or teacher. Many a mother stayed home until the children were in school and then arranged for a job that allowed her to be home when the children were home. The money that mom earned enabled the children to have extras that had never been part of the budget. They could take piano lessons and art lessons. They could play on teams that required uniforms and other costly items. Moms felt good about the extras they could provide because, as children reared during the Depression, they knew what it was to do without, and they didn't want their children to want for anything.

In the early 1950s, most families had the same set of rules. A child knew that if he misbehaved at the home of his friend, the parents in that house would handle it as if he were their own child. He also knew before he got home that he would be in trouble as soon as he walked through the door.

Teachers and principals were allowed to paddle disobedient children. Most children knew that if they got into trouble at school, they would get a spanking as soon as they got home.

Standard Rules Replaced

The 1960s and 1970s saw a lot of cultural changes. People were "finding themselves" and "doing their own thing." The *Feminist Movement* encouraged women to be more independent and to find fulfillment in the career world. The new philosophy encouraged selfishness and discouraged good parenting. Educational standards plummeted, and learning by exploring became popular. That philosophy wasn't good for parenting. These cultural changes meant that parents started exploring their way through parenting. They made it up as they went, so the rules for behavior in one house were often different from those in the home next door.

Perhaps the biggest change was that more and more mothers left the home to go to work—some by choice, some of necessity. They discovered, sometimes far too late, that a person cannot give a hundred percent at work and a hundred percent at home. Parenting is a full-time job, but something had to give; the family usually got the leftover time and attention. Parenting done by those who can't give full attention to the job greatly increases the stress level in the family. Trying to have a secure family while treating parenting as a part-time responsibility is the main reason for the rising rate of divorce, teen pregnancy, and drug and alcohol abuse.

Parents learned the hard way that someone had to be devoted to the training of the children. Parenting requires a lot of time and attention to detail. If one of the parents cannot be at home with the children, the only way to do the job successfully is to find a faithful Christian who will serve as a substitute parent and be completely devoted to the training of the children. A daycare center is unacceptable. Parenting cannot be done by proxy. Someone being paid minimum wage to watch ten children is not going to be devoted to training your child properly.

> **Trying to have a secure family while treating parenting as a part-time responsibility is the main reason for the rising rate of divorce, teen pregnancy, and drug and alcohol abuse.**

Necessity or Luxury?

Because many of the folks becoming parents in the 1970s had been raised with lots of extras provided by parents who wanted them to have everything they wanted, the line between necessity and luxury became blurred. For years, if a family with a dozen children had a small house, an outhouse, water nearby, a garden, a few chickens, and a cow or pig, little else was needed. If each person had one outfit for Sunday and two changes of clothing for work or school, he had an adequate wardrobe. Clothes were passed down from child to child until they were worn out. Then the better pieces were used for making quilts and the rest for cleaning rags.

Because the line between necessity and luxury became so blurred, by the mid 1970s the requirements had grown. It was "necessary" to have at least a three-bedroom house if you had more than one child. It was "necessary" to have at least one television and at least two cars. It was "necessary" to have the right kind of clothes to blend in with the current fashion trends.

Here we are in the next century, and many folks consider the following items to be necessities: a TV in nearly every room, at least one computer, a VCR and DVD player, a microwave oven, at least two cars, and a wardrobe that conforms to the current style. It is necessary for each child to have his own bedroom and all the toys and video games he wants. It is necessary for children to take music lessons, art lessons, and dance lessons and to participate in sports activities. It is necessary to have a nice house. It is necessary to eat out often.

Compare the modern list of necessities with what the apostle Paul had to say.

> "But godliness actually is a means of great gain, when accompanied by contentment. For we have brought nothing into the world, so we cannot take anything out of it either. And if we have food and covering, with these we shall be content. But those who want to get rich fall into temptation and a snare and many foolish and harmful desires which plunge men into ruin and destruction. For the love of money is a root of all sorts of evil, and some by longing for it have wandered away from the faith, and pierced themselves with many a pang" (1 Timothy 6:6–10).

The Changing Standards for Parenting

Back in the early '50s, the Bible was read daily in many homes. The rules for parenting followed biblical guidelines, and parents were confident in their ability to rear children. Television programs honored family values. Dad was the head of his home, and Mom was there to support him and keep the household running smoothly. With the other cultural changes of the past few decades, television programming has made Dad look like the family idiot who has to be rescued by his wife and smart-aleck children. All forms of dysfunctional family life provide the humor for modern programs. That shift in what passes for entertainment has helped undermine the family.

With a more hectic lifestyle that has followed on the heels of cultural change, the Bible isn't being read consistently in most homes. Without that biblical standard, parenting philosophies change often. Parenting philosophies are based on what the pediatrician recommends, or on an article in some parenting magazine, or on what was presented on the parenting segment of the morning TV news program. Without a standard for parenting, many parents are less confident. They aren't sure how to handle the day-to-day situations that occur in the life of a family.

> Warning: A child always knows when you aren't sure about   .
> what you are doing.

The Relationship of Security and Confidence

When rules and ideas flip-flop based on the latest thing a parent has read or heard, two things happen: (1) parents are less confident about their ability to parent successfully; (2) children grow up without self-discipline because they have never had consistent discipline in their lives.

As the level of parental confidence decreases, insecurity increases both for the parents and the children. In the 1950s, if John's mom called Billy's mom to report Billy's misbehavior, Billy's mom would be grateful and handle the situation with confidence. She would also be comfortable calling John's mom if the situation were reversed. Because the boys knew their moms would be comparing notes and agreeing on disciplinary procedures, they were more apt to consider the consequences before choosing to misbehave.

When defensive parents attack the accuser instead of responding to the child's misbehavior with confidence, the child learns that his behavior is acceptable to his parents.

Modern parents generally have less confidence. If someone informs a parent about a child's disobedience, the parent is apt to be defensive. The parent may turn on the one reporting the misbehavior because it confirms what the parent already knows: "I don't know how to do this parenting thing very well, and I'm angry with you for making me even more aware that I don't know. I'm angry and embarrassed because now you are aware of my shortcomings, and I will be embarrassed every time I see you and am reminded that you think I am a lousy parent."

When defensive parents attack the accuser instead of responding to the child's misbehavior with confidence, the child learns that his behavior is acceptable to his parents. He knows that the next time he is accused of wrongdoing, his parents will attack the accuser instead of penalizing him. Confronting the accuser instead of the guilty child is one of the main reasons for the erosion of our nation's morality. As engineers, we must do our part to stop this trend; it must be done one family at a time.

Parenting Styles

The cultural changes that have rocked the United States in recent decades have left us with four basic parenting styles: (1) high control/high support, (2) low control/high support, (3) high control/low support, and (4) low control/low support. Let's look at each of these.

High Control/High Support

These parents are the most successful. The rockets entrusted to them can fly correctly because the wiring is secure. These parents are able to control the behavior of their children. They are also very supportive. They encourage their children to try new things and take reasonable risks. When mistakes occur, they move in to support and redirect the child. They are not intimidated or confused by misbehavior. They respond with confidence when their authority is challenged. These parents keep a close eye on the Assistant Engineers to make sure that they are helping to install the wiring properly. These engineers know the Master's Schematics and follow them closely. They are in close, daily contact with the Mission Specialist. The most faithful servants of God come from this type of home.

Low Control/High Support

These are the permissive parents. The wiring in the rockets entrusted to them is often loosely connected and not securely anchored. These parents have a laid-back leadership style. They usually have a very lenient plan of action when their authority is challenged. They love their children and are very supportive. The children from these homes often have behavior patterns that are annoying to those who prefer a more structured environment.

High Control/Low Support

This type of leadership is most commonly seen in parents from military backgrounds. Discipline is rigid and severe, but it isn't balanced with high support. Children wired by engineers with this parenting philosophy often have great difficulty giving and receiving love. They are emotionally insecure but may appear very tough on the outside. This "hit 'em fast and hit 'em hard" style of leadership often produces children who are unable to serve with the Kingdom Fleet. When children see parents as rigid and unloving, it's hard for them to conceive of a heavenly Father who expects to be obeyed and has serious penalties for the disobedient, but who balances those expectations with love and support beyond comprehension.

Low Control/Low Support

Rockets wired by these types of engineers often wind up in jails or mental institutions. Parents of this type often make babies but then do little, if anything, to prepare them for life. These rockets go through life as empty shells that tend to collect life's dirt and grime.

As Chief Engineers in the Father's service, we need to have special places in our lives for these children. As we have opportunity to interact with rockets from these situations, we need to do what we can to install whatever wiring time allows us to install.

Conclusion

With these four models in mind, in the next chapter we will take a look at how we can be more confident and how we can move our families closer to being the ones that produce the most capable, faithful servants of the Lord.

Drill for Skills

 Making Connections

1. Parents must learn to act with _____, even when humiliation and fear are the primary feelings.

2. One benefit to having children is that they do improve one's ____
   _____.

3. As Chief Engineers, we are to wire the next generation of the
   _____ _____.

4. The cycle of _____ _____ _____ instead of the guilty child is one of the main reasons for the erosion of our nation's morality.

5. The most faithful servants of the Lord are wired by engineers who follow the _____ control, _____ support model of leadership.

Troubleshooting

1. Why is it necessary to have "God-confidence" instead of "self-confidence"?

2. What is the goal of parenting?

3. What is one reason for the confidence level of today's parents being lower than that of parents in the first half of the twentieth century?

4. What two things happen when parenting rules flip flop based on the latest thing a parent has read or heard?

5. Discuss the four parenting styles.

6. Discuss some of the embarrassing things that have happened in your parenting career. Are you pleased with the way you handled those situations? What changes would you make if you you could relive those experiences?

7. How has parenting changed since the 1960s?

8. What are some things your parents did that you will choose to handle in a different way.

9. Why are parents of today less comfortable comparing notes and agreeing on the way to handle misbehavior?

10. Why is it important for the Chief Engineers to know the Assistant Engineers well?

2

The Chief Engineers

In order to properly wire the rockets that have been entrusted to us, each of the Chief Engineers must understand the Master's Schematics and must understand the role he or she is to play in the wiring of the rocket.

Fathers have a unique responsibility. Children get their first ideas about God from their fathers. Because God has given fathers the primary role of leadership in the family, it is very important for dads to do their job well. Counselors often encounter adults who have a hard time loving God as a heavenly Father because of their childhood experiences with earthly fathers who were harsh or unloving.

God's Instructions to Husbands and Fathers

"So husbands ought also to love their own wives as their own bodies. He who loves his own wife loves himself; for no one ever hated his own flesh, but nourishes and cherishes it, just as Christ also does the church" (Ephesians 5:28–29).

"Husbands, love your wives, and do not be embittered against them" (Colossians 3:19).

One of the most important ways a child learns about his dad's character is in the way Dad loves Mom. It gives a child enormous security to know that his parents love each other and are kind to each other. As children see the gentler side of Dad interacting in healthy ways with Mom, they perceive him as being more "user friendly."

Some dads have a hard time seeing things through the eyes of a child. Learning to view the world in this way is one of the most important skills a dad can develop. When Dad can see things from a child's viewpoint, it helps him understand what children see as amusing as well as frightening. When a dad can remember how it felt to be little, he can be more successful in effective communication with his children.

No matter what size a dad is in comparison to other men, a child thinks, "My daddy is *big!*" God made Dad bigger than Mom because Dad is a leader, protector, and provider. When there is a "monster under the bed," nothing is more reassuring for a child than to know he is safe in his dad's strong arms. When a child grows up knowing he can run to his dad for love and protection, growing into a faith relationship with God is easier. Faith is an abstract thing. Children don't do abstract things well until they are older. Dad can lay a very important faith foundation by being a concrete example of a father's love and protection. Later the child can separate God from Dad and know that God cares for him even more than Dad does.

> **In the training of children, Dad's larger size and deeper voice make him more intimidating than Mom.**

That faith foundation serves well, as Dad does his part of wiring the rocket. If Dad can accurately balance being a loving leader with being a strong authority figure, his children will gain a better understanding of God's nature.

In the training of children, Dad's larger size and deeper voice make him more intimidating than Mom. When used wisely, those unique characteristics can be very good things. Used unwisely, they can be disastrous. Dad needs to be aware that he can be intimidating, especially when dealing with small children. His "I mean business" voice can be a strong deterrent to a child whose behavior is out of line. If he has to spank a child, he needs to be very aware of his size and strength and make sure he is in complete control of his emotions.

Dad's yelling is appropriate when a child is heading for danger and is too far away to touch—for example, when a child's hand is going toward a hot stove or a child is rushing toward a busy street. Yelling is appropriate when the house is on fire and Dad needs to get the family up and out of harm's way. Yelling is not appropriate as a means of controlling a child's behavior. It warns a child that Dad is out of control. If Dad yells just before he spanks, the child will understand that he is in trouble because Dad is angry. He probably will not make the connection that he is in trouble because of his own misbehavior.

A stern look and a serious tone of voice are far more effective. A serious tone of voice can communicate, "I'm very disappointed with the way you have chosen to behave. I love you far too much to let you get by with that sort of behavior." When punishment follows that kind of communication, the child is more apt to connect the consequences to his own misconduct: "A fool always loses his temper, but a wise man holds it back" (Proverbs 29:11).

God has given dads very specific guidelines for the way they are to interact with the children entrusted to them: "And, ye fathers, provoke not your children to wrath: but bring them up in the nurture and admonition of the Lord" (Ephesians 6:4 KJV).

God's commandment is very important because if a child cannot love, respect, and obey the dad he has seen, it will be more difficult for him to love, worship, and obey the God he has not seen.

Bring Up Children in the Nurture of the Lord

As soon as your child is old enough to memorize, teach him Ephesians 6:4. Spend time pointing out the neat things God does for us. Help your child identify these things as proof of the love our heavenly Father has for us. Tell your child: "God sure must love me a lot. When He was picking out someone to be your daddy, He picked me. I know He must love me a lot to give me such a special child to love."

Every day, in one way or another, let your child know the special things that you see in him as gifts from God. For instance, "I'm so glad God gave me a little girl with such a giving heart. God likes cheerful givers and I'm glad you are one." Or "I'm glad God gave you such a kind heart. You are so kind and gentle with the baby. God likes that about you. I like it, too." As you see good things God made for us, say, "I'm glad God made the pretty flowers for us to enjoy. God loves us. He gives us good things."

Be a good listener. Be willing to listen to the endless things your child wants to tell you. If you want your child to talk to you during the teen years, listen now! If you want your child to know that he can tell God anything, don't overreact when he confesses what he did wrong or when he tells you something outrageous. Always be approachable.

Bring Up Children in the Admonition of the Lord

Teach your child that *admonish* means "to correct." Sometimes God corrects us with His words. Sometimes He uses action to correct us, depending on what we need at the time. Since family rules are based on God's rules, parents follow God's example in the way they correct their children—sometimes with words and sometimes with actions.

Teach your child, "God gave Daddy and Mommy a very important job. During the years that you are living in our house, we are supposed to teach you God's rules so you will know how He wants you to behave. Then when you are all grown up, you will be one of God's good helpers. He needs lots of Christian helpers, but they have to know His rules so they can work together to do the job He wants them to do."

The Result of Proper Training

Dad's leadership in the wiring of the rockets will be a major factor in whether or not the children will grow up prepared for eternity. Most dads are trying to serve as parents at the same time they are trying to build successful careers. When caught in the time crunch between parenting and career, remember that your career will end some day. Your children will be eternally in one of two places. Make sure they are prepared to meet the Lord.

Mother's Role as a Chief Engineer

While Dad has a God-given position of leadership in the family, Mom has an equally important but different role. Mom is the suitable helper that makes Dad's efforts more successful. Moms are usually more nurturing than dads. Most moms have a lot more experience with small children and interact very comfortably with them. When Mom and Dad work as a team, wiring the rocket is much easier.

One of the ways that Mom serves the family is to make sure Dad's job is being done when Dad is not with the family. This job is put in serious jeopardy if Mom works outside the home. Fatigue and time pressure are constant realities when Mom is trying to juggle a career with all the tasks required of her as a Chief Engineer and as a keeper at home (Titus 2:5 KJV). It's hard for Mom to give her best effort as a mother when the time crunch and "to do" list are always there to complicate life. No one can give a hundred percent at work and a hundred percent at home. Since Mom doesn't receive a pay check for what is done at home, those tasks usually go on the back burner until someone has time to deal with them.

The Pressure of Stress

A tired, stressed-out mom puts a lot of pressure on a marriage. Because Dad is an adult and can fend for himself, his needs are usually put at the very bottom of the priority list. Mom is more apt to take care of the stuff at work and do what she can with the stuff at home. When she gets the children in bed for the night, meeting the needs of her husband becomes just one more thing on the "to do" list. That is one of the reasons the divorce rate started to climb when more and more women began to pursue careers.

For moms who wait until the children are in school before going to work, life is a little better, but not by much. When children have needs, they have needs! If children come home to an empty house, no one is there to assess just by their body language whether or not they have had a good day. No one is there to provide a snack and listen to the events of the school day. Children have a much different perception of time than adults do. For a sixth grader to come home at 3:30 P.M. upset over an incident at school, waiting until 6:00 P.M. to talk about it when both parents get home isn't good. The parents are tired and stressed and trying to get dinner on the table. When is there time to hear about the day's heartache and offer words of consolation?

When Mom comes home at the end of the day stressed out and dead tired, she still has to deal with the mothering, the homework, the laundry, and the housework. The increased stress level of a dual income family is rarely balanced by the perks of having the extra paycheck.

The single parent is under constant stress trying to do Mom's job, Dad's job, and be the breadwinner—all at the same time. Essentially, a single parent is doing three full-time jobs. Emotional stability is not easily maintained by one who is sleep-deprived and overworked.

Emotional Hub and Routine Manager

Whether Mom is able to be a full-time keeper at home or has a career, one thing remains the same: Mom is the emotional hub of the home. The adage is true: "If Mama ain't happy, ain't nobody happy." The way Mom models godly attitudes and behavior has a lot of influence over how securely the rockets will be wired. Modeling is the conduit through which the wiring runs, and since Mom usually spends more time with the children than Dad does, the way she models these attributes is extremely important.

Moms also have a lot of influence in the way children view Dad as head of the home. Always speak respectfully to your husband and about your husband. If you disagree with him, do it in private, not in front of the children. Support his leadership and help him to be the man God has called him to be.

In most families, Mom is responsible for the daily routine. Consistency is an important key to secure wiring. If you do things the same way every day, your child will learn that you can be trusted. He will know what to expect from you and he will know what you expect from him. A well-ordered, structured environment is the best thing for a child, especially in the early years. Give clear instructions. Have a routine. When you give a child a job to do, check to see if he does it.

> Remember: Children do what you inspect, not what you expect.
> Always follow through.

The Family Calendar

In most homes, Mom is in charge of the family calendar and schedule. She knows who has to be where and at what time. Mom usually keeps track of the birthdays; she plans celebrations.

Besides having a child's birth date and launch date firmly in mind, Mom also needs to have another date firmly in her mind. A child's fifth birthday is a very important date for Mom to have on her mental calendar. Most psychologists agree that a child's personality is pretty well set by the fifth birthday. That's why wiring during the first five years is critical to later success. If a child is going to be obedient, respectful, loving, giving, and polite, those characteristics need to be in place by the fifth birthday. From that point on, the engineers will do some tweaking and readjust some of the wiring, but the basics will remain the way they were originally installed.

One way to help instill godly characteristics is to have a lot of control over the things that influence your child. Keep TV viewing to a minimum and monitor closely what he does watch. When deciding what videos or TV programs to let your child watch, here are some questions you need to ask yourself.

1. Does it support or undermine what we are teaching?

2. Are the characters being unkind or rude to one another?

3. Would I want my child to act like the characters they are seeing?

When enjoying entertainment together, check for content and watch for teachable moments. Is Dad being honored as the head of the family, or do Mom and the kids have to rescue him from his own stupidity? Are we contradicting ourselves by trying to teach godly characteristics while we are being entertained by the antics of ungodly characters? If you have to turn something off because of the content, ask the children if they can name which one of God's rules was being violated. Teach your children early to help you look up information in the Bible so they know how to follow God's rules.

The Importance of Assistant Engineers

The babysitters, daycare providers, teachers, coaches, and friends who spend lots of time with your children are Assistant Engineers. They will help you wire that rocket. It is vitally important that you have a lot of control over who is with your children, and it is important to know what they believe. God warns: "Do not be deceived: 'Bad company corrupts good morals'" (1 Corinthians 15:33).

Invite into your home and swap babysitting only with people who share your values. Letting your child spend time with those whose values and rules are radically different from yours is like dropping him off in a foreign country where he cannot speak the language and does not know the culture. Remember also that Assistant Engineers with values different from yours will install wiring that may be faulty.

Wiring rockets for the King's fleet requires a lot of time, diligence, and persistence. It takes a lot of room. Pray daily for each of your children. Pray that you and your mate will be the best engineers you can be and that the Lord will help you with the wiring project. Pray for the folks who are rearing the person your child will marry. Ask the Lord to help them to be very good Chief Engineers and to guide their wiring efforts.

> "If any of you lacks wisdom, let him ask of God, who gives to all men generously and without reproach, and it will be given to him" (James 1:5).

> "Teach me good discernment and knowledge, for I believe in Thy commandments" (Psalm 119:66).

"The effectual fervent prayer of a righteous man availeth much" (James 5:16 KJV).

Memory Verses for the Job at Hand

Memory verses are for parents to store in their own hearts to guide them. Through the years these are to be wired into the rocket so the child will have God's word to guide him in decision-making. Memorizing the following verses will also help prepare him to be a Chief Engineer.

» "Children, obey your parents in the Lord, for this is right" (Ephesians 6:1).

» "And ye fathers, provoke not your children to wrath: but bring them up in the nurture and admonition of the Lord" (Ephesians 6:4 KJV).

» "Hear, O Israel: The Lord our God is one Lord: And thou shalt love the Lord thy God with all of thy heart, and with all thy soul, and with all of thy might. And these words, which I command thee this day, shall be in thine heart; and thou shalt teach them diligently unto thy children, and shalt talk of them when thou sittest in thine house, and when thou walkest by the way, and when thou liest down, and when thou risest up" (Deuteronomy 6:4–7 KJV).

» "Thy word have I hid in mine heart, that I might not sin against thee" (Psalm 119:11 KJV).

» "Teach me good judgment and knowledge; for I have believed thy commandments" (Psalm 119:66 KJV).

Drill for Skills

 Making Connections

1. Each of the Chief Engineers must know the _____ _____ _____ and the role that he or she is to play in _____ the rocket.

2. Children get their first ideas about _____ from their fathers.

3. _____ have the primary role of leadership in the family.

4. _____ is not appropriate as a means of controlling a child's behavior.

5. If Mom works outside the home, it is very important that the Assistant Engineer be a faithful _____.

 # Troubleshooting

1. How does the interaction between parents affect the emotional security of children?

2. Why is it important for Dad to learn to see things from a child's point of view?

3. How does a father's example of loving leadership lay a foundation for faith development?

4. Quote Proverbs 29:11.

5. Discuss ways that a father can bring up a child in the nurture and admonition of the Lord.

6. Discuss how Mom's role as Chief Engineer is affected if she has to work outside the home.

7. Discuss the impact of a well-ordered routine and its effect on children.

8. Why is it important to be aware of the launch date during the first five years?

9. Why is it important to instill godly characteristics during the first five years?

10. Discuss the importance of outside influences on children.

3

Confident, Consistent Discipline

As we prepare our rockets for the Kingdom Fleet, discipline will be a very important part of the wiring. We need to remember that the word *discipline* comes from the word *disciple*. Our job is to train the next generation of the Lord's disciples. Discipline is not something we do to a child; it's something we do for a child until he can demonstrate self-discipline. The point of discipline is to help a child move from living in a loving, respectful, obedient relationship with his parents to having a loving, worshipful, obedient relationship with God. As we discipline our children, we need to remember the wisdom from Hebrews:

> "All discipline for the moment seems not to be joyful, but sorrowful; yet to those who have been trained by it, afterwards it yields the peaceful fruit of righteousness" (Hebrews 12:11).

Satan wants the souls of our children. He doesn't want their lives to produce a harvest of righteousness. He doesn't want them to be trained in such a way that they will have peace.

If Chief Engineers wisely follow the schematics for discipline, they will properly wire their rockets. They will also add a great deal of security to the lives of their children because they will daily answer the two most important questions in a child's life: "Who loves me?" and "Who is in control?"

The Importance of Shaping Attitudes

If we are going to wire our rockets to fly with the Kingdom Fleet, we have to work on attitudes. As you read through the Master's Schematics for your own training, pay attention to how much time is spent on right thoughts and right attitudes. If we are to follow the instructions of Ephe-

35

sians 6:4 and train children in the nurture and admonition of the Lord, we must conscientiously shape attitudes.

Satan doesn't want our rockets to fly with the Kingdom Fleet. He doesn't want them to be wired properly. Satan is always hovering near the launch pad, trying to sabotage the work of the engineers. He will take any opportunity to mess with the wiring. We cannot be so foolish as to give Satan opportunities by bringing sinful entertainment into our homes. If we do that, we are aiding and abetting the saboteur. That is why it is so important to screen very carefully what our children see on TV and in videos and to monitor what they read.

It's also important for us to have a lot of control over the friendships our children form. We need to make sure they have close fellowship with people who support what we are teaching and avoid people who undermine what we are teaching. Satan will use friendships and entertainment to sabotage the wiring. We must not give him access, especially during the formative years.

Nip It in the Bud

Often, the first sign we have of sabotage is when a bad attitude surfaces. The mind of a child houses the intellect, the emotions, and the will. When Satan uses sinful thoughts to tamper with the wiring, the *intellect* of the child is aware of it. The *emotions* decide how the child will feel about it. The *will* decides how the child will respond to it.

An attitude is a pre-packaged decision. When sparks start to fly, the engineers know there is an underlying problem. Bad attitudes that are not corrected become actions. Actions give birth to habits. Habits become life patterns that will leave Satan's tracks all over the inside of the rocket. When a bad attitude surfaces, it needs immediate attention. In the training and disciplining of our children, it is very important to start by carefully shaping attitudes.

A bad attitude is the first evidence of sinful behavior. We are very fortunate to have the loving Creator on our side as we shape our attitudes. He left us the Master's Schematics, but it is up to us to study. He also gives us hints. When an attitude surfaces that needs attention, that is God's way of tapping us on the shoulder and saying, "This week it's time to teach courtesy." If the child is showing an attitude of rebellion, it's time to teach submission and obedience. If the child is showing an attitude of hatefulness, it's time to teach kindness. If the child is showing an attitude of selfishness, it's time to teach unselfishness. Satan tells us through worldly psychologists: "It's just a phase. Ignore it and it will go away."

As engineers, we cannot afford to ignore attitudes. They give birth to actions. It is much easier to shape attitudes than to correct actions.

The Science of Shaping Attitudes

In order to shape attitudes properly, engineers must concentrate on three important areas. We will look at each of these in more detail as we explore the engineer's tool kit later in the chapter. Right now we will introduce the idea and see how these tools are used to shape attitudes.

» *Model the correct attitude.* Modeling is the conduit through which the wiring is run.

» *Teach the correct attitude.* Identify God's rules governing that particular attitude.

» *Enforce the right attitude.* Learn to assess the situation accurately. Then (1) respond with positive reinforcement or (2) correct and redirect.

The Wiring Basics
for Shaping Attitudes

Before an engineer can shape attitudes, he must have a clear mental image of what attitudes are important for a lifetime of service in the Kingdom Fleet.

> "But the fruit of the Spirit is love, joy, peace, patience, kindness, goodness, faithfulness, gentleness, self-control; against such things there is no law" (Galatians 5:22–23).

Most of the other good attitudes and behaviors mentioned in Scripture come under the umbrella of the nine characteristics of the fruit of the Spirit. Often there is an overlap and an attitude or behavior can be placed under more than one of these character traits. If we can wire these attitudes into our rockets, they will have a solid foundation for a lifetime in the Kingdom Fleet.

Growing in the fruit of the Spirit is a lifetime proposition. If engineers can secure the basic wiring for these characteristics early in a child's life, it will be much easier for the child to grow into a strong relationship with the Lord.

To understand better how to shape attitudes, let's take a look at the following bad attitude. We will see how to use the pattern of *model, teach,* and *enforce* to shape the attitude properly before it becomes an action that repeats itself.

Disrespectful Attitude: Negative Response

Respectful attitude and obedience can be classified under "goodness," "love," "kindness," or "self-control."

Clean It Up or Get a Spanking

It's dinner time at the Stewarts' house. Six-year-old Steven and four-year-old Mary are having a pleasant meal with Mom and Dad. Near the end of the meal Mom says, "Mary, I noticed that you left a mess in the bathroom. After dinner, please go pick up your clothes and put them in the hamper. Please put your shoes in your room."

(Mom has modeled the correct attitude by speaking politely and respectfully.)

Mary says, in a rude and hateful tone of voice, "It's not my mess and I won't clean it up!"

Dad says quietly, but sternly, "Young lady, that was a very disrespectful answer. The Bible says that you are to obey your parents. It also says you are to honor your father and your mother. I will not allow you to break God's laws or our family laws by talking to your mother that way."

(Dad has assessed the attitude. Now he must correct and redirect by (1) identifying the behavior, (2) stating the choices, and (3) delivering the consequences.)

"Since you were rude and disrespectful, you have two choices. You may apologize to your mother right now and then go take care of the mess in the bathroom, or you can choose for Daddy to give you a spanking. It's your choice."

(If Mary apologizes and takes care of the mess in the bathroom, Dad can follow through by giving Mary a hug and letting her know the conflict is resolved. If Mary just sits there, she has made her choice. Dad should address that choice immediately.)

"Since you chose not to apologize to Mommy, you have chosen to get a spanking." (He should take Mary to another room and follow through on his promise. After Mary quits crying, Dad needs to let her know that she is still responsible for apologizing to Mom and cleaning up the mess in the bathroom.)

Disrespectful Attitude: Positive Response

Let's look at some positive ways to help Mary correct her bad attitude before it has a chance to become a habit. Mary and Mom seem to be rubbing each other the wrong way this week. Mom is consistently modeling the correct attitude, but Mary isn't getting it. Dad, Mom, and Mary can sit down together and come up with a "contract" that is age-appropriate. The possibilities are limited only by the creativity of the parents. A star chart or sticker chart on the refrigerator works well. So does a jar for pennies, small candies, or chewy fruit.

Whichever method is chosen, every time Mary answers one of her parents in a polite, respectful tone of voice, she gets a reward. The hard part is that the plan requires constant adult supervision. Rewarding Mary immediately for good behavior will often be inconvenient, but good disciplinarians know that promised rewards should be given immediately. Likewise, promised punishment should be swift and sure. Little children perceive time in a very different way than adults do. The reward or punishment loses its effectiveness even after a small amount of time has passed. If rewarding immediately seems to be a nuisance, remember that a week or so of inconvenience is a very small price to pay for a lifetime of a child you can enjoy.

The Tool Kit for Confident, Consistent Discipline

Becoming a confident, consistent disciplinarian will come more naturally if your parents modeled that behavior. Since the majority of families are weak in this area, it may be more helpful to look for good role models. Find a family with teens you admire. Make friends with the parents and ask permission to call on them when you have a parenting problem. Get to know a couple whose adult children are faithful Christians so you can get advice from them when needed. Remember that you do not have to take all the advice you are given. When several folks look at the same situation from different angles, they will see different things. Talking over a difficult situation with someone who has "been there, done that" may give you some valuable insight. Hearing about the humiliating incidents that "perfect parent" has lived through will help you put your situation in perspective. Don't be embarrassed to confide your difficulty. Chances are that the folks who appear to be perfect parents have also cried in frustration over their children. They have learned through experience that one benefit to having children is that it improves the humility of the parents.

The Three Most Important Tools

As we look into the engineer's tool kit, we see three main tools. Some of these tools have "attachments" to make them more useful. The three main tools the engineers will use to install the wiring in the rockets are these: (1) model the rules, (2) teach the rules, and (3) enforce the rules.

Tool #1: Model the Rules

As we have stated before, modeling is the conduit through which the wires will run as we wire our rockets. Rules have no value if they are not modeled consistently. Children will do what you do far more often than they will do what you say. For instance, if you want your children to speak respectfully to you but you yell like a maniac at them, don't be surprised if they grow up yelling like maniacs.

Modeling the rules is a tough tool to master. There should be no difference in what people see of you in public and at church and what your family sees of you at home. That's tough. Home is where we can relax and be ourselves. We just have to make sure that when we are being ourselves, we are honoring the Father.

Tool #2: Teach the Rules

Teaching the rules, especially to preschool children, requires patience. As often as possible, give one of God's rules that is the foundation for the house rule you are teaching. With the exception of safety rules, most of the family rules should fit inside one of God's laws. Even safety rules come under the umbrella of Ephesians 6:1. Teaching a child to honor God's rules will make it easier for him to obey the family rules. It will also lay an important faith foundation for the future. Teach your children that parents also have to live in obedience to God.

When teaching a rule, wait until your child demonstrates full capability for the rule before you hold him accountable for obeying it. Here's one way to think of it.

"Sit on Your Bottom!"

Elizabeth babysits two preschool children. She has a child-size table and two child-size chairs. The safety rule for using those items is: *You have to sit on your bottom if you want to use the chairs.*

Three-year-old Samuel understands the rule. He is physically able to walk up to the chair and seat himself. Samuel spends a great deal of his time pretending to be a superhero. Superheroes don't sit on chairs. They fly through the air. Therefore, Samuel prefers to climb on the chair and jump to the ground or "fly" to the sofa.

The first time Samuel, the superhero, stands on the chair and jumps to the ground, Elizabeth calmly states. "Samuel, the rule in this house is '*You have to sit on your bottom if you want to use the chairs.*' Mrs. Elizabeth does not want you to get hurt. In this house, all superheroes fly from one spot on the floor to another spot on the floor."

Samuel considers that information. As soon as Elizabeth is busy with something else, Samuel climbs back on the chair and "flies" to the sofa.

Elizabeth immediately comes to Samuel and asks in a calm tone of voice, "Samuel, what did Mrs. Elizabeth tell you about the chair?"

"I don't know," Samuel replies.

"You are a very smart little boy and I know that you heard what I said. You have to sit on your bottom if you are going to use the chair. Since you did not obey me, you are not allowed to use the chair for a while. I'll go set the timer on the stove. In thirty minutes, the timer will buzz. Then we'll try again and see if you can use the chair correctly."

Sarah, Samuel's fifteen-month-old sister, is fascinated with the chair. Sarah can toddle over and put one pudgy little knee on the seat of the chair. She has learned how to hold on to the back of the chair and get the other knee up there. She is so pleased with herself! Seating herself correctly is beyond Sarah's capability. Elizabeth stays very close and steadies the chair while Sarah is learning. When Sarah gets both knees on the chair, Elizabeth says, "What a big girl! You need to turn around and sit on your bottom. I will help you." Elizabeth gently lifts Sarah and seats her. Sarah and Elizabeth smile and clap to celebrate.

Samuel is accountable for using the chair correctly because he understands the rule and is able to obey it. It will be quite a while before Sarah will be accountable for using the chair correctly because she is still incapable. When she can walk to the chair and seat herself properly, she will be accountable.

Tool #3: Enforce the Rules

Enforcing the rules is difficult for some engineers. This is one of those tools that can "lock up" at times but, with constant care, should be one of the most valuable tools in the engineer's tool kit. If an engineer can gain a good understanding of potential snags, the wiring will be much easier to install. One of the most common snags is lack of time. Enforcing rules is often inconvenient. If the family is running late and trying to get out the door, it is inconvenient to take time to enforce the rules. Rockets are very smart. If they learn from the engineers that it is more important to be on time than to obey, they will plan their disobedience for just before departure time. They know it's a penalty-free time zone. Engineers have to remember that being late will not likely have eternal significance. On the other hand, failure to enforce the rules may cause problems in the wiring that will have eternal consequences. Enforcing the rules during a time crunch may require some scheduling adjustment and some organizational adjustment, but it's worth it to eliminate a penalty-free time zone.

Embarrassment is another problem that may cause this tool to "lock up" when most needed. Engineers tend to be self-conscious. They want to make a good impression.

Rockets do not share the engineers' concerns. Rockets are more apt to cause a problem at the precise moment the engineer is trying to make a good impression than at any other time. In an attempt to avoid embarrassment, engineers often ignore the problem and hope no one else notices. That technique is doomed to fail. A better strategy is to remove the rocket from the situation and enforce the rules in the same way you would at home. Otherwise, you will have faulty wiring that will allow the rocket to malfunction when similar circumstances arise in the future.

Fatigue, stress, and illness can cause the enforcement tool to "lock up" and cause major problems. Some rockets will make an effort to help out and to fly right when the family stress level is high. Some will try to ease the load when fatigue and illness have the engineers functioning with less enthusiasm and efficiency. The aforementioned rockets are few and far between. Some degree of malfunctioning is normal during difficult situations. In order for the wiring to be anchored securely, enforcement must occur even if it takes energy the engineer can barely summon.

Keeping Family Boundaries Secure

Jack's wife, Jane, had been very ill. After two surgeries within a week, two days in an intensive care unit, and seven days in a regular hospital room, Jane was finally at home. Jane's mom came to help, but she did not want to babysit while Jane was in the hospital. She wanted to stay with Jane at the hospital and assist with her care. A sweet family from church had kept their daughters, nine-year-old Jackie and seven-year-old Julia, so Jack, as well as Jane's mom, could be at the hospital.

Jane was still very weak and would be for quite some time. She was still in a lot of pain. She could not get up without assistance; she still needed help with bathing, dressing, and eating. Jack had gone back to work and Jane's mom was there for several weeks to run the household until Jane was up and about again.

Jackie and Julia were showing some signs of anxiety. They spent a lot of time being where they could see or touch their mom. They didn't want to sleep in their room because they were still afraid their mom might die. Julia was having nightmares about her mom's dying. Jack and Jane were very understanding about the anxiety and did what they could to comfort and reassure. Jack helped the girls fix pallets in the master bedroom so they could be with their mom at night and hear her breathing. During the day, Jane rested on the couch and observed the household activity. One thing she observed was that her mother often had to ask the girls two or three times to do their chores. Jane knew that she couldn't do much about it herself, so she spoke to her mother: "Mom, you never let us get by with not coming the first time you called. My girls are supposed to obey the first time they are called. If you need to spank them to get their attention, feel free to do it."

Mom said that she didn't feel comfortable handling the discipline when a parent was around, even though she knew Jane was physically unable to do it.

Jane called Jack at work. It was almost his lunch hour so he came home. He sat down with Jackie and Julia and gave them a good "talking to." Then he had a family meeting with Jane, the girls, and Grandma. He explained to all of them that he had gone over the rules one more time with the girls. He made it clear that if the girls gave Grandma any more resistance or if she had to repeat herself one more time that he was to be called at work. He let the girls know that he was never too busy to come home and enforce the rules.

The girls improved in their response to Grandma for a few days. Toward the end of the week, they slipped back into their old pattern. Jane called Jack at work. Within thirty minutes he was home to spank a couple of disobedient girls. He had to prove himself only once. From then on, when Grandma spoke, the girls obeyed.

An unexpected fringe benefit was that the girls were less anxious. Jack proved that no matter what, they still had a parent on duty to keep the family boundaries secure. Dad's concern gave the girls a better sense of security. The rules were the same, they discovered, even when the stress level was high.

Consistency is the most critical part of good discipline. It is hardest to maintain, but most important, when the security of the family is at risk. After all, we want to wire these rockets to be able to fly successfully in fair weather and in a storm. That can happen only if the engineers are diligent when it is convenient and when it is not.

Since proper use of the enforcement tool is the most complicated, we will devote the rest of the chapter to it. The point of enforcement is to make sure the lesson is imprinted in the rocket's circuitry in order that self-discipline will be securely attached.

Enforcement uses wisely (1) natural consequences, (2) logical consequences, and (3) applied consequences. A child needs to learn early to count the cost and consider the consequences so he will learn to make good decisions.

Natural Consequences

Natural consequences allow a child to see what will happen if he does not listen to the engineers.

Jason's Choice

Mary Ann took her four-year-old Jason to a fast-food restaurant. Jason was enjoying the little toy that came with his meal, playing roughly with it. Mary Ann said, "Jason, play gently with your new toy. It's plastic. If you are rough with the toy, it will break." Jason ignored Mary Ann's instructions and the toy broke. He started whining, "Get me a new toy! Please!" Mary Ann said gently, "No, son. I warned you that the toy would break if you were too rough. We'll have to throw it away. We are not going to get a new toy. I'm sorry you chose not to listen."

Make Do or Do Without

Sue Ellen and her five-year-old twins, Alexis and Alana, were in the kitchen. The girls were playing with children's modeling clay while Sue Ellen fixed dinner. Sue Ellen reminded the girls to play with one color at a time. Alexis and Alana did not listen. They mixed all the colors. For a while, their creations were colorful, but by the time the twins were finished, the clay was a multi-colored mess.

"Mom, we need some new clay," Alexis said. "This is yucky." Sue Ellen explained, "I'm sorry you girls chose not to listen to me. I told you what would happen if you mixed the colors. Clay isn't on the shopping list this week. Maybe in a week or two it will be. Meantime, you will have to make do with what you have or do without."

Natural consequences can be a valuable attachment to the enforcement tool. By experiencing the natural consequences, a child learns that it is important to benefit from the experience of others. The child learns that the Chief Engineers know what they are doing. The child learns that if he doesn't follow instructions, he might not like the results. Normally, natural consequences are wonderful. But if the price is too high, then we move to another form of consequences.

Logical Consequences

Logical consequences allow the engineers to make the punishment fit the crime in a way that is logical.

Cindy Impounds a Tricycle

Three-year-old Rebecca insists on riding her tricycle down the sloping sidewalk and into the street. Her mom, Cindy, realizes the severity of the natural consequences. Rebecca might fall and get hurt. Rebecca might be hit by a car and be seriously injured or killed. That's too high a price to pay. It's time to move to the logical consequence: take the tricycle away for the rest of the morning.

Cindy says, "Rebecca, your listening ears are not working very well. Mommy said for you to keep your tricycle up here where you'll be safe. Since you are not obeying Mommy, we're going to put your tricycle in the garage. After nap time, we will try again and see if you can do a better job listening and obeying."

"Where's My Baseball Glove?"

For a long time, Jane has been frustrated by the state of her son's bedroom. One Saturday, she spends the day in Eric's room working with him to clean and organize his possessions. Jane tells Eric that once she helps him get it organized, he is to assume total responsibility for his room. He is ten years old and perfectly capable of managing the assignment.

Eric leaves for school on Monday morning. Jane checks his room. It looks like a pig sty. The natural consequence is that he lives that way. It may start to smell like the boy's locker room but that probably won't bother Eric. Since using natural consequences isn't apt to get his attention, Jane opts for logical consequences.

Jane does not touch Eric's room. When he comes home, she lets him know she is serious. Jane and Eric work together to make a checklist for Eric to use every day. Jane instructs Eric to set his room in order every morning before he leaves the house.

Jane outlines the consequences that will be enforced if Eric does not comply. Anything that isn't cared for properly will be confiscated. Eric will have to work to earn the privilege of using it again.

Tuesday morning, after Eric goes to school, Jane inspects his room. Eric's bed is unmade. His baseball glove is on the floor and his clothes are scattered. Jane puts the bedding, the clothes, the glove, and everything else that is out of place into a large box. Then she puts the box into her closet.

Eric comes dashing in after school, runs into his room, and then emerges immediately: "Mom, where's my baseball glove? The guys are waiting on me for practice!"

"Eric," Jane says quietly, "you didn't take care of your glove and it has been confiscated, as I promised. In order for you to have the privilege of practicing baseball tomorrow, you must spend thirty minutes pulling weeds in the yard this afternoon."

Jane is ready to stand her ground; she is determined not to give in to Eric's whining or temper tantrums. She knows Eric may hold out until his only possessions are the clothes on his back.

It is important to remember that childhood is an internship for adult life. Responsibility and accountability need to be taught early if the rocket is to fly well in later years. The wiring for this part of the rocket needs to be securely anchored well before the teen years. Otherwise, the teen years will be very long and filled with explosions, flying sparks, and other unpleasant events that make the launch pad an unhappy place to be.

Applied Consequences

Applied consequences are something you do to help a child remember the importance of obedience. Spanking is the most common form of applied consequences. Using a time-out chair and standing a child in the corner are also applied consequences. The hard part for most parents is knowing when to use which type of applied consequences.

A lot of people are hesitant to spank. False information from the Devil's Diagram has been in circulation for so many years that otherwise intelligent engineers have difficulty distinguishing between wisdom and foolishness when it comes to the concept of spanking.

Pediatricians and worldly parenting magazines have been bombarding us for years with the concept that spanking is child abuse. Worldly studies show that spanking doesn't work. All it does is prove that you are bigger than the child, so you have the right to win. Parents in the grocery store shouting at a screaming child, "If you don't shut up I'm gonna beat you!" gives corporal punishment a bad reputation.

However, an appropriate spanking administered by a loving parent in the right way and for the right reasons is a very effective tool. If it weren't, our heavenly Father wouldn't have authorized its use. Sometimes a well-deserved spanking is the best way to resolve a conflict and restore harmony to the home. Here are some verses from the Master's Schematics that we need to store in our memory banks.

>> "Whoever loves discipline loves knowledge, but he who hates reproof is stupid" (Proverbs 12:1).

>> "A wise son accepts his father's discipline, but a scoffer does not listen to rebuke" (Proverbs 13:1).

>> "He who spares his rod hates his son, but he who loves him disciplines him diligently" (Proverbs 13:24).

>> "Foolishness is bound up in the heart of a child; the rod of discipline will remove it far from him" (Proverbs 22:15).

» "And you have forgotten the exhortation which is addressed to you as sons, 'My son, do not regard lightly the discipline of the Lord, nor faint when you are reproved by Him; for those whom the Lord loves He disciplines, and He scourges every son whom He receives.' It is for discipline that you endure; God deals with you as with sons; for what son is there whom his father does not discipline? But if you are without discipline, of which all have become partakers, then you are illegitimate children and not sons. Furthermore, we had earthly fathers to discipline us, and we respected them; shall we not much rather be subject to the Father of spirits, and live?" (Hebrews 12:5–9).

Some Guidelines for Spanking

Behavior That Responds Well to Spanking

» *Deliberate disobedience:* This includes selective listening. A child ignores what you are saying in hopes that you won't notice. It's a quiet form of rebellion.

» *Defiance and disrespect:* This includes door slamming and temper tantrums.

» *Deliberately hurting another child.*

» *Dishonesty:* (Be careful here. Make sure the child is old enough to know the difference in what really happened and what he wishes had happened. Many children don't know the difference until they are six years old.)

When and Where to Spank

Spanking should be a private affair. Spanking in public can get you into trouble because some adults might think you are abusing your child. Also, discipline administered in public is likely to humiliate your child. So if your child misbehaves in public, go to the car and handle the problem as you would at home. If you are with other people, excuse yourself immediately and find a private place to reinforce the idea that there are no safe havens. The rules and consequences are the same no matter where you are or what is going on.

Take your child to a bedroom or bathroom and briefly explain why he is being spanked. Two to five swats is plenty for a child. Put him over your knee and deliver what he needs. After the spanking, hold him close until the tears have stopped. Do not say, "I'm sorry I spanked you." Apologizing sends a confusing message.

It's better to say: "I'm sorry you chose not to mind Mommy. I love you far too much to let you get by with ignoring me. I hope next time you will remember to listen to Mommy and obey."

What If Spanking Doesn't Work?

If you've tried spanking and it doesn't work for you, ask yourself these questions?

» *Am I being consistent?* If you spanked him for jumping out of the time-out chair yesterday and yelled at him today for doing it, spanking won't work. Do it every time he deliberately disobeys. Outlast him. Some children will keep pushing you, hoping you will give in. You are the parent. If you don't earn his respect now, you will be in trouble when he is bigger than you.

» *Am I spanking when I am angry?* If you are, you run the risk of being an abusive parent. He will probably get the message that you are hitting him because you are angry. A spanking should be administered when you are in complete control of your emotions, not when you are too angry and frustrated to do anything else. He needs to know that the spanking is in his best interest.

» If you are angry, it's okay to say, "You need a good spanking, but I'm too angry to do it right now. Go sit on my bed and wait. When I've calmed down, I'll come in there." Having to wait for the consequences can be a valuable part of the learning experience.

» *Am I communicating?* It isn't necessary or wise to beat a child into submission. A little pain goes a long way for a child. However, if you are spanking him with your hand through thick jeans and a thick diaper, he may not be getting the message. He needs to know he has been spanked. If it doesn't hurt, it's not worth avoiding next time. If he has on several layers, you may need to get down to bare skin to communicate effectively.

Training to Obey the First Time

An important concept to remember is that you can train a child to obey the first time you tell him to do something, or you can train him to obey the thirtieth time you tell him. It's your choice. It's much easier on everyone if you train him to obey the first time.

Counting

When used correctly, counting can be a helpful tool in wiring little rockets. It can also be used in a number of incorrect ways. We'll look at a few situations to get a feel for how to use this tool effectively with young rockets.

Waiting to Obey

Some engineers count while waiting for a child to decide whether or not to obey. That is not a good strategy since it usually just proves the engineer has mastered counting. It also lets the child know how much time will elapse before action, if any, is taken.

Incorrect:

"David, come here, please."

"David, did you hear me?"

"David, I said come here!"

"David! I am going to count to three and if you aren't over here, I'm going to spank you."

"One, two, two-and-a-half, two-and-three-quarters. David, are you listening to me?"

> **You can train a child to obey the first time you tell him to do something, or you can train him to obey the thirtieth time you tell him. It's your choice.**

Incorrect (In the grocery store):

"Linda, it's time to go."

"Linda, you have to come away from the mechanical horse now."

"Linda, we have to go. Now come on!"

"Linda, I'm going to count to five and then I'm going to leave you."

"Linda, do you want me to go off and leave you? I'm going to count. One, two, three, four, five. Okay, I'm leaving now. Linda, come on. We have to go!"

If a child is to be trained to obey the first time an instruction is given, counting is counterproductive. Give a command one time in a calm, steady voice. The child will either obey or disobey. If he obeys, say thank you and go on about your business. If he disobeys, handle it immediately.

Marking Time

Although counting while waiting for a child to decide whether or not to obey is not wise, counting can be used to mark time and help a small child make a transition. Remember that it is hard for children to stop something fun immediately and go home or do something else they had rather not do. In those cases, counting can ease the transition and prevent tantrums.

Correct:

"Tyler, in a little bit we'll have to go home. In just a couple of minutes, I'll count to ten and then we'll pick up the blocks and get ready to go."

Watch the time carefully and in two minutes count to ten. As soon as you get to ten, get up and start picking up blocks with Tyler. Don't get trapped into a long conversation with someone else at this point. Do what you said you would do.

Correct:

"Jennifer, I know you are enjoying your video tape. In just a few minutes, we'll need to stop and get ready to go. When it's time, I'll count to five and then we'll stop the tape. Maybe you can watch the rest of it later today."

Set the timer for three minutes. When it buzzes, turn the timer off and go stand by the TV. Count to five. Stop the tape and get ready to go.

Three-year-olds John and Tyler are having a lot of fun playing together at John's house while their moms visit. When Tyler's mom is almost ready to go home, she can tell the boys, "It's almost time for us to go home.

I'm going to count to ten, and then it will be time to pick up the toys." The break in their play to listen to Mom, and then the counting, gives the children an easier way of making the transition.

Counting can also be used when children are learning to share. Mom can say, "I'm going to count to ten, and then it will be John's turn to have the toy truck."

Discipline Problems
and Suggested Solutions

Let's look at some common discipline problems that occur during the wiring of a rocket: arguing with parents and siblings, complaining, fighting, name calling, selfishness, pouting and unhappiness, whining, and bedtime battles. We will state the rules from the Master's Schematics, along with a practical solution or two.

Arguing with Parents

God's Rule: "Do all things without grumbling or disputing" (Philippians 2:14) . . . "Children, obey your parents in the Lord, for this is right" (Ephesians 6:1).

Practical Solution: Make a chart that shows what Dad controls, what Mom controls, and what the child controls. Help the child make good decisions in the area he controls, but in the areas Dad and Mom control, he is to obey promptly and respectfully.

OR

Give him a jar with about fifty pennies. Every time he obeys promptly and without argument, he gets three more pennies to put into his jar. Every time he argues, he has to give up five of his pennies. Let him know it is more costly to argue.

Arguing with Siblings

God's Rule: "Do all things without grumbling or disputing" (Philippians 2:14).

Practical Solution: When children are arguing, have them sit in chairs facing each other but out of kicking and touching range. They are to sit quietly until they say something nice to each other. If one child complies quickly, he gets to go play. When the other child is ready to say something nice, call the first child to come and hear it.

OR

If a child refuses to sit quietly, he is being deliberately disobedient. Respond accordingly.

Complaining

God's Rule: "Do all things without grumbling or disputing" (Philippians 2:14) . . . "And if we have food and covering, with these we shall be content" (1 Timothy 6:8).

Practical Solution: If the child is old enough to write, have him put all complaints in writing. For every complaint listed, a blessing must be listed. Since writing is tedious for some children, most had much rather stop complaining than to have to write their complaints.

OR

For an older child who complains about not having the latest fashion, quote Steve Joiner: "It is your responsibility to cover her, not decorate her. If she wants to be decorated, she can earn the money to do it."

Fighting

God's Rule: "Be angry, and yet do not sin; do not let the sun go down on your anger, and do not give the devil an opportunity" (Ephesians 4:26–27) . . . "Be kind to one another, tender-hearted, forgiving each other, just as God in Christ also has forgiven you" (Ephesians 4:32).

Practical Solution: Make the child shadow-box while standing in the corner. Have him box long enough to make his arms too tired to box—five to ten minutes. For every minute he refuses to do it, he has to go to bed fifteen minutes earlier that night.

OR

Have the child write a nice letter to the person he was fighting, saying at least three nice things about that person. One of the parents must read the letter before it is given to the other party.

OR

Have younger children sit against the wall with their hands folded in their laps until they are ready to be nice. One minute per year of age is about the right amount of sitting time. If the child is four years old, after four minutes ask if he is ready to be nice. If so, he can play again. If he fights again, it's back up against the wall for another four minutes.

Name Calling

God's Rule: "Let no unwholesome word proceed from your mouth, but only such a word as is good for edification according to the need of the moment, that it may give grace to those who hear" (Ephesians 4:29).

Practical Solution: If the child is old enough to call names, he is old enough to quote the first phrase of this verse. If he is calling names, he has to quote the first part of this verse. Then he has to sit with his hands folded in his lap until he can say three nice things about the person he was bad-mouthing.

Selfishness

God's Rule: "Do nothing from selfishness or empty conceit" (Philippians 2:3).

Practical Solution: A child has to understand "mine" before he can understand "thine." Let him have a few things that are "mine for my very own that I don't have to share." A sense of ownership helps him become a good steward. All other possessions are to be shared with his siblings and friends. The things that are his alone are to be put away when other children are playing with him. Remember that home is the training ground for all human relations. Teach him to negotiate politely when sharing and playing with friends.

Pouting and Unhappiness

God's Rule: "How blessed are the people whose God is the Lord!" (Psalm 144:15) . . . "This is the day which the Lord has made; let us rejoice and be glad in it" (Psalm 118:24).

Practical Solution: Select a big chair to be used as the unhappy chair. Any child who is unhappy has to sit in the chair until she is ready to be a happy member of the family. She doesn't talk to anyone and no one talks to her when she's in the unhappy chair. If she wants to get out and try to be happy, let her. At the first sign of pouting or unhappiness, she goes back to the chair immediately. (Be sure to use a big chair so that if fatigue is the problem, she can curl up and go to sleep.)

Whining

God's Rule: "How blessed are the people whose God is the Lord!" (Psalm 144:15) . . . "Do all things without grumbling or disputing" (Philippians 2:14).

Practical Solution: Teach your child that you have funny ears. You simply cannot hear anything said in a whining tone of voice. Be incredibly consistent if you wish to eliminate the whining behavior.

A star chart or a sticker chart on the refrigerator is very good for this one. Break the day into small segments: wake up time to breakfast, breakfast to snack time, play time to lunchtime, lunchtime to nap time, nap time to time for Daddy to come home, supper time to bathtime, bathtime to bedtime. For every time period that the child does no whining, she gets to put a sticker on the chart. When she goes all week without whining, she gets a special outing with the parent of her choice.

Bedtime Battles

God's rule: "Children, obey your parents in the Lord, for this is right" (Ephesians 6:1).

Practical Solution: Have a good, calm bedtime routine. Your child should have a warm bath, get a drink, and brush her teeth. Read her a couple of stories, listen to her prayers, and turn the lights out. For a child who has trouble settling in for the night, tell her that the Penny Fairy lives in your house. She will be coming by in about fifteen minutes to do bed check. Any child who has been lying there very quietly with her eyes closed will wake up in the morning and find money under her pillow. (For a child who still puts things into her mouth, call it the Raisin Fairy and leave a little box of raisins under the pillow.)

Always Follow Through

Becoming a confident, capable disciplinarian takes a great deal of time, effort, and patience. It is one of the most important things an engineer can do because, without it, the wiring in the rocket cannot be secured.

When using the engineer's tool kit, it is always important to follow through. If rewards are promised, they should be given immediately. If punishment is promised, it should be given immediately. Do not promise something you do not intend to do.

» "I'm going to wring your neck!"

» "I'm going to kill you!"

» "I'm going to blister your bottom!"

» "I'm going to string you up by your heels!"

» "I'm going to give you away if you don't stop that!"

» "I'm going to call the police and tell them to take you to jail!"

Say exactly what is going to happen and follow through.

» "If you are very good when we go to Mrs. Linda's house, we'll get french fries on the way home."

» "If you are very good in worship today, I have some candy for a treat on the way home from worship."

» "If you cannot be nice at Mrs. Beth's house, we'll have to go home." (If the child keeps on misbehaving, pack up immediately and leave.)

» "If you do not obey me, I'm going to spank you."

» "If you are a good listener in Bible class today, I'll read you an extra story at naptime."

Pray daily for the strength and wisdom to be the confident, consistent disciplinarian God has called you to be. Pray daily for the ability to model self-discipline so the wiring will have a strong conduit through which to run. If you make a mistake, apologize to your child and try to do better next time. Hang in there; you can do this.

Drill for Skills

 ## Making Connections

1. We must carefully screen the things our children see on _____ and _____, and we need to monitor what they _____.

2. It is important to have a lot of control over _____ that our children form with others.

3. A _____ _____ is the first evidence we have of sinful behavior.

4. If _____ are promised, they should be given immediately. If _____ is promised, it should be _____ and _____.

5. Wait until a child demonstrates full _____ for a rule before you hold him _____ for obeying that rule.

 Troubleshooting

1. What are some ways you can improve your role as a confident, consistent, disciplinarian?

2. What three areas of a child's mind process sinful thoughts just before a bad attitude surfaces?

3. What is the danger in the attitude, "It's just a phase. Ignore it and it will go away."

4. In order to shape attitude properly, what three things must an engineer do faithfully?

5. What negative attitudes have surfaced at your house that need to be reshaped?

6. What are the three most important tools in an engineer's tool kit?

7. Discuss things that cause the enforcement tool to lock up.

8. List some penalty-free zones in your house. What can you do to eliminate them?

9. Discuss the importance of consistent discipline during periods of high stress.

10. Why is it important to see the launch pad as the training ground for all human relationships?

4

Preventive Maintenance

From Cute Car to Beat-Up Car

Eighteen-year-old Henrietta pulled her little car into the service station, smoke billowing and a dreadful clanging noise coming from under the hood. She was terrified.

Henrietta knew Jed, the mechanic at this station. Any time her dad came across a mechanical problem he couldn't solve, he took it to Jed. Henrietta was hoping Jed would find a simple problem that wouldn't cost much to fix. More important, she hoped she could persuade him not to mention the problem to her dad.

The little car was a present from her dad on her sixteenth birthday. "This car is your responsibility," he had told her. "Have the oil changed every three months or every three thousand miles, and check the oil every time you fill up with gas. Have the tires rotated every five thousand miles."

Henrietta's dad was paying her tuition at the community college. She was working part time as a waitress in the town's only cafe and living at home to save money.

When Jed heard Henrietta pull in, he scooted out from under a car, only to be greeted by smoke and ghastly noises.

"What happened, Henrietta?"

"I don't know. It just started making this terrible noise and pouring out smoke, and the heat thingamajig on the dash board is all the way up to the top of the red zone. Jed, you've got to fix this for me and you have to promise not to tell my dad!"

"Henrietta, your dad said he told you to bring your car to me when the oil needed changing. Since you never brought it in, I figured maybe your cousin was changing it. When is the last time you had the oil changed?"

"Jed, I've never had the oil changed! I know Dad told me to do it, but between school and homework and my job, there just wasn't time. It's not that important, is it? You can fix the car, can't you?" she pleaded.

"Henrietta, a car has to have oil to run. You have to change the oil and do the preventive maintenance, or you'll burn up the engine. You're my friend and I'd love to help, but you've burned up the engine on this little car, and it will be very expensive to replace. You can't drive it home. It would never make it. I'll take you home in my truck."

When a tearful Henrietta told her dad the bad news, he told her that she could borrow his old truck for a few days until she could find a used car she could afford. He told her that she would have to come up with the money for the used car but he would help her check it out to make sure she was getting the most for her money.

Dad and Jed were able to find an old beat-up car that still ran fairly well. So Henrietta had to go from driving a cute little car she enjoyed to driving a car she was embarrassed to own, all because she failed to do the preventive maintenance.

As engineers who are busily engaged in the wiring of rockets, we also have some preventive maintenance to do. In the last chapter, we looked at the nuts and bolts of shaping attitudes. We did some work on becoming confident, consistent disciplinarians. Now it's time to take a look at the things we can do to prevent problems in the wiring before they occur.

Watch for Triggers

An observant engineer can do a lot to prevent problems. Just as a man who does the maintenance on his automobile is sensitive to any changes in engine sounds or in the way a car handles, a good engineer is very sensitive to the actions of the rocket he is wiring. He quickly notices when something is not as it should be.

Rockets are a lot of fun to watch. Pay attention to what makes your rocket happy, sad, anxious, contented, or frightened. Learn to recognize the triggers that set off problems.

Mary's New Schedule

Linda and her three-year-old Mary go to ladies' Bible class on Tuesday mornings. After class, Linda stops by the discount store for half an hour of shopping before heading back to the farm where they live. Mary always throws a temper tantrum on these weekly trips to the store.

Linda is puzzled. Several months ago, Mary went through a brief period of throwing tantrums when she didn't get her way. Linda and her husband dealt with that misbehavior, and Mary stopped having tantrums. So why has she gone back to having tantrums? Why does this misbehavior occur only on Tuesdays? The rest of the week Mary is a pleasant companion.

Linda is also frustrated. She usually has to leave a full cart in the store, take Mary to the car, and spank her for having a tantrum. She waits until Mary is calm again before going back into the store. That delay in her schedule makes her have to rush like a crazy lady to get home in time to meet her kindergarten son's school bus. He can stay with a neighbor until she gets there, but she doesn't like to impose on the generosity of her neighbor.

Linda talks the situation over with an older mom, and together they search for the circumstances that are triggering the tantrums. The older mom figures it out first, since she went through it with one of her children. When Linda and Mary are home during the week, they have a very predictable routine. They get Dad off to work. They put Scott on the school bus, and then they spend some time reading together. While Mary plays, Linda gets her housework done. Around 11:30, they are ready to sit down for lunch. Mary goes down for her nap at noon. She sleeps for a couple of hours. Linda uses that time to welcome Scott home from kindergarten, give him his lunch, and talk about his morning at school. While Scott plays in his room, Linda has her quiet time with God.

Tuesdays are different. Ladies' Bible class starts at 10:00. After refreshments are served, the children go to the nursery to play with Miss Amy while the ladies have their class. By the time they finish, it's 11:45. Linda gets to the store at noon and doesn't get home until nearly 1:00. By then Mary has had her tantrum and has been spanked at least once.

The trigger is the disrupted schedule. Mary is one of those rockets who needs a consistent schedule. Taking her to the store when she is hungry and sleepy is the trigger that causes the tantrum.

With that new knowledge, Linda rearranged her schedule a bit. She started leaving home an hour earlier for Bible class. She carried an ice chest to store the perishables, because she began shopping before class, when Mary was rested, happy, and had a full tummy. Mary was a joy to have along on these earlier shopping trips.

Linda started bringing lunch from home. She and Mary would have a picnic under one of the trees at the church building as soon as class was over. Mary was usually asleep by the time Linda got home, so Linda would carry her into the house and put her into bed. Then she could unload the car and put groceries away while Mary rested. Tuesday's were much nicer once Linda figured out what was triggering the problem.

The Persistent Trigger

Sometimes an engineer and a rocket go into a situation that triggers problems and the trigger can't be eliminated.

Captain Courageous

Jack has always been terrified about going to the doctor. He has had several health problems in his four years and he knows that a trip to the doctor means getting a shot or having blood drawn. *Fear is the trigger for Jack.* When Mom and Jack pull into the parking lot, Jack starts to cry. Mom has to drag him, kicking and screaming, into the doctor's office. She knows he is afraid but she also knows the visit is necessary. Mom may be frustrated enough to tell Jack to act like a big boy and to spank him as they cross the parking lot, but that would just make him cry and kick more.

After one particularly disastrous visit, Mom and the doctor have a telephone conference. The doctor isn't thrilled with Jack's actions because they upset the other children in the office. It's also very hard to examine and treat a child who has to be held down by three nurses and one mom. Mom dreads these sessions because she hates for Jack to be afraid. She knows she will be physically and emotionally drained by the time she gets home.

Mom and Doc come up with a workable plan. Mom makes a special "Captain Courageous" cape for Jack. She makes a construction paper "medal" to pin on Jack's shirt. When it's time to go to the doctor, she shows him his new cape and talks about being courageous. Since Jack loves new words, he likes the idea of the cape and the new word. Mom pins his medal to his shirt. She tells him that every time they come to a stop light or a stop sign, if he is still being courageous, she will hand him a star to put on his medal.

The doctor has his staff get ready for Jack's visit. The receptionist notices Jack's cape and medal. She gives him a star for his medal for coming into the office so courageously. She takes time to count how many stars he already has and to brag on him for being courageous on the way to the office.

When the nurse calls Jack's name, she brags on his cape and medals. She gives him a star for being so brave when it's time to come back to the examination room. The doctor continues the positive reinforcement. He tells Jack that only courageous patients are allowed to listen to the doctor's heart with the stethoscope or to look in the doctor's ears with the special light.

The doctor promises Jack there will be no surprises. He reassures Jack that if something is going to hurt, he will let Jack know ahead of time and give him time to make sure he has his courage attached. Jack is allowed to sit in Mom's lap for the part that's going to hurt. Captain Courageous does not kick and scream when something hurts, but he is allowed to cry if he needs to, or better yet to give a courageous shout that scares the hurtful things away. With that kind of positive reinforcement, Jack will soon learn that he can face his fears successfully.

Wise engineers use observation and attentiveness to be aware of things that trigger difficulties. They make sure their tool kits are well equipped to handle any potential problems.

Positive Parenting Is Preventive Maintenance

As we wire our rockets, one of the most important ways we can head off discipline problems is to have a positive environment on the launch pad. If the engineers are happy and confident, the rockets will pick up some very healthy attitudes.

Family life is a lot like a game of "Follow the Leader." In order for the game to go well, the leader has to be one that people will follow. God must have designed the family on that format because Christianity is the ultimate game of "Follow the Leader." Our leader is Jesus, and He shows us how to live, how to die, and how to get to the home we will share with Him eternally. In order for our rockets to follow the Lord's leadership, they first have to learn to follow the leaders God has placed at the launch pad.

If all we do is nag, scold, or punish our children for the wrong things they do, their wiring will be faulty.

As we concentrate on discipline and on training our children, it is easy to fall into a trap. If all we do is nag, scold, or punish our children for the wrong things they do, their wiring will be very faulty. We need to balance the negative things with a lot of positive things. Our children will not be successful mentally, emotionally, or spiritually if they don't come off the launch pad knowing God loves them and gave them special abilities to use in His service. Rockets have to know that Mom and Dad love them and think they are capable.

So amid all the discipline and training, how do we go about having a positive atmosphere in our homes that will produce children with healthy self-esteem? In this chapter we are going to work on ways to help our children build a healthy self-concept. We are not trying to rear egotistical children with an over inflated sense of their own importance. A healthy self-concept is not produced by letting the child be the center of his own universe, with everyone working to make sure he is always happy.

A healthy self-concept comes from the child's knowing that God made him, God loves him, and God has plans for him. It comes from knowing that God will never leave him—no matter how badly he messes up. He can choose to leave God, but God will never leave him. A healthy self-concept comes from knowing we have nothing to fear as long as we are walking with the Lord. With that said, let's start looking at ways to have positive, happy homes where the joy of the Lord is a daily reality.

 ## Master's Schematics

The Scriptures clearly teach that God intends for His people to be joyful. Let's look at a few of the examples in Scripture that talk about joy.

» "Be glad in the Lord and rejoice, you righteous ones, and shout for joy, all you who are upright in heart" (Psalm 32:11).

» "He loves righteousness and justice; the earth is full of the lovingkindness of the Lord" (Psalm 33:5).

» "The Lord has done great things for us; we are glad" (Psalm 126:3).

» "Blessed are the people whose God is the Lord!" (Psalm 144:15).

» "For the kingdom of God is not eating and drinking, but righteousness and peace and joy in the Holy Spirit. For he who in this way serves Christ is acceptable to God and approved by men" (Romans 14:17–18).

» "But the fruit of the Spirit is love, joy, peace, patience, kindness, goodness, faithfulness, gentleness, self-control; against such things there is no law" (Galatians 5:22–23).

Ideas for a More Joyful Climate in the Home

1. Make sure the children see Mom and Dad showing affection for one another. Make sure Mom and Dad speak lovingly and respectfully to one another and to the children.

2. Share jokes or funny incidents.

3. Be playful. When Dad drops an ice cube down the back of Mom's shirt, everyone enjoys the game of chase and the tickle fight that follows.

4. Do the unexpected. If you are coming out of church and find the cars covered with snow, have an impromptu snowball fight on the parking lot, Sunday clothes and all.

5. After an activity or after a normal day, ask each child, "What was the happiest thing that happened today?" or "What was your favorite thing about today?"

6. Sing happy songs around the house. Have cheerful music playing in your house.

7. Laugh together but never at one another. Don't let someone's embarrassment or inconvenience be the brunt of family humor.

Things a Child Needs to Hear Often

If it is true that "nothing improves a child's hearing like praise," then praise needs to be in every engineer's tool box.

» "God loves you and made you to be very special."

» "Every child of God was created to be good at something. We're going to help you find out what you do well and help you master those things."

» "I love you. Even when you mess up, you are mine, and I love you."

» "I sure am glad God gave you to me. I enjoy having you around. I like you."

» "I'm proud of you, just the way you are."

» "You are my good helper. Thank you for working with me."

» "You can handle this job. You are very responsible."

» "When I count my blessings, I count you twice."

» "I'm glad I can count on you to be where I need you to be and to do what I need you to do."

» "I'm glad I can trust you."

Fun Self-Esteem Builders

1. Play the "Who Loves You" game. While dressing a small child say, "Who loves you?" As he names people you can say, "That's right. And who else loves you?" At the end say, "Who loves you best of all?" (God and Jesus love you best of all!)

2. Play favorites. Ask a small child, "Who's my favorite little boy?" or "Who's my favorite two-year-old?" If you have several children, you can still have favorites. "Who's my favorite oldest child?" "Who's my favorite little girl in a blue dress?" Lots of hugging and cuddling with this simple game will help a child know he has a spot in the hearts of his parents that no one else can occupy.

3. Small children love to see themselves in the mirror. Stand at the mirror with them and point out all the special features you see:

   a. Fun, sparkly eyes

   b. Quick, listening ears

   c. Hair to decorate a quick-thinking brain

   d. A delightful smile

   e. Good, helping hands

   f. Feet that are quick to obey

4. Teach your children that when they look in the mirror, they are looking at someone God created to be very special and dearly loved.

Positive Directives

One way to make the mood of your home more joyful is to rethink the way you talk to your children. Make it positive instead of negative, whenever possible. Here are some examples to get you started.

Say:	Instead of:
"Hold it steady."	"Don't drop it!"
"Use your inside voice."	"Stop yelling."

"Feet go on the floor."	"Get your feet off the couch."
"Go sit on the couch while Daddy and I bring the groceries inside	"Move!" or "Get out of the way!"
"Use your walking feet."	"Stop running!"
"Hands go in your pockets while we're in the store"	"Don't touch anything in the store."
"Hold my hand when we go out by the cars."	"Don't go on the parking lot alone."
"Stay where I can see you."	"Get back in here!"
"Hold onto the grocery cart while we do the shopping."	"Stop running. Come back here!"
"Please pick up your toys."	"Stop making messes."

Catch 'Em Being Good

A lot of our time in training our children is spent redirecting when they get off course. But what about reinforcing when they are on target? Reinforcement is often overlooked. Some parents raise praise addicts. They spend so much time on praise and flattery that the kids become insecure and can't move without asking, "Do you like what I'm doing?" There is a better way to handle positive reinforcement. Here is one way to do it right.

Rewarding Good Behavior

One Saturday Tom and Carol were having a family from church come over for the afternoon. Tom and Carol had four very well-behaved children, ages fourteen, twelve, eight, and four. The family coming to visit had three rowdy, annoying children, ages ten, eight, and six. Tom and Carol sat down with their four during lunch to talk about how to handle potential difficulties with the three rowdies. They talked about being good examples and getting parental help with anything they couldn't handle.

When the guests arrived, Tom gave the children about forty-five minutes of togetherness. He had been watching and observing that his children were doing well with a difficult situation, so he went outside carrying ice cream treats. He told the seven children that they were all doing so well, he thought their behavior should be recognized and celebrated. He brought all the adults out to celebrate the seven children playing nicely with each other. He accomplished a couple of things with that strategy. He used a treat and adult attention to reinforce the good he saw.

Having four adults outside gave his kids a brief break and let them relax a bit. It helped the other kids see that good behavior will be rewarded. The adults hung around to visit outside and supervise. Tom's kids got to slip into the house one or two at a time for a sanity break. With this positive parenting strategy, Tom taught his kids that he appreciated their efforts. He also taught them that he would be there with some parental power to give them a break from a tough situation.

Use Creative Problem Solving

Henry's Separation Anxiety

One day Henry, the fourteen-year-old son of Tom and Carol, came home from his private school with a note from the teacher. He had been talking and goofing off when he was supposed to be listening. This was new behavior from a young man who had always been a good student. Henry's mom put him on room restriction until his dad came home. After they had discussed the matter, they would come to Henry's room to deal with him.

Henry was grounded for a week and had to write an apology to his teacher that both parents read and initialed. Henry was warned that he would be in real trouble if he didn't get his act together.

On the next Friday, Henry brought home another note from the same teacher. Henry had not improved his behavior. Carol gave him a "young man you are in big trouble" speech and put him on room restriction until Tom came home. When Tom came home, Carol showed him the note, and they discussed potential ways to handle the situation. They went to Henry's room to give him their verdict. It went something like this.

Carol said, "Son, we are very worried about you. Misbehaving in school isn't like you. Dad and I have discussed this, and we think we've discovered the problem. You are suffering from separation anxiety. It is too stressful for you to be away from us all day, and that stress is being reflected in your behavior. Dad and I aren't willing to see you suffer like this so we have the perfect answer. Monday morning, your little sister and I are going to school with you. I'll take my folding chair and sit right beside you in every class. Janie can take her baby dolls and play at our feet during class. When we go down the hall, Janie will hold your hand and I will have my arm around you. Everyone in that school will know 'this is my precious son that I love so dearly.' We love you so much that we are willing to do this for as many days as necessary until you quit suffering from separation anxiety."

Of course, Henry was about to die. He had rather have his dad take away his allowance or ground him for the rest of the year than to suffer the humiliation of having his mommy and little sister tagging around school with him.

Henry begged. He pleaded. He told his folks, "Mom, please don't do that. I'll never act up in class again. I'll get my act together—I promise! Please don't come to school with me."

Carol said, "All right, son. Dad and I are willing to give you one more chance to handle this separation anxiety on your own, but if we see any more symptoms that indicate you aren't handling it, then Janie and I will be there for you because we love you."

As you can imagine, Henry was a model student for the rest of his school career. His younger brothers got the word; they, too, were model students.

Creative problem solving can make a big difference in the way a rocket is wired. It is a valuable tool that will help a child during the wiring stage of his development, and it will help him fly straight when he encounters the storms of life.

Traditions

Traditions bind a child to the family and give him a sense of belonging. When there is a problem, you can pull the family in for a tradition, and tensions start to melt. Consider making up a strange tradition that is unique to your family.

» Be the only family on the block that celebrates the first snowfall of every year by running barefoot around the house in the snow.

» Celebrate a strange holiday. National Pig Day is on March 22. You could celebrate with pig-related foods and activities.

» Find a weird holiday to celebrate just for fun. Make up a story about the origin of that holiday and retell the story every holiday. Decorate the house for that holiday, and invite another family to share the fun with you.

Ways to Have Fun at No Cost

Build a child's self-esteem by giving him happy memories of home. Here are a few things you can do that don't cost any money.

1. Throw a sheet over the dining room table and let it become a cave. Give the kids a few kitchen things and a few blankets or sleeping bags and let them go "camping."

2. Find a dark hallway. Plug in a lamp or use the camping lantern for a campfire. Have a picnic around the "campfire." Make shadow pictures on the wall. Tell stories and sing songs around the "campfire."

3. Go for a walk. Stop to see some of the pretty things God made. If you have a preschooler, he may want to bring back rocks and "critters" from your walk. Set up a nature center on the front porch made of the pretty sticks and rocks he has collected. Any bugs, worms, snails, toads, and other critters can be put in the nature center. If they wish, they can stay in the nature center. If they want to crawl away and be with their other animal friends, they can do that and you may see them another day.

4. Jump into a pile of autumn leaves.

5. Collect pine cones and pine branches. See what pretty things you can make with what you find.

6. If it snows and you don't feel like taking the little kids outside, bring a big dishpan of snow inside and empty it in the bathtub. Let the children sit in the tub and make little snowmen. Put the snowmen into the freezer or line them up on the front porch for Daddy to see when he comes home.

7. If you have a couch with removable cushions, take them off and let the kids build a fort. The cushions can stand on their sides on a clean floor and not be damaged by being the walls of a fort. (Teach you children not to walk or bounce on cushions.)

8. Line up some chairs to make a train and go on a trip. Let the kids tell you about the trip and what they saw on their journey.

9. Keep a junk drawer of fabric scraps, buttons, ribbon, and such like that the kids can use for their cutting and gluing projects.

10. Play "finish the story." Mom or Dad can start a make-believe story. Pause at a good spot and have one of the children tell more of the story. It's fun to see how a plot develops when it's passed around the family. When the story starts to drag, Mom or Dad should give it a snazzy ending.

11. Have tickle fights.

12. Have pillow fights.

13. On a hot day, wash the car as a family and let the project turn into a water fight.

14. Give the kids a cardboard box and see what they do with it.

15. Make up songs about what you see and do.

16. Make mud pies. Decorate with dandelions, clover, and other things found in the yard. Line them up to dry in the sun.

17. Get old appliance boxes from the throw-away pile at an appliance store and let the kids turn them into tunnels, castles, airports, or other creations.

18. Read to the children every day. Even when they are in grade school, read aloud to the family. *Mrs. Piggle Wiggle, Owls in the Family, Meet the Austins,* and *Boxcar Children* are some fun read-

aloud books that grade-school children will enjoy on trips. While Dad drives, Mom can read to the family.

19. Get a movie from the library or borrow one from friends. Gather around the popcorn bowl and watch the movie together.

20. Keep a bag or box with adult clothes that aren't being used. Let the kids use them for dress-up. Moms, don't throw away those makeup samples you will never use. The little girls will love to have them when they play dress-up.

21. Go to a park and play on the equipment. Take a walk. Have a Pooh Bear picnic—peanut butter and honey sandwiches.

22. Save your old dish detergent or shampoo bottles and lids for the kids to fill with water on hot days. Let them go outside in their old clothes or swimsuits and squirt each other.

23. Hide all the stuffed animals around the house. Turn off the lights, grab the flashlights, and go on a jungle adventure of helping the children look for the animals.

24. Keep socks that have lost their mates. Let the kids make sock puppets and act out stories with them.

25. Go outside and play "Shadow Tag." Let the shadows chase each other. Instead of tagging the child, have your shadow touch his shadow. Then it will be his turn to chase you. Try jumping on each others' shadows. Hide in each others' shadows or in the shadows of trees and other objects.

Drill for Skills

Making Connections

1. An observant engineer needs to be able to recognize _____ _____ that set off discipline problems.

2. Wise engineers use _____ to be aware of things that trigger difficulties.

3. Family life is a lot like a game of _____ _____ _____.

4. Our rockets need to know that God gave them special _____ _____ to use in His service.

5. Mom and Dad need to speak _____ and _____ to each other and to the children.

 ## Troubleshooting

1. Discuss a problem you've had with a rocket and try to find the trigger.

2. How does a positive environment relate to the development of healthy attitudes?

3. Discuss ways to foster a happy, healthy atmosphere in the home.

4. How can doing the unexpected increase the level of joy and fun in a family?

5. Discuss the difference in laughing together and teasing.

6. List six ways to say "You are special" or "I love you" to a child.

7. How can rewards and parental power reinforce good behavior?

8. Discuss a situation in your family where creative problem solving was useful.

9. Discuss traditions that are important to your family.

10. Share some of the fun things you remember from your child-hood.

Section

2

Securing the Wiring

5

Wiring to Grow in Wisdom

In the first section of this book, we looked at the Chief Engineers and the tools they will need to wire the rockets entrusted to them. Now it's time to get down to the specifics of wiring our rockets. God gave us the master plan for rocket wiring when He told us about the four important areas that comprised the development of Jesus when He was a child. "And Jesus kept increasing in wisdom and stature, and in favor with God and men" (Luke 2:52). In this section we will look at how to wire our rockets in each of these important areas. We will compare the Devil's Diagram to the Master's Schematics in order to see more clearly which way the wiring must be run.

Wiring for Wisdom

Through the Bible, God speaks a lot about wisdom—encouraging wisdom, and outlining the blessings that come from wise living, as well as the consequences of foolish behavior.

Modeling is the conduit through which these wires will run. Model consistency, self-discipline, and a firm reliance on God's word. Let your children hear you pray for wisdom—for yourself and for them. Don't be afraid to let your children know when you make a mistake. Model for them how to own up to mistakes. Do what you can to correct the situation and continue the journey a little wiser because of what you learned from the mistake.

There is a serious shortage of wisdom in our society. Common sense is not very common any more. We are living in the information age. Most people in our society are inundated with information but starving for wisdom. We must make sure that from infancy our children are learning the Holy Scriptures that will make them wise (2 Timothy 3:15). It is the only way to make sure they know the difference in godly wisdom and worldly wisdom.

Because worldly wisdom is all around us, we need to check the source and see worldly wisdom as it really is, not as the world presents it. We need to look at the Devil's Diagram so we can recognize dangerous thinking and keep it from finding its way into the wiring of our rockets.

 ## Devil's Diagram

>> "Look out for number one."

>> "Be number one."

>> "Don't let anyone get ahead of you."

>> "If it feels good, do it!"

>> "If it's right for you, then it's right."

>> "Be your own master."

>> "Who cares who you step on while climbing the ladder of success?"

>> "Demand your rights."

>> "It's not my fault!"

>> "I can't help it!"

The predominant theme of the Devil's Diagram is selfishness. People who are wired according to the Devil's Diagram live selfish lives based on the foolish thinking of worldly people. People who live by the standards of evil may seem to be doing all right, but the Lord has given us some warnings we need to heed regarding the "wisdom" of man.

>> "There is a way which seems right to a man, but its end is the way of death" (Proverbs 14:12).

>> "The wicked strut about on every side, when vileness is exalted among the sons of men" (Psalm 12:8).

 ## Master's Schematics

Before we can start the work of wiring for wisdom, we need to take a close look at the Master's Schematics. The Bible has a lot to say about wisdom, especially in the book of Proverbs. As engineers, we need to appreciate the value our Father has placed on wisdom and give it the same priority in our lives. We need to make sure our rockets know that we expect them to grow in wisdom.

» "It is He who made the earth by His power, who established the world by His wisdom; and by His understanding He has stretched out the heavens" (Jeremiah 10:12).

» "The Lord possessed me at the beginning of His way, before His works of old. From everlasting I was established, from the beginning, from the earliest times of the earth. When there were no depths I was brought forth, when there were no springs abounding with water. Before the mountains were settled, before the hills I was brought forth; while He had not yet made the earth and the fields, nor the first dust of the world. When He established the heavens, I was there, when He inscribed a circle on the face of the deep, when He made firm the skies above, when the springs of the deep became fixed, when He set for the sea its boundary, so that the water should not transgress His command, when He marked out the foundations of the earth; then I was beside Him, as a master workman; and I was daily His delight, rejoicing always before Him, rejoicing in the world, His earth, and having my delight in the sons of men" (Proverbs 8:22–31).

Appreciate the value our Father has placed on wisdom and give it priority. We need to make sure our rockets know that we expect them to grow in wisdom.

» "The fear of the Lord is the beginning of wisdom; a good understanding have all those who do His commandments; His praise endures forever" (Psalm 111:10).

» "But the wisdom from above is first pure, then peaceable, gentle, reasonable, full of mercy and good fruits, unwavering, without hypocrisy" (James 3:17).

» "But if any of you lacks wisdom, let him ask of God, who gives to all men generously and without reproach, and it will be given to him. But let him ask in faith without any doubting, for the one who doubts is like the surf of the sea driven and tossed by the wind. For let not that man expect that he will receive anything from the Lord, being a double-minded man, unstable in all his ways" (James 1:5–8).

» "For the Lord gives wisdom; from His mouth come knowledge and understanding" (Proverbs 2:6).

» "Study to show thyself approved unto God, a workman that needeth not to be ashamed, rightly dividing the word of truth" (2 Timothy 2:15 KJV).

» "Do not be afraid of sudden fear, nor of the onslaught of the wicked when it comes; for the Lord will be your confidence, and will keep your foot from being caught" (Proverbs 3:25–26).

For the rest of this chapter we will be looking at the Master's Schematics and how to use it in the day-to-day wiring of our rockets. Fortunate for us, the Mission Specialist we serve has wisdom as one of His primary characteristics. He knew how much we would need that wisdom in order to serve Him faithfully, and so He shares it generously with those who ask. Let's look at some of the previous Scriptures that tell us of our Father's wisdom and of its importance.

In Proverbs chapter 8, a beautiful description of wisdom is given. It is described as a separate entity with a life of its own. It is so important that wisdom was the first of His works when God began the process of creation. Wisdom was there as a witness when God created the earth and established boundaries and the laws of nature. Although we realize that this is poetic, it still gives a vivid image of wisdom and its importance to the Creator. If wisdom is that important to Him, surely it should be very important to us.

Also, in the passage from Proverbs 8 we can see the place of honor that God has given to wisdom. God did not begin the important work of creation until wisdom was firmly established. As engineers, we must make sure that we are developing wisdom in our own lives because wisdom, like all the other characteristics wired into our rockets, must be modeled. The stronger the model, the easier the wiring installation.

Psalm 111:10 teaches that wisdom begins by fearing the Lord. The fear that we have for the Lord is not the same kind of fear that we have of monster hurricanes, tornadoes, and earthquakes. Those fears come from the knowledge that something beyond our control is coming and all we can do is try to get out of the way.

Fear of the Lord is tremendous respect for who He is, what He has done, and fear of the consequences He has in store for the disobedient. It is kin to the feeling you have in the pit of your stomach when a policeman pulls you over and you have been driving 65 in a 25 mile-per-hour speed zone. The anticipation of the action he is about to take causes fear and dread. Multiply that feeling one hundred times, and you have an idea of the fear of the Lord.

Just as we have nothing to fear from a policeman if we are obedient to the laws of the land, we have nothing to fear from the Lord if we are living in an obedient relationship with Him. If we step outside His laws, there is great reason to fear. "It is a terrifying thing to fall into the hands of the living God" (Hebrews 10:31).

> **We can't put the Bible on the shelf and expect to know it. Our children need to see us reading the Bible every day.**

In order to live in an obedient relationship with the God of heaven, we must partake of His wisdom. Godly wisdom is described for us in the book of James.

Wisdom can be obtained by asking, according to James 1:5–8. The asking must be accompanied by faith that God will answer in the affirmative.

Wisdom can be obtained by careful and diligent study of God's word. Unlike people in the ancient world, each one of us has easy access to the word of God. Much of His wisdom is available to us in the Bible.

We can't put the Bible on the shelf and expect to know it. We have to work at it. Our children need to see us reading the Bible every day. They need to see that when the engineers are confronted with a problem, the first response is to talk to God and ask for guidance. The second response is to open God's word for comfort and instruction. If we consult God only in private, our children won't know about it. Model the wise handling of problems so the wiring for that part of the rocket will be secure.

Facts about Wisdom

> » *Wisdom can be obtained by memorizing portions of God's Word:* "Thy word have I hid in mine heart, that I might not sin against thee" (Psalm 119:11 KJV); "Let the word of Christ dwell in you richly in all wisdom" (Colossians 3:16 KJV).

> » *Wisdom is reinforced by using what has been learned.* The more you say it, the more deeply ingrained it will be: "The mouth of the righ-

teous utters wisdom, and his tongue speaks justice. The law of his God is in his heart; his steps do not slip" (Psalm 37:30–31).

» *Wisdom can be obtained through prayer and careful Bible study.* Engineers must be diligent in prayer and in Bible study so that the conduit will be strong enough to support the wiring that must be installed in the rockets. Engineers must pray daily for the rockets in their care. Ask the Lord to help the wiring to be secure, especially in this area. If the wisdom wiring is faulty, the rest of the wiring in the rocket will be flawed.

Installing the Wiring

We have looked at some ways to make sure the conduit for the wiring is strong and secure. Now we will take a look at how to install the wiring in the rockets entrusted to us.

There are several things we can do to make sure our rockets are properly wired for wisdom. One very important way is to have a lot of control over the close friendships your rocket enjoys. Know those Assistant Engineers and check what they install in the rocket. Have the courage to separate your child from companions who will harm him spiritually. Be willing to lose an adult friendship, if necessary, to guard the soul of your child.

» "He who walks with wise men will be wise, but the companion of fools will suffer harm" (Proverbs 13:20).

» "Do not be deceived: 'Bad company corrupts good morals' " (1 Corinthians 15:33).

Another important way to teach wisdom is to begin very early in life helping a child make good choices. Use the words *decision, choice,* and *responsibility* in conversation with your preschool child. In one household, the parents worked hard with their three-year-old daughter on the concept of responsibility. Their eighteen-month-old daughter proved that she had been listening to those conversations. Her first sentence was, "I do it by myself, it's my 'sponsibiwity."

Decision-making can be taught to small children by involving them in the process. You can say to a small child, "We need to make a decision. Do you think you should wear the red shirt today or the blue one?"

Let your preschool child decide whether to go outside and play before you read stories or after. Let him help decide whether the family will have macaroni and cheese for dinner or spaghetti. The more opportunities he has to make choices and decisions, the better equipped he will be for making decisions when the outcome matters.

It is important to foster independent thinking skills by encouraging responsibility. In any task that a child must learn, an adult should do it with the child until the new skill is mastered. Encourage effort. For instance, after nap-time, Mom and her two-year-old John make the bed together. Mom is on one side of the bed, and John is on the other. Mom does her side of the bed and then goes to the other side to help John pull up the covers and straighten out the wrinkles. The day will come when John will let Mom know he wants to do his side by himself. Let him. He isn't tall enough to see it from Mom's perspective, so it probably won't be done very neatly. Praise the effort and thank him for his help. Don't go behind him and fix it because, if you tell him it's good and then you go fix it, your actions have made your words a falsehood. Wrinkled bed linens won't keep a person out of heaven, so they aren't high on the priority list.

> **Praise the effort and thank him for his help. Don't go behind him and fix it because, if you tell him it's good and then you go fix it, your actions have made your words a falsehood.**

Once a child is proficient in doing a task, it becomes his responsibility. When a two-year-old starts dumping her toys in the floor, remind her that it is her responsibility to pick them up. She can ask for help, if needed, and an adult will help—especially if it's a big mess. A child should hear often, "I'll be glad to help you with any job that is difficult for you, but I expect you to do what you can do for yourself."

A major component of wisdom is the ability to think through a problem and solve it. The earlier a child learns responsibility, the easier it will be for him to solve problems. Because he has some experience with the steps involved in doing a job well, he will be better equipped to think through the steps required to solve a problem. He will also be better prepared to anticipate consequences. Those who are wise know how to evaluate a situation and anticipate consequences, and this helps them avoid many of the problems that come with life on this planet.

One important way to install wisdom-wiring is to teach at a very early age that each person is to do his or her own thinking. Do not allow your rocket to learn to follow the crowd.

"They're Just Babies"

Bob and Joan had two sweet little girls. Jennifer was three years old and Julie was almost two. Bob had to work one Sunday and Joan was alone at church with the girls. Worship was over and the adults were visiting in the foyer. The doors to the auditorium were open. The kindergarten crowd was enjoying a game of "Chase" up and down the aisles, over and under the pews. Joan looked up to see Jennifer and Julie running with the other children. She stopped her girls and reminded them of the family rule: "We use our walking feet when we are in the church building. No running." Some of the other moms stopped their children and offered similar instructions. The children took off running as if their parents had uttered not a word. The other parents shrugged helplessly and went back to their conversations.

Joan handled the situation a bit more wisely. She caught her little girls, took them into an empty classroom, and gave each of them a spanking. She told Jennifer and Julie that if she couldn't trust them to obey her, they would have to stand by her side until she was finished visiting.

One of the moms criticized Joan's behavior: "Joan, they're just babies. They were just following the crowd. You shouldn't have spanked them." Joan replied, "My children are going to learn at an early age that we do not allow the crowd to do our thinking for us. They are intelligent girls. They hear very well. They knew our rule, and they knew what I meant when I told them to quit running. They made a poor decision and had to take the consequences of that decision."

Joan had learned from her friend, Pam O'Neal, how to handle that sort of confrontation. Pam had a better grasp of how to install the wiring for wisdom than did most mothers because she was more familiar with the Master's Schematics. She had shared her wisdom with her friend.

Both of Joan's girls had already memorized Ephesians 6:1: "Children, obey your parents in the Lord, for this is right." Another verse that the girls would learn is, "You shall not follow a multitude in doing evil" (Exodus 23:2).

Joan is modeling wisdom and the courage to do the right thing, regardless of the foolishness around her. She won't be stumped when her children are older and come home saying, "Mom, why can't we? Everyone else is allowed to do it! Pleeeeze?" She has learned from Pam the correct answer to that question. She will have the courage to answer her girls wisely: "And aren't you glad that God gave you parents with better sense than that!" Joan is learning from Pam how to be like the worthy woman Solomon describes. "She opens her mouth in wisdom, and the teaching of kindness is on her tongue" (Proverbs 31:26).

The proper use of discipline will be very important in the wisdom-wiring of our rockets. One very wise engineer was once asked how it came to be that she had such good little boys. She replied, "It takes a lot of talk and a strong right arm." That's another way to state: "The rod and reproof give wisdom: but a child left to himself bringeth his mother to shame" (Proverbs 29:15 KJV). It takes a lot of talking and teaching to wire a wise child. It also requires the wisdom to know when psychology needs to be "applied" to be effective. Good engineers must be willing and able to apply some "psychology" to a child's backside when talking isn't getting the job done.

> **"The rod and reproof give wisdom: but a child left to himself bringeth his mother to shame"** (Proverbs 29:15 KJV).

Earlier in this book, we looked at the process of shaping attitudes before they have a chance to give birth to sinful actions. When installing the wiring for wisdom, attitudes will have to be monitored carefully. Solomon said it to his son in the following verse. "My son, give attention to my wisdom, incline your ear to my understanding; that you may observe discretion, and your lips may reserve knowledge" (Proverbs 5:1–2).

Rockets will need to pay attention and listen in order to cooperate with the wiring process. From time to time, an engineer's teaching will probably be met with stubborn resistance. It may be necessary for an engineer to respond as one dad did. He quietly told his stubborn little girl, "My dear, your attitude needs to be adjusted. Would you like to adjust it, or do I need to do it for you?" The little girl knew from past experience that

Daddy would put her over his knee to adjust her attitude. She chose to change her attitude before it became necessary for Daddy to do it for her. Daddy noticed her wise choice and commended her for choosing wisdom instead of foolishness.

Engineers need to make sure that wisdom is a frequent topic of conversation. When the family is observing different situations—for example, in Bible stories, in books being read, and in movies and TV shows—the engineers should point out folks who made wise choices and folks who need to rethink their decisions.

Rockets need to learn early in life to respect the engineers and listen to what they can teach them. One good way to do this is to share stories about past mistakes, especially the ones that got you into trouble as a child. Not only will children enjoy hearing about that part of your life, but they will also learn from your mistakes.

Solomon instructed his son to listen and remember what had been taught.

> "Hear, my son, and accept my sayings, and the years of your life will be many. I have directed you in the way of wisdom; I have led you in upright paths. When you walk, your steps will not be impeded; and if you run, you will not stumble. Take hold of instruction; do not let go. Guard her, for she is your life" (Proverbs 4:10–13).

Inspecting the Wiring

Jesus said, "Wisdom is vindicated by her deeds" (Matthew 11:19).

As engineers, we will need to inspect the wiring in our rockets periodically to see that it is secure. Since wisdom is proved right by her actions, it makes sense that we will be able to see wisdom in action in our rockets. Growing in wisdom takes many years, but there are some things you should see in a rocket whose wisdom-wiring is secure. Here are some guidelines to help with that process.

1. A wise child knows the rules.

2. A wise child can anticipate consequences.

3. A wise child knows to consult his parents when he isn't sure what to do.

4. A wise child does his own thinking. He does not follow the crowd.

5. A wise child usually makes good decisions. He learns from the consequences of his poor decisions.

6. A wise child trusts God to help him do what is right.

7. A wise child considers the effects his actions will have on others.

8. A wise child cares about being right with God. He wants to please God.

9. A wise child accepts the consequences when he makes a mistake.

10. A wise child accepts the teaching of his parents in a respectful manner.

11. A wise child brings joy to his parents because they see him growing to be more like the Father every day.

Memory Verses to Help with Wisdom-Wiring

» "The fear of the Lord is the instruction for wisdom, and before honor comes humility" (Proverbs 15:33).

» "Teach me good discernment and knowledge, for I believe in Thy commandments" (Psalm 119:66).

» "A wise son makes a father glad, but a foolish son is a grief to his mother" (Proverbs 10:1).

» "Wise men store up knowledge, but with the mouth of the foolish, ruin is at hand" (Proverbs 10:14).

» "The heart of the wise teaches his mouth, and adds persuasiveness to his lips" (Proverbs 16:23).

» "The rod and reproof give wisdom, but a child who gets his own way brings shame to his mother" (Proverbs 29:15).

» "Get wisdom! Get understanding! Do not forget, nor turn away from the words of my mouth. Do not forsake her, and she will guard you; love her, and she will watch over you" (Proverbs 4:5–6).

Drill for Skills

Making Connections

1. "And Jesus kept _____ in _____ and _____, and in favor with God and men" (Luke 2:52).

2. _____ is the conduit through which the wiring for wisdom will be run.

3. In our society, we're inundated with information, but we're starving for _____.

4. Wisdom begins with the _____ of the _____ (Psalm 111:10).

5. Good _____ making can be taught to small children by involving them in the process.

Troubleshooting

1. Why must wisdom be modeled by the engineers?

2. Why is worldly wisdom dangerous?

3. What elements of truth, if any, are hidden in worldly wisdom?

4. Why should wisdom be one of the primary characteristics wired into our rockets?

5. How does the fear of the Lord differ from other fears?

6. How can wisdom be obtained?

7. Why is it important to have a lot of control over the Assistant Engineers who assist in wiring our rockets?

8. Discuss ways to transfer responsibility from parent to child.

9. Discuss ways to incorporate the subject of wisdom into family conversations.

6

Wiring to Grow in Stature

Less Than Perfect

A tearful Robert sat on the hospital bed and held his sobbing wife against his chest. It wasn't supposed to be this way. The birth of a baby should be a happy time. This special day had started off the way the books said it might. Nicole had called Robert at work to tell him she had started labor. She kept him posted during the day. They were prepared and Nicole wasn't frightened. Robert spent the day finishing a few details so he could turn his project over to the man who would cover for him for a couple of weeks. Robert got home about 5:00 P.M. and Nicole was ready to go to the hospital.

Labor was long and exhausting, but they knew that was often the case with first babies. Nicole came through like a trouper. They were anxious to see little Hannah and hold her. Which of them would she most resemble? Robert was six-three. He had broad shoulders, a trim waist, jet black hair, and bright blue eyes. He was always handsome, even as a child. Nicole was stunning. She had that rare combination of beautiful auburn red hair, bright green eyes, and a flawless peaches-and-cream complexion. At five-six, she had a very nicely proportioned figure. Friends and strangers had always told her she was beautiful. Friends and relatives had often mentioned that Hannah was going to be a very beautiful baby.

Everything was fine, right up to the moment of delivery. As soon as Hannah's head appeared, the doctor's tone of voice changed. When the birth was completed, a nurse whisked Hannah away. Robert was at the head of the table holding Nicole's hand. Why wasn't Hannah given to them to touch and to hold? The doctor said that he just wanted to make sure Hannah was all right before he let the parents hold her. Everything would be fine.

As the nurses cleaned Nicole and helped her into a fresh gown, they chatted about the weather and upcoming plans for the week. They avoided questions about Hannah. Nicole had counted on holding and nursing her baby right away, but she and Robert saw that would not be the case. The more the nurses chatted, the more anxious Robert and Nicole felt. Why wouldn't someone tell them what was happening with their baby? Where was she?

Why wouldn't someone tell them what was happening with their baby? Where was she?

The nurses got Robert and Nicole settled in a hospital room and finally, a new doctor came in. "I'm Dr. Jack Sanders," he said politely. "I'm a pediatrician, and your little Hannah has a couple of problems we need to discuss. You need to know that I'm a specialist. I work with children who have birth defects."

Robert and Nicole gasped simultaneously. Dr. Sanders gave them a moment to absorb what he had said, then continued. "The good news is that Hannah does not have a life threatening condition. She does have a cleft lip and a cleft palate. If you've never seen a child with this kind of birth defect, it can be pretty shocking. Hannah will need a series of surgeries over the next five years, and after that her appearance will improve dramatically. She may need speech therapy for a couple of years, but most children do quite well with that sort of thing.

"Because of the hole in her palate, Hannah will not be able to nurse. Nicole, Hannah will do better if you are willing to use a pump to supply milk for her. Both you and Robert will have to learn how to feed her so she won't choke. Our nurses are trained to deal with little ones like Hannah, and we won't send you home with her until you've learned to feed and care for her."

Dr. Sanders paused, and then asked, "Are you ready to see Hannah?" Robert and Nicole nodded. The nurse brought her in and gently placed her in Nicole's arms. The new parents were heartbroken. They knew with their heads they would love her just the way she was, but it was very hard to get their hearts on board right away.

The phone rang; Robert answered it. One of the ladies from church had heard that Hannah had been born, and she wanted to visit. Robert explained that they weren't quite up to visitors right now and asked her to wait a few days.

The nurse took Hannah back to the nursery. The doctor left his card and told Robert and Nicole to call if they had any questions. He knew from experience that Robert and Nicole were going to need some "falling apart" time as they mourned the loss of their dream child and accepted the reality of a deformed baby. Robert held Nicole close, as together they began to deal with their disappointment and frustration.

How would they tell the grandparents and the rest of the family? How would those unusually attractive family members react to a child who was going to be unattractive for quite some time— maybe always? How would the folks at church react? Robert and Nicole had been there when the other new moms brought their babies in. They had joined the chorus of "ooh's" and "aah's" as each new baby was admired. How would people react to a baby who wasn't cute and adorable?

Robert and Nicole would have a lot of adjusting to do. They would have to do a very good job wiring little Hannah, especially wiring her for stature, simply because Hannah was born into a society obsessed with physical beauty.

The Obsession

Next time you go out in public, pay attention to how people use beauty as a standard for worthiness. Monitor your own responses to people. If you need directions, will you ask a person who is well dressed and attractive, or will you ask someone who is rather homely? If you see someone who is attractive, do you automatically credit that person with success and high intelligence? If you see someone who is unattractive, do you automatically assume that person is probably not the brightest bulb in the box? When meeting people, do you give the same level of respect to the man who drives the garbage truck as you do to the corporate lawyer?

Watch how people respond to children in public. If a cute little girl smiles at an adult, that adult will probably smile and speak to the child. If a little girl who has uncombed hair and a messy face smiles at an adult, the adult is likely to look the other way and ignore the child. Some studies say that even school teachers are often guilty of giving more positive attention to cute children than to homely ones.

The next time you go to church, pay attention to the way those around you respond to beauty. Monitor your own responses to beauty. If an attractive visitor comes in, how many people rush to greet that visitor? If someone comes in who isn't well dressed, may not smell freshly bathed, and has three scruffy looking little ones in tow, how many folks rush to greet that visitor and make the little ones feel loved and welcome?

As an engineer, start monitoring your responses to people, and especially to children. Are you more apt to interact in healthy ways with attractive people and ignore the less attractive ones? If you see a person in a wheelchair or with some disability, do you look the other way? Can you comfortably converse with someone who has a physical deformity or disability?

In our society, beauty, brains, and wealth are the three main tools used to assess a person's worthiness. As engineers, we must carefully evaluate ourselves to make sure we view these characteristics the way God does so we can properly wire our rockets.

Wiring to Grow in Stature

Since modeling is the conduit through which the wires run, engineers must make sure their attitude toward the physical is in accordance with God's will before the wiring can be installed in the rockets. When God sent Samuel to anoint the second king of Israel, Samuel saw Eliab and thought surely he had found the new king.

> "But the Lord said to Samuel, 'Do not look at his appearance or at the height of his stature, because I have rejected him; for God sees not as man sees, for man looks at the outward appearance, but the Lord looks at the heart'" (1 Samuel 16:7).

Years ago, mothers told their daughters, "Pretty is as pretty does." We have all known people who are nice to look at, but when we get down past the surface beauty, we find some unlovely character traits. Most of us have also known people who would never win a beauty contest but who have hearts that are so good we can't help but think of them as beautiful. Beauty truly is in the eye of the beholder, and we must learn to behold people from God's point of view instead of from the world's flawed value system.

Again, we will compare the Devil's Diagram with the Master's Schematics to make sure we understand how to install the wiring.

 ## Devil's Diagram

» Only the beautiful people can be part of the "in" crowd.

» He can't do this job. He doesn't have the charm or charisma necessary.

» You ought to compete in the next beauty pageant.

» You should be a model. With that sexy body, you could do very well.

» Don't pick her to be on our team. She isn't smart enough. She'll pull us down.

» Don't let him know about tryouts. We don't want that klutz on our team.

» We can't let her come to the party. She doesn't have the right kind of clothes.

» Don't invite him. He won't fit in.

» Don't let her know about our get-together. She's so dull and boring.

People who operate from the Devil's Diagram follow a very selfish pattern. People are valued if they are witty, intelligent, beautiful, charming, well dressed, or if they are wealthy enough to contribute money or talent. Someone operating from this system will form friendships carefully and surround themselves with beautiful people in order to increase their own value in the eyes of the world. If someone loses his money, has an accident and loses his good looks, or does something embarrassing, his friendships can be severed. When people lose their value, they are disposable.

The entertainment industry keeps these false values in good standing. Pay attention to current television programming. If a woman is in danger and needs to be rescued, the odds are very good that she will be in fine physical condition and that she will be gorgeous, even if she's just been mugged. Her clothes, even if torn, will be sexy. The man doing the rescuing will certainly be a tall, handsome, muscle-bound fella who just happened to be at the right place at the right time. He won't be wearing paint-splattered overalls or look like he just came from overhauling a car engine. He won't smell like he just came from mucking out the barn. He will be very handsome. Even after the car chase or the fight scene, he will still be looking good.

There are a few fat folks on TV, but most of them are in minor roles or cast as local idiots. The sheriff who is lazy or dishonest is almost always fat. Most of the fat women we see on TV are either cooks, maids, or house-keepers. Most of them would not do well on an intelligence test. They are there to be ridiculed. Only the gorgeous are cast in roles to be admired.

God has a different standard, and we need to value people the way He values them. Remember that every single person you meet was personally created by the Master of the universe. His goal is that every person will choose to prepare for an eternity with Him. Our job as engineers in His service is to see people the way God sees them and to value them accordingly. We are to treat each person as a precious soul who was created with tender-loving care. Every child that God creates has some kind of talent. Each child is valuable to the Creator and, for that reason, should be valuable to us. We need to appreciate the good we see in each person and do what we can to be a source of encouragement. Everyone we meet is carrying some kind of burden. Let's not add to that burden by using a flawed system to evaluate their worth. Let's make it a point to value people the way our Father values them.

Master's Schematics

>> "For Thou didst form my inward parts; Thou didst weave me in my mother's womb. I will give thanks to Thee, for I am fearfully and wonderfully made; wonderful are Thy works, and my soul knows it very well. My frame was not hidden from Thee, when I was made in secret, and skillfully wrought in the depths of the earth. Thine eyes have seen my unformed substance; and in Thy book they were all written, the days that were ordained for me" (Psalm 139:13–16).

» "He has made everything appropriate in its time" (Ecclesiastes 3:11).

» "How lovely on the mountains are the feet of him who brings good news, who announces peace and brings good news of happiness, who announces salvation, and says to Zion, 'Your God reigns!'" (Isaiah 52:7).

» "For the Lord taketh pleasure in His people: He will beautify the meek with salvation" (Psalm 149:4 KJV).

» "Give unto the Lord the glory due unto His name: bring an offering, and come before Him: worship the Lord in the beauty of holiness" (1 Chronicles 16:29 KJV).

» "Charm is deceitful and beauty is vain, but a woman who fears the Lord, she shall be praised" (Proverbs 31:30).

We can see a lot of beauty in God's creation. He made some people very lovely on the outside. Others who aren't quite as lovely from our point of view are just as valuable to God.

We can see from the Master's Schematics that God has a different standard for beauty. Feet that carry good news are beautiful to Him. People who worship Him in the beauty of holiness are special to Him. He promises to beautify the meek with salvation. Those who fear the Lord are to be praised.

We learn from Proverbs 31:30 that physical beauty is a fleeting thing. It has been said that most women reach the peak of their beauty in their early thirties. After that, the sands of time start to sink, and most women aren't amused at where those sands choose to settle. Many women spend the bulk of their adult lives fighting a losing battle with the effects of gravity.

For both men and women, whatever physical attractiveness came with the original equipment, the ravages of time will equalize. Visit a nursing home. A rare few of those who live there are still physically attractive, but most who still have hair have seen it thin and yellow over the years. Hands once soft and smooth are gnarled, wrinkled, and spotted. Bodies once trim and toned have settled into wrinkled, bent-over shapes that move very carefully, if at all.

If God grants us a long life, the beauty that was ours in youth will fade. That is one reason we need to see beauty from His perspective—so we make sure we are beautiful in His eyes. We need to be like the women commended in the New Testament for their beauty.

> "And let not your adornment be merely external—braiding the hair, and wearing gold jewelry, or putting on dresses; but let it be the hidden person of the heart, with the imperishable quality of a gentle and quiet spirit, which is precious in the sight of God" (1 Peter 3:3–4).

As Chief Engineers, we need to model the things that are beautiful to the Lord, because they are the only things of true value. Our bodies will wear out and lose their attractiveness. The quiet and gentle spirit that is beautiful to the Lord will grow more beautiful during the years to come, if we care for it properly.

Installing the Wiring

Usually when we think of stature, we think of physical growth and development. In this book, we're going to assume that if you feed and water them, children will grow. When wiring for stature, we will concentrate on helping our rockets see the world's value system from the Master's point of view. We need to teach our children that being pretty or handsome is not a sin, but it is a sin to be vain and conceited. "Do nothing from selfishness or empty conceit, but with humility of mind let each of you regard one another as more important than himself" (Philippians 2:3).

Most engineers consider their child to be quite attractive, but children in school may pick on that child and say unkind things about his physical characteristics. It's good for a child to know that his folks think he's good looking. Even children who are blessed with very attractive features will go through an awkward stage when hands and feet are too big for the frame, coordination is off, and nothing seems to work quite right. Especially during those periods, children need to hear positive remarks that help to assure them that their awkwardness will pass.

One good way to compliment physical features without emphasizing beauty is to appreciate the value of different parts of the child's body. Stand in front of a mirror with your young child and talk about his sparkly eyes and other characteristics we discussed in chapter 4 (page 67) when we were working on ways to build self-esteem.

Moms are very important to the secure wiring when it comes to stature, because women are more prone than men to worry about physical appearances.

Scruffy Ed, Pretty Elaine

If Ed and Elaine are working on a Saturday plumbing project, it is almost certain that something will break or they will have forgotten a necessary part. If Ed makes the trip to the hardware store, he will wash the biggest part of the grunge off his hands and jump into the truck. It won't matter to him that his clothes are dirty and he looks pretty scruffy. It won't matter that he hasn't showered or shaved that day. From his perspective there is no point in getting cleaned up when he's going to come back and get dirty finishing the project. The folks at the hardware store are used to people coming in wearing their grubbies. Dirt doesn't seem to bother them.

However, if Elaine is going to the store, she will have to take a quick shower and put on clean clothes, provided Ed hasn't got the water for that part of the house turned off. Even if she has no water, she will clean up as best she can and brush her hair. She'll put on a dab of lipstick so she doesn't scare the natives when she enters the store.

As a general rule, appearance matters more to women than to men. If Dad is taking Junior on an outing, he probably won't notice if Junior's clothes match or if his hair is combed. They will just go on their outing. If Mom is taking Junior on an outing, she will make sure he has on a matching outfit and that his face and hands are clean. She will make sure his hair is combed.

The male Chief Engineer enjoys hearing his wife say he is handsome. The female Chief Engineer needs to hear from time to time that her husband thinks she's pretty. For one, it's a pleasure and good for the ego. For the other, it is a need. Appearance matters more to Mom. She needs to know her husband appreciates her efforts to be attractive to him. Commenting on his wife's beauty is another way a husband says "I love you."

Chief Engineers have to understand the differences in the way men and women are wired because it is important to the different ways we wire male and female rockets.

A little girl needs to hear Daddy tell her that she is pretty. A little boy needs to hear Mom say that he is handsome and getting to be big and strong like Daddy.

The difference in the way men and women are wired is the reason Mom will have a stronger influence over the way the rocket is wired in regards to attitudes about physical appearance. Dad will be important in reinforcing what Mom models and teaches.

One way to model correct attitudes toward the physical is to express contentment with your physical characteristics over which you have no control. Express gratitude for the good health you enjoy, eyes that can see, and ears that can hear.

Do's and Don'ts for Wiring for Stature

» Do what you can to make the most of your attractive features.

» Don't spend a lot of money on beauty products.

» Don't spend a great deal of time primping. Keep it simple and move on.

» Don't have a "bad hair day" more often than not.

» Don't complain about every laugh line, wrinkle, and physical flaw.

» Don't obsess over the extra weight you are carrying.

» Do what you can with diet and exercise and get on with life.

» Don't admire athletes and movie stars for their good looks, regardless of their character or lack thereof.

» Don't criticize others for what they are wearing, or for a hairstyle that you see as unbecoming.

» Do express thankfulness that your body works as well as it does.

» Do teach your rockets that God gave us our bodies, and we need to take good care of them so we can serve the Lord more easily.

» Do teach that if we have food and clothing, we are to be content.

» Don't give in to pressure to buy the latest fads just because everyone else is doing it.

» Don't give in to pressure to "fit in" by having the same style everyone else has.

» Do teach your children to assess others according to character, not fashion.

» Do teach them to use whatever God has given them for a lifetime in His service.

Modesty

Years ago, we heard a lot about modest apparel and immodest apparel. We don't hear much about it any more. Here are a few things we need to consider as we wire our rockets. There is no verse in the Bible that indicates how long a skirt should be or how low is too low for a neckline. There are no Scriptures that condemn wearing shorts or swimsuits. There are no Scriptures that forbid the wearing of spaghetti straps and tube tops. Every person must answer to God for the decisions made in regard to those things. We have been given some guidelines to help us in making wise decisions about the clothing we choose.

> "Likewise, I want women to adorn themselves with proper clothing, modestly and discreetly, not with braided hair and gold or pearls or costly garments; but rather by means of good works, as befits women making a claim to godliness" (1 Timothy 2:9–10).

> "In the same way, you wives, be submissive to your own husbands so that even if any of them are disobedient to the word, they may be won without a word by the behavior of their wives, as they observe your chaste and respectful behavior. And let not your adornment be merely external—braiding the hair, and wearing gold jewelry, or putting on dresses; but let it be the hidden person of the heart, with the imperishable quality of a gentle and quiet spirit, which is precious in the sight of God" (1 Peter 3:1–4).

Sending Mixed Messages

When wiring our rockets in regard to modest apparel, here are some things we need to consider. Women are to choose garments that are appropriate for women who profess to worship God. We are to dress so as to influence the unbelieving by our purity and reverence. We are to dress so that our beauty will be seen in our gentle and quiet spirits.

Those who teach communication skills sometimes talk about mixed messages. When going into a high-level business meeting, one would be advised to wear a "power suit." The suit communicates a high level of professionalism and a serious attitude toward the subject at hand. When going to a funeral, one would not be advised to wear bright, festive colors; that would send a mixed message. From your mouth could come the words, "I'm so sorry for your loss," but the flashy, festive garment would communicate celebration.

> Sexy clothing on a person who professes godliness sends a very confusing message. Most people are more influenced by what they see than by what they hear.

As we wire our rockets in the area of modesty, we must model and teach our rockets how to send clear messages into the world we are trying to win for Christ. Sexy clothing on a person who professes godliness sends a very confusing message. Since most people are more influenced by what they see than by what they hear, the sexy clothing will communicate more clearly than the spoken words.

The sight of a scantily clad woman is sexually stimulating to many men. As moms train their daughters, there are a couple of important things to consider. Jesus said, "But I say to you, that everyone who looks on a woman to lust for her has committed adultery with her already in his heart" (Matthew 5:28).

If a woman loves her brother in Christ and wants him to go to heaven, she will not dress in a way that tempts him to lust. Just as she would expect her brother in Christ to protect her from physical danger, she will protect him from spiritual danger by doing what she can to help him keep his heart pure. We must not let those operating from the Devil's Diagram dictate what is beautiful. We must let the holiness of our Father do the dictating and dress in a way that honors Him.

As engineers, it is wise to decide very early in the wiring process what the standard will be. We are told: "Train up a child in the way he should go, even when he is old he will not depart from it" (Proverbs 22:6). It is important to train from the beginning. If the standard is to be no short shorts, no tube tops, no spaghetti straps, and no skin-tight clothing, then that standard needs to be taught and maintained from the beginning. It's incredibly confusing to install the wiring one way when a child is small and then, when she starts to develop a figure, change the rules and hold her to a higher standard. Tell the truth in all things. Install the wiring from the beginning the way you want it to be when it's time for the launch date.

Teaching Contentment

One of the ways Satan will mess with the wiring in a rocket is to try to instill a lust for more things. We must teach the importance of being content with what we already have. Squelch the constant need to have something new.

> "But godliness actually is a means of great gain, when accompanied by contentment. For we have brought nothing into the world, so we cannot take anything out of it either. And if we have food and covering, with these we shall be content" (1 Timothy 6:6–8).

Another way Satan tries to mess with the wiring is to tempt us with so many activities that we lose all control over our time. One of the biggest temptations comes in the wide variety of extracurricular activities available to our children. While organized sports can be very helpful—especially for little boys who will use their energy inappropriately if not given a safe outlet—that extracurricular activity is among the biggest time stealers.

It is all right for our children to participate in extracurricular activities as long as those activities do not become an obsession that interferes with worship, Bible class, or service to the Lord. Participation in physical sports should not be allowed to destroy family time. Sports can take over the life of a family to the point that some families eat meals together only on holidays. At other times, they eat and live in shifts. Mom is busy rushing kids from practice to practice while Dad is doing his own thing. The inside of Mom's car looks and smells like hamburgers and french fries. Such families wear themselves out with hectic sports schedules. They don't have time to be real families. They push God and His agenda into the background where they are considered unworthy of time and attention.

In many of these families, children have little contact with the head of the family. Proper installation of the wiring is left for another day. Rivers of chaos flow through many of these homes, and time is sucked into that river, never to be seen again. When the family is rarely together, correct wiring installation becomes an impossible dream.

The family that refuses to join the rat race is much healthier, emotionally and spiritually. Members spend more time together, stress levels remain low, financial pressures are fewer, and the family is in a much better position to serve the Lord together.

We must train our children to be spiritual athletes. They must know about the spiritual race and the "finish line."

> "Therefore, since we have so great a cloud of witnesses surrounding us, let us also lay aside every encumbrance, and the sin which so easily entangles us, and let us run with endurance the race that is set before us, fixing our eyes on Jesus, the author and perfecter of faith, who for the joy set before Him endured the cross, despising the shame, and has sat down at the right hand of the throne of God" (Hebrews 12:1–2).

Inspecting the Wiring

As we work our way through the wiring project, here are some characteristics we should see in rockets whose stature wiring is secure. All these characteristics should continue to develop during the wiring process. The closer the launch date, the more apparent these character traits should be.

1. A properly wired rocket will value people according to character, not beauty, intelligence, or athletic ability.

2. A properly wired rocket will see himself as a valuable person specially designed by the Master of the universe.

3. A properly wired rocket will know about his talents and see them as God-given gifts to be used in the Father's service.

4. A properly wired rocket will not be swayed by current fashion trends.

5. A properly wired rocket will befriend those who are seen as less valuable by worldly standards.

6. A properly wired rocket will make time for the most important things in life.

7. A properly wired rocket will make family time a top priority.

8. A properly wired rocket will become a spiritual athlete who is preparing for the spiritual race.

9. A properly wired rocket will assess situations from a godly perspective.

10. A properly wired rocket will be cheerful. He will recognize that of all the things one can wear, facial expression is the most important.

Memory Verses to Help with Stature Wiring

» "For Thou didst form my inward parts; Thou didst weave me in my mother's womb. I will give thanks to Thee, for I am fearfully and wonderfully made; wonderful are Thy works, and my soul knows it very well" (Psalm 139:13–14).

» "But the Lord said to Samuel, 'Do not look at his appearance or at the height of his stature, because I have rejected him; for God sees not as man sees, for man looks at the outward appearance, but the Lord looks at the heart'" (1 Samuel 16:7).

» "Charm is deceitful and beauty is vain, but a woman who fears the Lord, she shall be praised" (Proverbs 31:30).

» "A gray head is a crown of glory; it is found in the way of righteousness" (Proverbs 16:31).

» "But godliness actually is a means of great gain, when accompanied by contentment. For we have brought nothing into the world, so we cannot take anything out of it either. And if we have food and covering, with these we shall be content" (1 Timothy 6:6–8).

Drill for Skills

 ## Making Connections

1. In our society, people use _____, _____, and _____ to measure worthiness.

2. In 1 Samuel 16:7 we are told that man looks at the _____ __ _____, but the Lord looks at the heart.

3. In 1 Peter 3:3–4 women are commended for the unfading beauty of their _____ and _____ spirits.

4. It is not a sin to be pretty or handsome. It is a sin to be _____ and _____.

5. When complimenting children, emphasize _____, not physical attributes over which he had no control.

 ## Troubleshooting

1. How does the appearance of another influence your interaction with that person?

2. How much time and effort do you spend trying to improve the physical characteristics God gave you?

3. How can we retrain ourselves to see people as God sees them?

4. How does the entertainment industry generate false values about beauty?

5. List some of the things God considers to be beautiful.

6. Why is Mom very important when it comes to wiring for stature?

7. What are some of the "do's" and "don'ts" for wiring for stature?

8. How does our attitude toward modest apparel affect the gospel message we have been commanded to communicate?

9. How do we resist the world's standard of beauty and teach modest dress and behavior?

10. Discuss ways to keep extracurricular activities from devouring all our time.

11. In what areas do we need to model for our children the ability to resist peer pressure?

7

Wiring to Grow in Favor with God

He was just a little boy, not much more than a toddler when his parents took him to his new home. He probably understood that his parents loved him very much. He knew they would come to see him from time to time. He probably didn't understand much about this thing called a vow that his mother had made to the Lord. He probably didn't understand why this man called Eli would now be responsible for him.

The Bible doesn't give us any information about how Samuel felt or about how Hannah and Elkanah felt as they left Samuel with Eli. The story in 1 Samuel 1 tells of the man Elkanah and his two wives. Peninnah had children, but Hannah had none, and childlessness was a source of great grief to her. One time while worshiping in Shiloh, Hannah prayed to the Lord and promised that if God would give her a son, she would give that child back to God for all the days of his life.

God answered Hannah's prayer and gave her Samuel. She kept him at home until he was weaned. Then she took him, along with flour, wine, and a three-year-old bull, to the meeting place at Shiloh. After they had worshiped, Samuel stayed with Eli to serve before the Lord (1 Samuel 2:11). Every year when his mother went to Shiloh to worship, she took a new robe she had made for him. Because of Hannah's dedication, Eli asked the Lord to give her more children to take the place of Samuel. God answered that prayer and gave her three sons and two daughters (1 Samuel 2:21).

Although we will not be asked to transfer physical custody of our children to prepare them for the Lord's service, we are to be just as devoted as Hannah was to the spiritual training of our children.

A common fault among engineers is their inability to think long term. Sometimes engineers get so bogged down in the daily parenting challenges that they forget to look at the project as a twenty-year commitment. Engineers tend to forget that at different times in our lives, we are called upon to serve the Lord in different ways. When we were young and single, it was all right to have Bible studies and church activities going every free minute. With just ourselves to consider, the way we used our time didn't have much of an impact on anyone else.

Many young couples serve the Lord with great joy and enthusiasm during the time when they have no children. They accomplish much in the Lord's service. But life changes when children come along. Wise engineers lower the stress level for themselves and their families when they recognize that parenting changes the way we serve the Lord.

Cindy Wants to Serve

Cindy called Anna one Monday morning. "Anna, I just feel so guilty I have to talk to someone! Bob had a good sermon yesterday on serving the Lord with gladness. After listening to his lesson, I feel even more guilty and don't know what to do."

"Cindy, I suspect I know where we're going with this discussion, but help me out. Why are you feeling so guilty?"

"Well, when I see all that you and Mary and Caroline do for the Lord, I feel guilty because I feel like I'm not serving like I should. You take food every time someone is sick. You sing for funerals. You go stay with Elizabeth when she's afraid to spend the night alone. You go to visit folks in the hospital. You've been so good to look after Evelyn since she had to go to the nursing home. You teach a Bible class. I watch you and just feel like I'm not doing anything in the Lord's service!"

Anna replied with a gentle smile in her voice. "I thought I knew where you were going with your question, and I was right. You see, I had this same conversation with an elder's wife about twenty-five years ago. Let me give you an updated version of what Mildred told me. Maybe it will help you deal with what you are feeling.

"Cindy, have you figured out how Mary, Caroline, and I have the time to serve the Lord in the ways you've mentioned?"

"I guess it's because all your children are married or away in college. You don't work outside the home, so you have more time," Cindy replied.

"That's right. You have four children under the age of six, and two of them are in diapers. When Mary, Caroline, and I had little ones at home, we didn't do all the going and doing kinds of service. We stayed home, wiped noses, changed diapers, and cleaned up messes. We read stories, ran through water sprinklers, and cleaned up messes. We played in the mud, chased frogs, and cleaned up messes. We nursed sick kids, did mountains of laundry, and cleaned up messes. We refereed squabbles, spanked little bottoms, and cleaned up messes. We read Bible stories, sang songs, taught memory verses, and cleaned up messes. We cooked a million meals, gave countless baths, and cleaned up messes. We did just what you do all day every day. We were full-time wives and mothers.

"We sometimes felt guilty, too, when we saw the other ladies going and doing. Sometimes we felt a little jealous that we were cooped up at home with little kids when it would have been fun to have the fellowship of our sisters as we worked together for the Lord."

Cindy said, "I love being a stay-at-home mom, but I often feel left out of the fellowship that comes when serving the Lord with the other ladies."

Anna said, "I've 'been there, done that.' I remember how it feels to be home all day with little ones. The most helpful thing Mildred told me, when we had this conversation years ago, was that my children were gifts from God, as well as my new mission field. Mildred reminded me that if I served the Lord well in my own home, there would be three more servants in the Kingdom when my children were grown. Mildred's advice helped me cope with the guilt I was feeling. When I began to see my children as a mission field, I realized I was serving the Lord by training my children."

"I never thought of it from that point of view," Cindy said.

Anna said, "You are serving the Lord very faithfully. You are at worship with your children every time the doors open. You are training them to behave correctly during worship. You make sure that they are learning godly principles every single day.

"Your little Kayla is in my Bible class, and she knows nearly every story before I tell it. She's my Bible time helper because you've done such a good job teaching God's word. I wish all the little ones in my class had the benefit of a mom who teaches diligently.

"You are doing one of the most important jobs in the Kingdom. Keep doing it well and in about twenty years we'll be ready for you and the servants you're training to take over the going-and-doing kinds of ministry. Mary, Caroline, and I will have slowed down tremendously due to age and failing health. We'll be counting on you to take over for us so we can do the less physically demanding jobs. We don't plan to retire but our aging bodies will probably be ready for some of the more sedate jobs in the Lord's service."

Imagine Cindy's relief after hearing Anna's words. Sometimes, we forget that parenting is one of the most important jobs in the Kingdom because we are training the next generation of the Lord's servants. They won't be prepared to live in favor with God if we don't do a good job installing the wiring. For the years that we have rockets on the launch pad, we can serve the Lord with our families, as long as we don't get so busy with the going and doing that we are too tired or too busy to install the wiring.

As with all the other areas we will wire, we will look at the Devil's Diagram and at the Master's Schematics to make sure we have a clear picture in our minds of how to install the wiring.

 ## Devil's Diagram

» It doesn't really matter what you believe, as long as you are a nice person.

» God loves us all. All of us will go to heaven when we die.

» There is no hell.

» Don't worry about religion. One is as good as another.

» If you force kids to go to church, they'll hate it. When they're grown, they can choose.

» If you decide to take your kids to church, let them play during worship.

» Kids can't get anything out of worship.

» Why bother taking kids to church? You'll be worn out when you get home.

» How can you listen in church when you're wrestling little kids?

» God is within us and around us. We don't need a church to worship God.

» Religion is worthless. You don't need an organized religion to talk to God.

» Be your own master. God is too far away to be of any earthly value.

» You decide what's right for you. Don't let some church tell you what to believe.

» As long as your name is on a church membership list somewhere, you have a relationship with God.

» The only reason a church wants you is so it can get your money.

» You're too busy to bother with God right now. Do it later, when you have more time.

» Church is for people who are too weak to make it on their own.

» Church is just a social club with a cross on top of the building.

 ## Master's Schematics

» "Ascribe to the Lord the glory due to His name; worship the Lord in holy array" (Psalm 29:2).

» "God is our refuge and strength, a very present help in trouble. Therefore we will not fear, though the earth should change, and though the mountains slip into the heart of the sea" (Psalm 46:1–2).

» "The fool has said in his heart, 'There is no God'" (Psalm 53:1).

» "When I am afraid, I will put my trust in Thee. In God, whose word I praise, in God I have put my trust; I shall not be afraid. What can mere man do to me?" (Psalm 56:3–4).

» "My soul waits in silence for God only; from Him is my salvation. He only is my rock and my salvation, my stronghold; I shall not be greatly shaken" (Psalm 62:1–2).

» "Blessed be the Lord, who daily bears our burden, the God who is our salvation" (Psalm 68:19).

» "He has fixed a day in which He will judge the world in righteousness through a Man whom He has appointed, having furnished proof to all men by raising Him from the dead" (Acts 17:31).

» "I am the way, and the truth, and the life; no one comes to the Father, but through Me" (John 14:6).

» "If you love Me, you will keep My commandments" (John 14:15).

» "There is one body and one Spirit, just as also you were called in one hope of your calling; one Lord, one faith, one baptism, one God and Father of all who is over all and through all and in all" (Ephesians 4:4–6).

» "And as it is appointed unto men once to die, but after this the judgment: so Christ was once offered to bear the sins of many; and unto them that look for Him shall He appear the second time without sin unto salvation" (Hebrews 9:27–28 KJV).

» "And I saw a great white throne and Him who sat upon it, from whose presence earth and heaven fled away, and no place was found for them. And I saw the dead, the great and the small, standing before the throne, and books were opened; and another book was opened, which is the book of life; and the dead were judged from the things which were written in the books, according to their deeds. And the sea gave up the dead which were in it, and death and Hades gave up the dead which were in them; and they were judged, every one of them according to their deeds. And death and Hades were thrown into the lake of fire. This is the second death, the lake of fire. And if anyone's name was not found written in the book of life, he was thrown into the lake of fire" (Revelation 20:11–15).

Wiring to Grow in Favor with God

It is vitally important that we model complete devotion to the Lord since we, and our children, will spend a few short years on this earth. In eternity we will be either in the presence of the Lord who was worthy of our love and service or forever separated from Him. Because the concept of being separated from His love, His protection, and His blessings is an unbearable thought, we must do what He commands in order to be able to live with Him forever.

Devotion to the Lord is modeled in many ways. Our children need to know that God is not someone we know only on Sundays. He isn't someone we dress up to go see at our convenience. He is the one we walk with daily. He is the one we talk to all throughout the day. He is the one we talk about as we come and go. We recognize His blessings and we thank Him for all He does for us. Every day we open His word to learn about His nature and His wishes for us.

We show our love and devotion to Him in the way we serve one another. Our homes are practice fields where we develop the characteristics God wants us to have as a permanent part of our natures. The more deeply rooted godly characteristics become in our lives, the more effective we will be in doing the main job He has given us—taking the gospel.

Installing the Wiring

When humans form healthy relationships with one another, they find areas of common interest. As they work around their individual likes and dislikes, they become more and more alike.

Selflessness

Horton and Hilda have been married for almost sixty years. Their friends say they look alike, even though there is little physical resemblance. Horton is six-two, 230 pounds of sun-weathered farmer. His large, gnarled, and wrinkled hands haven't lost much of the strength they had when he was running the farm by himself. Hilda is five-two and wouldn't tip the scales at a hundred pounds, dripping wet. Her hair provides a beautiful silver frame for her small face. Horton's hair abandoned him so many years ago that he would be hard-pressed to describe its color and texture. He has a liberal assortment of "age spots" to decorate the top of his head. A favorite game of the grandchildren is to take an ink pen and play "dot to dot" when Horton is reclining in his big chair. They love to see the pictures they can make when they connect the freckles and age spots on Grandpa's head.

Since there is little physical resemblance, why do people say Horton and Hilda look alike? Because their facial expressions and mannerisms cause them to be mirror images of each other. They often finish each other's sentences. They reared six children during the Great Depression. During their sixty years, they've suffered financial hardship, the death of a child, the loss of their parents and siblings, and Hilda's battle with cancer. They've enjoyed times of having a comfortable income, celebrated the birth of twenty grandchildren, and enjoyed the years that Hilda's cancer has been in remission. They've learned to give and take. Hilda learned to fish with Horton, although putting a worm on a hook always did make her feel a bit squeamish. She never really enjoyed spending hours on the lake in the boat, but she took along a book and lovingly spent the time with Horton because it pleased him to have her near while he enjoyed his favorite pastime.

Horton built a quilting frame for Hilda. He spent hours sitting in the spare bedroom reading to her while she worked on quilts for the grandchildren. When she needed a special visual aid for her Bible class, he went to his workshop and created the very thing she needed to make the story come alive for the children.

Because of their love for each other, they often put personal preferences aside to do what would bring joy and contentment to the other. Their love has matured and deepened with the years. The things that caused heated battles in the early years are now the source of family jokes. They can glance at one another and immediately know what the other is thinking. The years and the experiences they shared have blended two individuals into a couple that is truly one in heart and in spirit.

Healthy human relationships grow and mature as we learn to set our own preferences aside to do what is in the best interest of another. That is good practice for living in relationship with God. The ability to renounce all forms of selfishness is the key to a successful relationship with God. Our personal likes and dislikes must be set aside so we can concentrate on what He likes and dislikes.

God's Likes and Dislikes

As we prepare our children to grow in favor with God, we need to examine what God likes and dislikes. We need to know what He wants us to be in order to model for our children the most important relationship we will ever have. We have to be able to model before we can do the wiring installation.

Let's start with the negative side. This list will not be comprehensive but hopefully it will serve as a springboard for your private study of the nature of God.

> "There are six things which the Lord hates, yes, seven which are an abomination to Him: haughty eyes, a lying tongue, and hands that shed innocent blood, a heart that devises wicked plans, feet that run rapidly to evil, a false witness who utters lies, and one who spreads strife among brothers" (Proverbs 6:16–19).

God also detests false worship. When we come before Him, we are to worship the way He dictates, not the way that suits us. The main reason Israel and Judah were sent into captivity was because of their false worship. They did what pleased themselves rather than what God had ordained.

> " 'I hate, I reject your festivals, nor do I delight in your solemn assemblies. Even though you offer up to Me burnt offerings and your grain offerings, I will not accept them; and I will not even look at the peace offerings of your fatlings. Take away from Me the noise of your songs; I will not even listen to the sound of your harps . . . Therefore, I will make you go into exile beyond Damascus,' says the Lord, whose name is the God of hosts" (Amos 5:21–27).

Wiring for Honesty and Integrity

Did you notice how many of the things on God's "hate" list have to do with honesty and integrity? The other things have to do with worship and the way we deal with others. If the integrity-wiring and the worship-wiring are secure, most of the other things God hates will not be a problem in the lives of our rockets.

Wiring the honesty and integrity part of growing in favor with God requires diligent work over several years. As with all other parts of wiring installation, the key is to model honesty and integrity. Start very early introducing these concepts to the children, but be very patient. It takes a while for these to develop fully.

Modeling Honesty

The Chief Engineers model honesty and integrity in many ways. When the phone rings and Dad really doesn't want to talk, Mom doesn't cover by saying, "He's not home. May I take a message?" Mom models honesty by saying in a pleasant tone of voice, "Sam really doesn't want to talk right now. May I take a message?"

> **Many people allow themselves to become abrupt and abrasive in their speech. They use their version of honesty as a cover-up for some very rude behavior.**

If cousin Serena calls to say that she and her three rambunctious children are coming for the week, Dad doesn't have to be rude and say, "I'm sorry, but your kids are brats and we really don't want you to come." A very important part of modeling honesty is modeling the practice of "speaking the truth in love" (Ephesians 4:15). Dad can say, "It is very kind of you to want to spend some time with us. However, it isn't going to work out for you to stay at our house for a week. If you'd like to get a motel in the area, we'd be glad to have you over for supper once or twice while you are in town."

Many people allow themselves to become abrupt and abrasive in their speech. They use their version of honesty as a cover-up for some very rude behavior. The book of James has a lot to say about the proper use of the tongue. Engineers must know that book well and follow those guidelines carefully as we model honest behavior and speech.

Modeling Integrity

Engineers model integrity by the meticulous way they keep promises. If they promise to bring home ice cream, they will bring it. If they promise to be home at 8:00 P.M., they will be there or call to explain why they are delayed. If they promised to feed the neighbor's dog for a week, they will do it without complaining. If Mom promises to let the kids do an art project after supper, she will let them, even if it turns out to be inconvenient.

Imagination vs. Honesty

Honesty and integrity are developed over the years by consistent modeling and by patient teaching. One of the most fascinating and entertaining things about little rockets is that each one comes equipped with a marvelous imagination. If cultivated properly, that imagination can be a source of delight for the family, and it can help a rocket amuse himself for long periods of time. When this little one learns to read, he will go on many wonderful imaginary adventures as he explores different kinds of books. Imagination is the precursor to creativity in later years. Managed properly, it can be a wonderful blessing.

Imagination causes problems for some engineers when they try to wire honesty into a rocket. One thing engineers have to understand is that many children, until they are about five years old, do not know the difference in what happened and what they wish had happened. The difference is not known automatically; it has to be taught.

There are many ways to help a small child use his imagination and still work on honesty.

Building an Honesty Foundation

David is two-and-a-half years old. His mom has to work part-time, so he stays at Aunt Sarah's house while Mom is gone. David is blessed with a really close-knit family. He is dearly loved. The adults in his family talk to him, read to him, and sing to him. Because of that positive interaction with adults, David is above average in his ability to talk. He can sing simple songs. He loves to pretend. When he's at Aunt Sarah's, he often rides his indoor tricycle around in the house. When Aunt Sarah says, "Where are you going?" David will reply, "I'm going to Paw Paw's. I'm rounding up cows." Aunt Sarah will tell him to have a safe trip and to let her know when he gets back.

Aunt Sarah is encouraging a good imagination by "playing along" with whatever David is pretending. When David "comes back" Aunt Sarah will ask, "Did you have a good time at Paw

Paw's?" After David tells her about his trip, then she says, "It's fun to pretend to go see Paw Paw and Maw Maw." By using the word "pretend," she is laying a foundation for honesty. Little by little he will learn which things are "pretend" and which ones are not.

David's maternal grandparents have a cattle ranch in Texas, and he has been there several times in his short life. He knows that Paw Paw always saves some of the more interesting ranch chores until David can be there to help him. Paw Paw calls David his "favorite little cowboy." When David pretends to go see Paw Paw and Maw Maw, he is using a combination of imagination and memory to enjoy being with his family.

When they watch videos or read fairy tales, Aunt Sarah reminds David that these stories are for pretend. Little by little, David is learning that "true" and "pretend" are different.

Another good way Aunt Sarah helps David learn honesty is by reading stories and watching videos. David loves the story in Aunt Sarah's big Bible about David and Goliath. She reads it to him nearly every day. David knows that any story from the Bible is a true story. Every day before they read the Bible, they sing a little song.

> Every word in the Bible is true.
> Every word in the Bible is true.
> I know, I know, I know, I know
> That every word in the Bible is true.

After every Bible story, Aunt Sarah reminds David that it is a true story. Even though David doesn't completely understand what "true" means, Aunt Sarah is laying a very important foundation. When they watch videos or read fairy tales, they talk about the stories, and Aunt Sarah reminds David that these stories are "just pretend." Little by little, David is learning that "true" and "pretend" are very different.

The same idea can be used when discussing Santa Claus, the Easter Bunny, and the Tooth Fairy. Children and engineers can have a wonderful time enjoying the fanfare surrounding those special characters and still understand that they are just pretend.

A just-pretend Santa is important. Otherwise, when a child asks Santa for a huge gift, the parents feel pressured not to disappoint the child. If the child understands that it's a wonderful game of pretend and that Mom and Dad buy the gifts, it helps prevent the urge to put expensive gifts on the credit card and spend the rest of the year paying for them.

Another important way David's family is helping him learn honesty is in the way they support each other in matters of discipline. One day David was at Aunt Sarah's. They were playing outside when David started running toward the street. Aunt Sarah called to him: "Come here!" David laughed at her and continued running. Aunt Sarah caught him and gave him a spanking. After he quit crying and was able to listen, she explained to him that he must never do that again. She made sure he understood why he got in trouble.

An hour later, David's mom came for him. When she asked him about his day, David said, "Aunt Sarah 'panked me."

Mom asked, "Why did Aunt Sarah spank you?"

David said, "I ran to the street. I not come back when Aunt Sarah say 'come back.'" Mom picked David up and said, "Thank you for telling me the truth about what you did. You must always obey Aunt Sarah so she can keep you safe. Go give Aunt Sarah a hug to show her you are sorry you did not obey." By presenting a united front, the adults are modeling integrity.

By the time David is old enough to go to school, he will know the difference between what is true and what is pretend because his family has done a good job teaching him. At that time, he will be old enough to be held to a higher standard. "If you get in trouble at school, you are in trouble when you get home." By the time he's school-age, the wiring will be secure enough to handle a higher standard. Before the age of six, it's better to tread gently while the wiring is being installed.

Teachable Moments

When wiring for honesty and integrity, it's important to watch for "teachable moments." If the clerk gives an engineer too much change, it's a good time to model honesty by politely pointing out the error and returning the extra change. If you are at church and find a quarter on the pew, have one of the children give it to one of the church leaders.

People who are growing in favor with God do not follow the adage, "finders keepers, losers weepers." Rockets need to learn to respect the property of others because it is one of the foundation principles for honest behavior. A good family rule is: "If it doesn't belong to me, I do not touch it without permission."

Respect the property of others because it is one of the foundation principles for honest behavior. A good family rule is: "If it doesn't belong to me, I do not touch it without permission."

By the time a rocket is ready for school, honesty can be taught regarding homework and tests. Each person is to do his or her own work. A parent or teacher can be helpful, but the final responsibility for the work belongs to the student. Do as one wise teacher did. When she was passing out the math tests, she said, "Today each one of you will be taking two tests. One test will be in math; the other will be in honesty. Even if you fail the math test, be sure you pass the honesty test."

Teach your children to do their very best in whatever they do. Don't push for super achiever grades. If a child brings home a bad grade on a report card, he should be in trouble if he got a bad grade because he was goofing off and didn't do his work. He should not be in trouble if he did his very best. We can't all be terrific in every area. Reward effort, not success.

Wiring for Worship

Teaching a child to worship at home is one of the most important ways to wire a child to grow in favor with God. As you go through the day with your child, point out God's blessings and thank Him. Children need to learn that sometimes it's appropriate to fold hands and bow heads to talk to God. They also need to learn that it's fine to do one-liner prayers.

One-Liner Prayers

When Mom takes her toddlers out to play, one of the children notices a pretty butterfly. Mom says, "Thank you, God, for pretty butterflies." Those one-liner prayers throughout the day help our children be aware that God is the source of all good things and that we express our appreciation to Him. It also helps them develop the ability to "pray without ceasing" (1 Thessalonians 5:17 KJV). If they get in the habit of praying one-liners all through the day, they will grow up knowing how to talk to God anytime, anywhere, and under any circumstances.

Many families try to do regular family devotionals. Some are more successful than others.

Family Bible Time

Nick and Natalie had three children: five-year-old Amy, three-year-old Bobby, and two-year-old Roxanna. Natalie had taught children's Bible classes for years. She was very comfortable singing about God as she interacted with the children during the day. Nick and Natalie knew it was important for the children to see Nick taking the lead in spiritual matters, so they came up with this solution: Natalie would continue the teaching she did with the children during the day, but at night, Nick would take the lead.

Each evening, the family remained at the dinner table until everyone finished eating. If little Roxanna became too restless, they let her go play with her toys for a while. When it was Bible time, Roxana came back to the table to sit in Natalie's lap while Nick read a short story from his Bible.

Nick did a bit of skipping, leaving out some details to develop a story line the children could follow. That approach worked well for a year or two, but as the children grew, so did Bible time. Nick started reading a chapter at a time. Roxanna got to choose the book of the Bible Nick read first. When that book was done, Bobby picked a book, then Amy. They followed that progression all the way up through Natalie and Nick. Natalie and Nick kept it easy and picked Ruth or Esther or another book of interest to the children.

By the time the children were all in grade school, the whole family looked forward to evening Bible time. One night they had a planned activity. They ate supper quickly, and Nick read the next chapter from the book of Acts. When he got to the end of the chapter, he instructed his children to get ready for their outing. Roxanna said, "Daddy, you can't stop reading now. We have to know what happened to Paul!" Nick promised to bring his Bible along so Natalie could finish reading to the family while he drove. Nick and Natalie's program was doing what it was designed to do. Their children were learning to be hungry for the word of God. They were growing in favor with God.

Rewards of Family Bible Time

Learning to worship does begin at home, and if engineers are diligent, worship will be a time the family learns to enjoy. Besides drawing closer to God and to each other, it gives tremendous security in times of crisis. For years, Nick made it a point to join each child at bedtime. He sat on the side of each bed and offered a short prayer. As the children grew older, that prayer time became more special. The children knew they could share their concerns and Dad would pray with them.

At church one Sunday, an announcement was made that Holly and June, on their way back to college, had been in a bad accident. During worship, several prayers were offered on their behalf. Holly and June were special to Nick, Natalie, and their children because both of them had been baby sitters for the children. Shortly after lunch that day, an elder called Nick and Natalie with the news that June had died and Holly was in intensive care.

Because this family was accustomed to worshiping together, it was very natural to turn to God with this terrible heartache. Natalie and the children were all in tears. Nick gathered his family close. He wrapped his arms around them as he talked to God. Not only did his prayer and the physical closeness give comfort to his family, but he also taught by example that in a crisis, the first response is to talk to God.

Families that grow in favor with God at home have a much easier time training children to worship when it is time to assemble with other Christians.

Wiring for the Worship Assembly

Wiring a child for public worship is a very important task, if he is to grow in favor with God. Organization is necessary so the family will not be frazzled and frustrated when it is time to go to Bible class or worship. Modeling is also important.

Make it a priority to meet with the brethren every time they assemble. If there is a vacation Bible school or a gospel meeting, make sure you and your children are there. That type of modeling doesn't teach legalism if it's done with the right attitude. Teach your children what a treat it is to go to worship. "I was glad when they said to me, 'Let us go to the house of the Lord'" (Psalm 122:1).

Prepare Sunday clothes and shoes on Saturday night. Make sure all the Bibles and money for contribution are by the door. Make sure Bible class homework is done and memory verses have been learned.

A rushed and frazzled family will not worship well. Sing as you dress for worship. Prepare your minds for worship by listening to gospel singing.

Get to bed on time. Set the alarms to get up on time. Teach children that worship is top priority and that the family must prepare for worship. When children become old enough to attend sleepovers, allow sleepovers only on Friday night. Set aside Saturday night as the time to prepare for worship. Get up on Sunday in time to have breakfast. A hungry, out-of-sorts child is not going to be a joy in Bible class or in worship. A rushed and frazzled family will not worship well. Sing as you dress for worship. Prepare your minds for worship by listening to gospel singing.

Ages and Stages—In the Worship Assembly

Here are some suggestions to help with the wiring of your rocket. Each rocket is different and will need individual wiring for the worship assembly. Many parents bring books and toys for small children. For some children, that works very well. For others, it creates discipline problems.

Kevin Learns Quiet Play

Tom was serving at the Lord's table, so Elaine was on her own with three little ones. Her daughters, three-year-old Katie and five-year-old Konnie, knew how to behave during worship. Elaine had a couple of books in her bag to amuse eighteen-month-old Kevin. Kevin pulled out the book on animals and promptly started mooing like the cow and barking like the dog. Elaine tried unsuccessfully to get him to be quiet. She took the book away from him and he started screaming. She had to carry a screaming Kevin out the door while making sure Katie and Konnie were right behind her. Elaine spanked Kevin, hid the books, and returned to worship. On the way home, Tom and Elaine discussed the incident.

Here is what they decided. From Kevin's point of view, his behavior made sense. At home when they read that book, Elaine always encouraged Kevin to say the name of each animal and imitate the sound each animal makes. It was hard for Kevin to understand that he was supposed to look at the book quietly when he was "reading" during worship. Tom and Elaine decided that Kevin would be better off without books and toys during worship. He learned that he could play quietly with his dad's tie or with his mom's watch, but he was not allowed to "read" or have toys during worship because he wanted to interact with them.

Babies

Consider quiet toys, a bottle, and a pacifier for babies less than a year. If she starts "talking," rub her back quietly. Whisper and encourage her to be quiet. You might need to stand in the foyer with her at times. That's all right. Try to stay in a separate place where you can participate in worship. Don't give in to the temptation to visit with other parents in the same situation. Set an example of worship, even under difficult circumstances.

Toddlers

Help your toddler sit on the pew or in your lap. Bring one or two quiet toys or books and a quiet snack. Do not entertain him. Train him early that the assembly is for worship. Little legs need to be stretched. Let him stand quietly on the floor beside you if he is not disturbing others. Encourage him to sing when it's singing time. Have him bow his head during the prayers. Give him some money, just before the collection plate arrives and let him participate in the contribution.

Twos and Threes

Take her to the restroom before worship. Get a drink before worship. Give her a little snack between Bible class and worship. Do not train her to need to go potty three times during the sermon. Toys and books stay at home. Have your child sit quietly on the pew or in your lap during worship. Do not entertain her. The church assembles for worship. Encourage her to sing at appropriate times. Reward good behavior. Quietly explain the importance of different parts of the assembly. Encourage participation.

Fours and Fives

The child should hold his song book and sing with the congregation. He should be able to sit quietly with his head bowed during the prayer. He should sit quietly during the Lord's supper. Teach him to take "notes" during the sermon. Write "God," "Jesus," and "Bible" on a page of a notebook. Have him make a mark every time the preacher says one of those words. At the end of the sermon, count the number of times the preacher said each word. This activity promotes good listening skills and encourages involvement in the longest portion of worship. On the way home, ask questions about the sermon. Praise good listeners. Worship is God's time. Honor it.

Managing Discipline Problems During Worship

Parental Opposition

The biggest obstacle to training may very well be opposition from other parents who think you are being much too hard on your children.

Natasha's Broken Promise

When Natasha was five, she begged her parents to let her sit with friends during worship. Natasha's mom, Stephanie, said, "You can sit with Heather and Caitlin, but you must remember that we are here to worship God. I expect you to sit in the pew and sing when it's time to sing. I expect you to listen when it's time to listen. Can I count on you to obey our rules for worship?"

Natasha was excited. "I can do it, Mom. I promise." So Natasha went to sit with her friends. Ed and Stephanie, with their other two children, sat a couple of rows behind them with Natasha and her friends in full view.

Caitlin's parents were on one side of the children and Heather's parents were on the other side. The four adults were aware of the three little girls and what they were doing, but none of them saw a problem with the behavior. Heather, Natasha, and Caitlin were down on their knees in front of the pew. They had their coloring books spread out and were happily whispering and giggling as they passed crayons back and forth. The girls, in a world of their own, were completely ignoring the main reason for the assembly.

Even if every other child in the congregation was allowed to behave that way during worship, Natasha knew better. Stephanie went down the side aisle to remove Natasha from the group of gigglers. When she motioned for Natasha to "come here," the other four parents glared at her. They had no clue why she would remove Natasha from that situation. They felt that Stephanie was insulting their parenting skills.

Stephanie took Natasha out a side door and found privacy in an empty classroom. "Natasha, you broke your promise to me," Stephanie said firmly. "You promised me that you could obey our rules for worship. Not only did you disobey me, you disobeyed God. God expects our full attention and our respect when we come to worship. Do you think that it was respectful to play and whisper and giggle during the time that we were supposed to be praising God in song?"

Natasha hung her little head. "No, ma'am."

Stephanie continued: "Back in the days of Moses, when God's people came together to hear the law being read, they stood in the presence of the Lord. Since you were not able to sit in the presence of the Lord and show your respect, you and I will find a place where we can see and hear but won't disturb others. We will stand at attention in the presence of the Lord until the end of the worship assembly this morning."

Stephanie found a private place at the back of the auditorium. They stood there during the remainder of worship. Never again did Natasha's parents have to remove her from the assembly.

Ed and Stephanie found one other couple in the congregation who believed in training children to worship. Those two families let their children sit together during worship, and the parents enforced the rules for proper behavior. These wise engineers understood that training starts early. If the wiring for worship was to be done correctly, it couldn't wait until the children were old enough to "get something out of worship." Worship is our gift to God, not an entertainment opportunity.

Inconsistency

Another obstacle to managing problem behavior during worship is inconsistency. Children who do not obey at home will not miraculously obey during worship. Very few children learn to worship without challenging the rules. When a little rocket challenges the engineer's authority to set the rules, the response should be very predictable, whether that challenge occurs at home, at an elegant restaurant, in the grocery store, or in the worship assembly.

The prime training time is between fourteen and thirty-six months. It's the time when a little one learns, "I can sit in Daddy's lap during church and be good, or I can go outside with Daddy and get a spanking. It's my choice."

Engineers err in judgment when they are afraid to handle disobedience that occurs during worship. The theory is, "I don't want my child to hate coming to worship." Does your child hate going to the discount store because he got a spanking for having a temper tantrum in the checkout line? Is he afraid of an elegant restaurant because Mom took him to the bathroom and spanked him for telling the waiter to shut up? A very important part of securing the wiring is to eliminate any penalty-free zones. Wherever he is, whatever the situation, he is to be obedient and respectful.

Wiring for worship takes time, patience, consistency, and diligence. Worship training is much easier in two-parent families who worship together. If an engineer is on her own with the children, it can still be done. Try to "adopt" an older couple as pew parents or pew grandparents. Go over the rules so all the adults are in agreement. If you have to take one child out, the other adults can care for the ones who are behaving well.

Inspecting the Wiring

If the wiring for growing in favor with God is being properly installed, here are some things your child will know by the time he is five.

1. The Bible has two big parts—the Old Testament and the New Testament.

2. The names of all the books in the Bible.

3. God's love and constant care for him.

4. At least fifty basic Bible stories.

5. Some information about Adam, Enoch, Noah, Abraham, Jacob, Joseph, Moses, David, Elijah, Elisha, Ruth, Esther, Deborah, Samson, Jesus, Mary, Martha, Lazarus, Peter, Dorcas, and Paul.

6. Several verses he can quote from memory.

7. God's plan of salvation:

   Hear the word of God (Romans 10:17)
   Believe and obey the word of God (Mark 16:16; John 14:15)
   Repent (Luke 13:3; Acts 3:19)
   Confess that Jesus is the Son of God (Matthew 10:32–33)
   Be baptized into Christ (Matthew 28:18–20)
   Be faithful unto death (Revelation 2:10)

In homes where children are well-wired, questions about baptism will come up fairly early.

Jeremy Learns about Baptism

Jason and Amy were doing an excellent job securing the wiring of the four little rockets entrusted to them. One day, six-year-old Jeremy asked, "Daddy, can I be baptized?

Jason asked, "Why do you want to be baptized, son?"

"Because I know I need to hear the word of God, believe it with all my heart, repent of my sins, confess that Jesus is the Son of God, and be baptized to take my sins away."

"I am so proud of you for knowing what you need to do to become a Christian," Jason complimented. "In a few years, you will be ready to follow through on the things you know you need to do. For right now, you are completely safe. Do you know why?"

"No, sir."

"God has given Daddy and Mommy a very important job. For the years you live with us, God expects us to be teaching you about God. We are supposed to teach you what God expects of His people. We are to prepare you to walk faithfully before God all the days of your life. You are off to a really good start and we are proud of you.

"Right now, you are still learning about right and wrong. If you do something wrong, you answer to me or to Mommy. In a few years, you'll do something wrong and you'll feel terrible about it. You won't feel bad because you are afraid I'll find out and you'll get a spanking. You'll be upset because you will know that you sinned against God. You will want to make things right with God. When that time comes, you come and tell me about it, and we will talk more about being baptized. For now, Mommy and I are responsible for your behavior and God expects us to spend a few more years helping you get ready for the time when you are old enough to be accountable to God."

"How old do I have to be before I'm accountable to God?" Jeremy asked.

"The Bible doesn't tell us the answer to that question. Most children have to be at least eleven years old before they really understand what it means to be accountable to God. Even when you're accountable, Mommy and I will still be responsible for teaching you and helping you do the right thing."

In a home where children are being wired to grow in favor with God, similar discussions will come up from time to time. Wise engineers think through those situations ahead of time so they will be prepared for those discussions.

When guiding a child toward becoming a Christian, several things need to be considered. A child must have a loving, respectful, obedient relationship with his parents before he can have a worshipful, loving, obedient relationship with God. A young person must also be mature enough to understand the concept of eternity and the idea of a lifetime commitment.

For a small child, eternity is how long it is from Thanksgiving to Christmas. An older child has a better handle on time, eternity, and the consequences for his behavior. An older child is in a better position to make the most important decision a person can make.

We started this chapter by discussing the things God hates so that we could properly install the wiring to grow in favor with God. The Bible is full of good characteristics that God wants us to wire into the rockets entrusted to us. Most of those good characteristics relate to how we show our love to God by loving our fellow man. They will be discussed in the next chapter. We will close this chapter with a list of memory verses for Mom and Dad that need to be wired firmly into little rockets during the first five years. Even if the rocket doesn't fully understand each one, hiding God's word inside is one of the most important ways to secure the wiring. It will serve him well for a lifetime.

Memory Verses for the Engineers

» "He has told you, O man, what is good; and what does the Lord require of you but to do justice, to love kindness, and to walk humbly with your God?" (Micah 6:8).

» "But an hour is coming, and now is, when the true worshipers shall worship the Father in spirit and truth; for such people the Father seeks to be His worshipers" (John 4:23).

Preschool Memory Verses

» "Children, obey your parents in the Lord, for this is right" (Ephesians 6:1).

» "Be kind to one another" (Ephesians 4:32).

» "In the beginning God created the heavens and the earth" (Genesis 1:1).

» "You shall not steal, nor deal falsely, nor lie to one another" (Leviticus 19:11).

» "And you shall love the Lord your God with all your heart and with all your soul and with all your might" (Deuteronomy 6:5).

» "Thy word I have treasured in my heart, that I may not sin against Thee" (Psalm 119:11).

» "Teach me good discernment and knowledge, for I believe in Thy commandments" (Psalm 119:66).

» "The Lord is my helper, I will not be afraid" (Hebrews 13:6).

» "It is by his deeds that a lad distinguishes himself if his conduct is pure and right" (Proverbs 20:11).

Drill for Skills

Making Connections

1. We are to be just as dedicated as _____ was to making sure our children are trained to be the Lord's servants.

2. _____ is one of the most important jobs in the Kingdom.

3. Strong relationships are formed when we set aside our preferences to do what is in the _____ _____ of another.

4. The ability to renounce all forms of _____ is the key to a successful relationship with God.

5. Worship is our gift to God, not an _____ opportunity.

Troubleshooting

1. How does parenting change the way we serve the Lord?

2. Why is good parenting such a valuable job in the Lord's service?

3. What are some ways we model complete devotion to the Lord?

4. Why is it important to model unswerving devotion to God?

5. Why is it necessary to put our own preferences aside and concentrate on obedience to God's commands?

6. What is the most important relationship that we will ever have?

7. How does an engineer appreciate a child's vivid imagination and still wire for honesty and integrity?

8. In what way is respect for the property of others a foundation principle for honesty and integrity?

9. Discuss some ways to prepare a child for a daily relationship with God.

10. How can daily devotionals create a hunger for the word of God?

11. How does a strong relationship with God prepare a family to handle a crisis?

12. How does worship at home prepare a family for the worship assemblies at the church building?

13. What is the most difficult aspect of behavior management for you to handle during worship?

8

Wiring to Grow in Favor with Man

Shallow Kendra

Kendra was a social butterfly. She was pretty, poised, and confident, flitting from friendship to friendship in the blink of an eye. Mrs. Jones, Kendra's third-grade teacher, loved Kendra, but sometimes she worried about her and those left in her wake. Moreover, Mrs. Jones was especially concerned about the powerful influence Kendra wielded over her peers. Kendra had a first best friend, a second best friend, and a third best friend. Those friendships changed from week to week as the other children in the class did what they could to be on Kendra's best-friend list.

Mrs. Jones was ill at ease with the methods Kendra employed to maintain her popularity. Kendra had surface-level friendliness, but deep down she was very selfish. She was often unkind to the other children. She always wore the latest fashions and had the most sought-after toys; she looked down her nose at those who were not so fortunate. Mrs. Jones insisted on kindness and respect in her classroom, but she knew that Kendra said hurtful things to the less fortunate when the teacher was not around.

Kendra was popular, but she was not being wired to grow in favor with man. There is a huge difference between the worldly view of popularity and being in favor with man.

In the Scriptures we have two references to growing in favor with man.

» "Now the boy Samuel was growing in stature and in favor both with the Lord and with men" (1 Samuel 2:26).

» "And Jesus kept increasing in wisdom and stature, and in favor with God and men" (Luke 2:52).

Any engineer who has studied the Scriptures knows that Samuel was loved and appreciated, but we have no evidence that he was in favor with all men at all times. Even a casual reading of the life of Christ shows He was well loved by those He helped and by many He taught. On the other hand, some hated Him and sought to have Him put to death. If the Son of God was not in favor with all men at all times, then we can hardly expect to be. Growing in favor with men is much deeper than an attempt to be liked by everyone.

God's "To Do" List

If engineers are to be successful in wiring this characteristic into our young rockets, we must have a strong grasp of what it means to grow in favor with man. God has given many lists in the Bible of things that are good and things that are evil. He didn't give long "to do" lists for His children. If we had to put God's "to do" list in writing, it would look something like this:

» Teach and make disciples (Matthew 28:18–20; Mark 16:15–16).

» Do good to all men, especially fellow Christians (Galatians 6:10).

» Do every job as if you were doing it for the Lord (Colossians 3:23).

» Study so you can do the job the Lord assigned (2 Timothy 2:15).

» Learn to worship God and do it well (John 4:23–24).

» Imitate God. Live a life of love (Ephesians 5:1–2).

It is important to have in our minds the things that are important to God. As we stated in our last chapter, setting aside our own preferences and accepting His is the basis for living in relationship with God. There is a lot of overlap between growing in favor with God and growing in favor with man. As we wire our rockets to grow in favor with man, we must do it in a way that keeps them in favor with God.

As engineers, we must model the ability to grow in favor with man, but we must do it with God's priorities firmly in mind. Let's take a look at

Devil's Diagram

>> Truth is whatever you want it to be at the moment.

>> There are no absolutes.

>> If it's right for you, it's right.

>> Look out for number one!

>> Be your own master.

>> If you hurt someone, they'll get over it.

>> Whatever!

>> Say what you think people want to hear. Don't worry if it's not true.

>> Listen to gossip. That information may be handy if you want to manipulate a situation.

>> People are tools to be used.

>> Make friends only with people who will raise your social status.

>> Friendships are expendable. If someone loses status, dump him.

 ## Master's Schematics

>> "So then, while we have opportunity, let us do good to all men, and especially to those who are of the household of the faith" (Galatians 6:10).

>> "Do not love the world, nor the things in the world. If anyone loves the world, the love of the Father is not in him" (1 John 2:15).

>> "Little children, let us not love with word or with tongue, but in deed and truth" (1 John 3:18).

>> "If someone says, 'I love God,' and hates his brother, he is a liar; for the one who does not love his brother whom he has seen, cannot love God whom he has not seen. And this commandment we have from Him, that the one who loves God should love his brother also" (1 John 4:20–21).

» "It is by his deeds that a lad distinguishes himself if his conduct is pure and right" (Proverbs 20:11).

» "And I say to you, that every careless word that men shall speak, they shall render account for it in the day of judgment. For by your words you shall be justified, and by your words you shall be condemned" (Matthew 12:36–37).

» "You are the salt of the earth" (Matthew 5:13).

» "You are the light of the world" (Matthew 5:14).

» "Let your light so shine before men, that they may see your good works, and glorify your Father which is in heaven" (Matthew 5:16 KJV).

» "A new commandment I give to you, that you love one another, even as I have loved you, that you also love one another. By this all men will know that you are My disciples, if you have love for one another" (John 13:34–35).

» "And so, as those who have been chosen of God, holy and beloved, put on a heart of compassion, kindness, humility, gentleness, and patience; bearing with one another, and forgiving each other, whoever has a complaint against anyone; just as the Lord forgave you, so also should you. And beyond all these things put on love, which is the perfect bond of unity" (Colossians 3:12–14).

» "But sanctify Christ as Lord in your hearts, always being ready to make a defense to everyone who asks you to give an account for the hope that is in you, yet with gentleness and reverence" (1 Peter 3:15).

Modeling and Wiring

As we wire our rockets, we must carefully model the ability to live in favor with man. We will need to model good people-skills in the areas of wisdom, love, kindness, and communication. We have to teach our rockets how to live in the world without being of the world. We have to model for them how to use the godly characteristics being developed. Those characteristics in our lives stand out because they are so different from what is seen in worldly people. Godly character honors our Father and helps attract people to Him. The forming of relationships prompts outsiders to ask questions and gives us an opportunity to share the gospel.

We must teach our children to be mission-minded. The main job on God's "to do" list is for His children to take the gospel to others. We need to wire our rockets to look beyond surface friendships. We need to teach them that everyone with whom we have a relationship is a soul that God longs to save. Our influence, our friendship, and our teaching may be the only opportunity that person has to come to Jesus. That is why we must wisely model the right way to deal with people.

Wiring our rockets to grow in favor with man takes a long time; mistakes come with the territory. Engineers must model how to own up to mistakes, clean up the messes, and move on a little wiser. It is also an area where engineers will need to take the time to teach good thinking skills. It is time-consuming but it is necessary. Children need to be taught to weigh the pros and cons when a decision must be made, so they can make wise choices.

Installing the Wiring

Installing the wiring to grow in favor with man is probably the trickiest and the most time-consuming job for engineers. It requires a great deal of wisdom and patience to secure this wiring. There are three critical questions to consider as we wire our rockets to deal wisely with people.

» How can I set boundaries wisely?

» What is the loving thing to do in this situation?

» What is in the best interest of the person with whom I am dealing?

Remember that the launch pad is the training ground for all human relationships. Home is the place where we can relax and be ourselves. However, we must make sure that even in our most relaxed moments, we are still honoring and obeying our heavenly Father.

Home is the place where rockets learn and practice people skills. Many engineers allow their little rockets to fuss, fight, argue, and treat each other hatefully. One reason is that engineers sometimes allow fatigue to overrule their responsibility to require and enforce better behavior. Others contend that fighting with siblings teaches children to stand up for themselves. Wise engineers use relationships between siblings as a practice field for dealing with those outside the family. Learning godly relationships with siblings and parents will help a child deal wisely with people in the world.

Learning to Set Healthy Boundaries

As children develop good people-skills, they must learn to set boundaries. Engineers must teach their rockets how to assess situations and set boundaries. Many of those teachable moments occur after a mistake has been made. Many engineers get frustrated by the mistakes their rockets make and respond too harshly. That is a communication killer. If a rocket knows an engineer will explode in anger, he is not apt to be forthcoming with the details of a mistake. Ignorance of boundaries is not deliberate disobedience and should not be handled sternly. Engineers must recognize that most mistakes of this kind are caused by a lack of experience. The only way to get experience is to mess up, back off, and try again. Respond to such mistakes with patient teaching.

Start early by establishing physical boundaries. Then the foundation will be there when it is time to move from the concept of physical boundaries to the abstract concepts of emotional boundaries and boundaries in service.

John Learns about Boundaries

Cindy and her two-year-old son John are sitting on the floor playing with blocks. Cindy builds a tower and John knocks it down.

Cindy says, "John, that was my tower. I didn't want you to knock it down. Next time, ask me before you knock down what I built."

In reality, Cindy doesn't care if John knocks down her blocks. Since John is an only child, it is up to Cindy to teach him how another child would feel about having his space invaded. Cindy is laying the groundwork for healthy boundaries by giving John physical boundaries.

When John and Cindy play blocks together, she plays in her space and has him play in his space. She asks before reaching over into his space to get a block. He has to ask her when he wants to reach into her space to get a block. It will take John a while to learn this behavior because he is immature and impulsive. Cindy patiently teaches him.

Remember that a child cannot understand "thine" until he understands "mine." If a child has a sense of ownership and if he is learning to take good care of his things, he will have a strong foundation for good stewardship. Learning to respect another person's things and space and learning to protect his own things and space are good ways to lay a foundation for emotional boundaries. Small children understand concrete ideas, not abstract ones. Using concrete examples, as Cindy does with John, will lay the foundation for setting appropriate time and emotion boundaries when a rocket reaches that stage of development.

Here is a good family rule: "If it doesn't belong to me, I don't touch it without permission." This rule establishes physical boundaries. If it is enforced, children will learn to ask for permission to use a sibling's possessions, a courtesy that will eliminate a lot of squabbles. Each child should have a few special things he does not have to share. The things to be shared stay in the sharing domain, as long as the person borrowing an item takes good care of it. If the borrower is irresponsible, he loses the privilege of borrowing for a while.

Personal Space

Modeling and teaching about physical boundaries is the conduit that will support the wiring when knowledge of physical space does matter.

Children do have to learn how to protect their bodies and other things of value. Most engineers are familiar with the concept of personal space. We all have an area around our bodies that is our personal space. We usually allow our mates and our children to come all the way into that space. When interacting with others, we all have a certain space we like to keep between ourselves and them. That distance varies from person to person. People who hug and touch other people easily usually have a small personal space. A shy person usually prefers to have more space between himself and another person. Personal space can vary depending on the circumstances.

Adults adjust the size of personal space from situation to situation almost automatically. For instance, if you are sitting on a pew at church with your best friend, you will probably sit fairly close together, but if you are sitting with a person you do not know, you will probably not sit very close. You may hug your best friend, but you probably will not hug the person you just met.

An engineer has years of experience with personal space. A rocket does not have those years of experience. He adjusts personal space more on the mood at the moment. He gains experience and confidence with time. Because of his inexperience, it is important to teach a child that you respect his space. Encourage him to speak politely to others, but do not require him to make physical contact with other people. The exception would be if a child has hurt someone he is quite comfortable touching. Then it's all right to require an "I'm sorry" hug. Otherwise, affection should be given to people at the times and under the circumstances that a child chooses to give it.

Grandma Invades Kenneth's Space

Gloria hasn't visited her daughter, son-in-law, and grandson in more than a year. She can hardly wait to see them. Two-year-old Kenneth and Mom have talked a lot about Grandma, and Grandma has sent him gifts by mail. He has seen her picture. He picks up on his parents' excitement; he is glad she is coming. When Grandma arrives, Jana and Rick welcome her with open arms. She brings with her a year full of hugs and kisses she has saved for this special little boy. Kenneth does not remember this lady that is in his house. His words may have indicated excitement about Grandma, but the reality is that he doesn't know her. He hides behind Mom and cries when she tries to force him to give Grandma a big hug. From the actions of the adults, Kenneth thinks he has done something bad because he doesn't want to hug this stranger. Grandma acts like her feelings are hurt because he doesn't love her.

The engineers in this example put Kenneth in a situation he has neither the experience nor the verbal skills to handle. Kenneth knew what he was feeling. He was feeling a little shy. He wanted to have some time to study this lady called "Grandma" before deciding whether or not to let her inside his space.

The engineers in this situation have installed some very faulty wiring that could endanger Kenneth. If they continue to use the same behavior in similar situations, they are sabotaging the wisdom-wiring that was designed to protect Kenneth.

Being nagged, prodded, and pressured into giving a reluctant hug teaches Kenneth that adults do not have to respect his space or his feelings. If he knows from past experience that he has to override his feelings and give hugs and kisses on demand, he may put himself in serious danger when the appropriate response is to choose safety over politeness.

God gave us instincts for our protection. Wise engineers teach a child to "trust your gut." If your tummy is telling you this isn't a good idea, err on the side of safety and do what you can to get out of the situation.

Engineers need to model respect for a child's personal space, just as they expect the child to respect the space of others. The situation with Gloria and her family should have been handled differently. Here is an example.

Grandma Respects Kenneth's Space

Rick and Jana meet Gloria at the door and are thrilled to see her. For the first few seconds, everyone is talking at once. Gloria enters the kitchen and sees little Kenneth standing by the refrigerator.

She quietly says, "Kenneth, I'm your grandma and I'm glad to see you. I brought a present for you. I'm going to put it over here by your chair and you can open it when you want to."

As Kenneth approaches the table to get his gift, Grandma sits down in a chair on the other side of the table. He can see her, but she isn't in touching distance. As he struggles with the gift, she says, "If you need some help, Grandma can help you or Mommy and Daddy can help you."

Kenneth takes the present to Mommy and lets her help him. Mommy says, "What are the nice words we need to tell Grandma?"

"Thank you," comes the shy reply.

"You're welcome," Grandma says. "In my Grandma Bag, I brought some books that you might like. When you want to, I will read with you. I'll put my bag on the floor so you can have the books when you want them."

Gloria sets her Grandma Bag on the floor beside her chair. Kenneth is now used to having Grandma in the room with him. He knows that Mommy and Daddy like her. He is brave enough to go sit on the floor and start taking books out of the bag. Gloria makes no attempt to touch him. As she visits with Rick and Jana, Kenneth gets a little more comfortable. He gets used to the sound of her voice. In a few minutes, he finds a book and puts it in Grandma's lap. She quietly picks it up and reads it to him while he leans against her. At the end of the book Grandma says, "Would you like to sit up here with me and read it again?" Kenneth reaches up and is happy to have Grandma hold him and read the book again.

All Kenneth had needed was a little time and a little space. Wise engineers take their cues from children when it comes to sharing physical space. Paying attention to a child is part of modeling respect for the boundaries a child has set.

Using Words for Boundary Protection

Children also have to be taught to respect the other's boundaries. It is easier for them to respect boundaries set by adults. Respecting boundaries set by other children is a little tougher, but it is important to the development of good people skills.

Brothers' Boundaries

Six-year-old Henry is an extrovert, and his brother Randy, five, is an introvert. Henry is like his dad; he likes to roughhouse. He is usually loud and boisterous. Randy is quiet. He loves books and likes to play by himself. He is very creative and spends a lot of time with his building set.

Henry loves surprises; Randy doesn't. Henry loves to sneak up behind Randy and tackle him. He likes to wrestle with Randy. Randy doesn't mind wrestling from time to time, but he doesn't like the sneak attacks. Randy doesn't put thoughts into words very well, so he uses his fists to express his displeasure when Henry tackles him. That usually escalates into a knock-down-drag-out fight with both boys getting into trouble.

Mom and Dad observed and discussed the situation. They sat down with the boys for a family meeting. Dad explained the concept of boundaries to the boys. He explained that he and Henry have pretty small personal-space boundaries. They don't mind being tackled and tickled and touched. Dad also explained that Mom and Randy have larger personal-space boundaries. He explained that personal-space boundaries come in different sizes and each person is allowed to define his own space. Dad explained the ground rules for respecting the space of each person in the house. Dad stated that he and Henry would quit teasing Mom by sneaking up on her. They did it to tease her, but Dad knew she didn't like it. Dad explained that it isn't a "good game" unless everyone involved is enjoying it.

Mom and Dad taught Randy that he could use his words to protect his space. Randy should tell Henry: "I don't like people to sneak up on me." Dad took some of the blame for the problem.

"Henry and I enjoy that game so much that sometimes I forget you don't," Dad explained to Randy. "So when I sneak up on you, instead of this game being fun, you become upset and I wind up apologizing. I like to wrestle with both of you, so any time Henry and I are wrestling and you want to join in, you are welcome. And if you want to wrestle me one on one, all you have to do is ask."

Dad then explained to Henry that he was to respect the boundary that Randy sets. Henry is welcome to sneak up on Dad and tackle him, but he is not to sneak up on Randy. Henry can ask Randy to wrestle and, if Randy agrees, they are welcome to have a free-for-all in the big open space in the den. When either calls "Stop!" the wrestling is to stop immediately.

"By the same token, Randy," Dad continued, "you must respect your brother's boundary. When Henry is not around, do not 'borrow' Henry's things to add to your latest construction project. That makes Henry angry. You must respect his boundary by waiting to get permission to borrow his things."

This strategy, with parental enforcement as necessary, will help the boys learn that their boundaries are set in different places. They must learn to respect another person's boundary, even if it isn't the one they would have set under similar conditions.

Children should be taught to use their words to protect their space. Teach them that if words aren't getting the job done, they are allowed to call in some parental power to enforce the boundary. If they are in danger, they are allowed to use physical force to protect themselves.

Boundaries in Service

One of the most valuable things we can do within our families is to learn to serve the Lord together. We grow in favor with man by being representatives of God's love. We show our love for God in the way we serve other people. There are many going-and-doing types of service that will have to wait until the rockets have been launched. Engineers should not feel guilty for letting others in the Kingdom do those things while they devote themselves to the wiring project. It is one way engineers model healthy boundary-setting.

Even though many of the going-and-doing things will need to wait, there are many ways families can serve together. The key is to do it together. When it's "work day" at the church building, the whole family can go. Creative adults can usually find jobs that allow even the toddlers to be good helpers. Rather than letting the kids run aimlessly through the building, involve them in the jobs to be done. They won't be very efficient at first, but if their efforts are acknowledged and appreciated, it won't be long before they are genuinely helpful. Serving together is an important way to connect children to the church family and help ensure their faithfulness as adults.

There are many ways children can learn to serve. Children love to make things for other people. A two-year-old can "color a pretty picture" to send as a "thank you" card. Childish works of art can be sent in the mail to brighten the day of someone who is sick or bereaved.

Mom Encourages an "Artist"

Belinda and her three-year-old Kristin worked for a couple of hours each morning at the church building while Karen's older sister was in kindergarten. Belinda worked on the Bible correspondence program with brother Sanders. Kristin had a little desk beside her mom's. Kristin played with her dolls until it was time to do stamps. Her job was to put stamps on the envelopes to tell people about Jesus. She took her job very seriously. During the year as they worked in the program, Belinda and Kristin often prayed for brother Sanders and his family; his mom was old and very sick.

Belinda's family was transferred out of state. They still got the church bulletin from the congregation, and one day the expected announcement came. Brother Sanders' mother had passed away. Belinda told Kristin about it and they prayed for brother Sanders. After they had prayed, Kristin disappeared for a few minutes. When she came back, she was carrying a picture of a horse that she had drawn. She told Belinda that it was for brother Sanders to "help him not be so sad that his mommy had died." Belinda sent the picture to brother Sanders along with a note stating that Kristin had drawn it for him to help him not be so sad. In a few days, Kristin got a letter from brother Sanders. He told her that of all the cards he had received, hers was the one he appreciated the most because it came from the heart of a little one. He assured her that her pretty picture was hanging on the wall in his office and that it was helping him feel better and not be so sad.

Another way engineers can teach children to serve is by connecting prayer to service. It is one thing to pray for people. It is another to look for ways to serve and encourage those for whom we have prayed.

Carolyn's Prayer Poster

Carolyn put a big posterboard with a rainbow at the top on the wall of her kitchen. Beneath the rainbow were the words: "God Is Answering Our Prayers." Carolyn and her children wrote the names of people who were sick or who needed encouragement on little cloud-shaped pieces of paper. Each day, Carolyn and the children prayed for each of those people. When God answered a prayer, one of the children would put the cloud with that prayer request on the poster. In a year's time, that poster was covered with little clouds.

One evening, an elder and his wife came for supper. They saw the poster on the wall and went to look at it. The elder turned to Carolyn with tears in his eyes. He told her how much it meant to him to know that her children were praying every day when his father was so ill. He also told her how much he appreciated the pretty pictures the children had colored and sent to him when he was mourning the loss of his dad.

Opportunities for Small Hearts

Because stay-at-home mothers have more flexibility in their sched-ules, they have excellent opportunities to help their children learn to serve the Lord. They can minister together when one of the ladies at church or in the neighborhood has a baby. They can share their living space with the children from the other family while Mom is in the hospital.

Children can help prepare a meal for someone who is ill or bereaved. They can also make cookies and cards of encouragement for each of the church leaders or for the Bible class teachers.

Children younger than twelve should not visit hospitals and should visit nursing homes cautiously. Staph infections are easy to catch in hos-pitals and nursing homes. Younger children have not developed the resis-tance to infections that teens and adults have developed.

However, children can learn to love and serve the elderly by befriending widows and widowers who are still living at home. A small basket of fruit and homemade cards make a lovely gift for someone who is lonely. If the children like to sing, let them sing a song or two for the one being visited. Let them say one of the memory verses they have learned. In our society, family members are often far away from their loved ones. Letting children adopt grandparents from church or from the neighborhood can be a blessing for both generations.

Families who are surviving on one paycheck generally don't have much extra money. Children can learn creative gift-giving by providing services rather than a store-bought gift. When making Christmas gifts for the widows at church, one mother and her little girls gave homemade coupons that said,

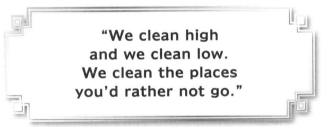

**"We clean high
and we clean low.
We clean the places
you'd rather not go."**

The widows loved redeeming those coupons, and the girls loved pulling old treasures from under someone's bed, dusting them carefully, and putting them away as instructed.

Mom had carefully coached her girls on how to clean and how to respect the property of other people. She had instructed them in the use of good manners when going into someone else's home. The time they spent with the elderly richly blessed the children. They got to hear the neat stories of childhood from those aged saints. The girls learned about the nature and needs of the elderly. They learned not to be afraid of oxygen tanks and tubes. They learned that some elderly people have take-out teeth. They learned not to comment when an adult's teeth fall out unexpectedly. They learned that sometimes elderly people don't hear well. They learned to look directly at the person to whom they were speaking and speak a little more slowly in order to be understood.

Blessings and Mistakes

Children who grow up learning to serve the Lord by serving others will be richly blessed by their encounters. They will make some mistakes along the way, but good engineers will know those mistakes provide teachable moments. Remember that the rockets are very inexperienced. The only way to get experience is to be willing to take a risk. Mistakes come with the territory. A mistake can be very profitable when it is properly managed. As he learns to rethink a situation, a child learns how to do constructive damage control. Since mistakes will always be a part of life, it is wise to learn to handle them honestly. When rockets misfire, a patient and loving response from the engineers will secure the wiring and strengthen the bond of love between the parent and child.

A Victim or Just Irresponsible?

Nine-year-old Samantha was selling candy to raise money for the elementary school chorus. Each member had to sell at least twenty boxes of candy in three weeks to raise enough money for the special trip the chorus was planning. Samantha worked very hard and turned in her money a week early. The night before all the money was due, Dad saw Samantha coming up the sidewalk lugging twenty new boxes of candy. He went out to help her and asked why she had all the candy.

"This is Jeremy's candy," Samantha explained. "His mom is in the hospital, and he isn't going to be able to sell it, so he asked me to do it for him."

"What's wrong with Jeremy's mom, and how long has she been in the hospital?"

"She fell off a ladder this afternoon and broke her wrist. She's in the emergency room, and Jeremy's dad had to pick him up from school. That's why I have to sell his candy."

"Honey, we need to think this through together before you start selling candy. Let's stash this in the den and go sit at the table."

Dad fixed an after-school snack, got a couple of pens and some paper, and joined Samantha at the table.

"I'm sorry Jeremy's mother got hurt this afternoon. I'm proud of you for wanting to help Jeremy. We need to determine what is the best thing to do. Remember that we've been talking about setting healthy boundaries. Let's look at the boundaries and see if that's what you've done in this case. Can you tell me what it means to set a boundary?"

Samantha replied thoughtfully, "It means to decide where to draw the limits on where we will serve. It means that anything inside the boundary is a good thing to do and anything outside is something to avoid."

"That's right. Let's draw a big circle on this piece of paper and let that be our boundary. In this situation, who needs to be helped?"

"Jeremy's mom needs some help. She broke her right wrist and she's right-handed."

"Okay. How could we serve Jeremy's mom?"

"We could take dinner to them tonight so she won't have to cook."

"Good idea. Mom had asked me to pick up pizza for us tonight, so I could get pizza for them, too, and you can go with me to deliver it. Who else needs to be served?"

"Jeremy. His mom isn't going to feel like taking him to sell candy tonight, and his dad has a meeting."

"How long has Jeremy known about selling candy?"

"Three weeks."

"Why did he wait until the last minute to sell his candy?"

"I don't know."

"What happens if Jeremy's candy isn't sold?"

"He has to give it back to Mrs. Perkins, and he won't get to go on the trip with us," Samantha said.

> He chose not to do his job. Now at the last minute, he wants you to do it for him so he won't have to take the consequences.

"Sometimes setting a healthy boundary is hard, but I think that's what we need to do in this case. Jeremy had the same length of time as everyone else to sell his candy. He put it off. He knew that if he didn't sell his candy, he wouldn't be able to go on the trip. He made a choice. He chose not to do his job. Now at the last minute, he wants you to do it for him so he won't have to take the consequences of his poor decision. Do you think it is best for Jeremy for you to bail him out, or is it better for him to learn that he has to take the consequences when he is irresponsible?"

"He'll be mad at me if I tell him I changed my mind. I already said I'd do it."

"That's not what I asked. Which choice do you think is better for Jeremy?"

"Probably to learn from his mistake. But how do I get out of this?"

"That's one reason you are going with me to deliver the pizza. You can tell Jeremy that you spoke too quickly when you said you'd sell the candy for him. You made a mistake. When you had a chance to rethink it, you realized your mistake. Now you will have to let Jeremy take care of his own candy. You can apologize for not thinking it through before committing yourself."

"What if he gets mad at me?"

"He'll just have to be angry. It's not your fault that he chose to be irresponsible, and it's not your job to bail him out. The other thing we have to think about is that boundaries also protect you. What do you have planned for tonight?"

"We have a big test in math tomorrow, and I need to work on fractions. I still have trouble with them, and I was going to see if you'd help me tonight."

"Setting a boundary is going to be best for Jeremy because he will learn from his mistake. It will also protect you because if you work all evening selling candy, you won't be ready for that test. Your first responsibility is to take care of the things you are supposed to do. Then you can worry about extra things that need to be done. Now, let's load that candy into the car and head for the pizza place. We can deliver the pizza and be home in plenty of time to eat and work on fractions."

Conclusion

Learning how to recognize boundaries, respect the boundaries of others, and set healthy boundaries are skills that take years to develop. The earlier the process begins, the stronger the wiring will be in this aspect of growing in favor with man.

Setting appropriate boundaries is another way to put Scripture into action. If we are operating from the Master's Schematics, boundaries will be set according to what is in the best interest of those with whom we come in contact. Boundaries will be determined by behavior that honors God and draws people to Him. Boundaries will be drawn in a way that respects the overall mission of leading people to Jesus.

Strong wiring in the area of healthy boundaries will help a rocket fly right when he encounters the winds of peer pressure. He will have a better chance of drawing the boundaries correctly if he has been doing it for years.

Connecting service to others with a strong prayer life provides a rocket with a very good safety plan. He will know how to contact the Mission Specialist when he sees trouble on the horizon. The skills and experiences gained while serving people will be of great benefit when resisting peer pressure. A rocket who has been able to serve in the family unit will have an experience base that other rockets don't have. A rocket who has a strong experience base will be more capable of independent thinking. The experience he has gained from mistakes will help him recognize a situation that will lead to a mistake. If a rocket can learn to anticipate a mistake, the odds are much higher that he will steer around it. The time he has spent with his engineers will let him know he has a powerful resource on the launch pad if he runs into a situation he can't handle on his own.

A rocket who has had daily practice using godly characteristics on the launch pad will be in a much better position to grow in favor with man. Godly speech patterns, kindness, speaking the truth in love, respect for authority, time spent learning God's word, and practice putting love into action will equip him to grow in favor with man in a way that honors God.

Drill for Skills

Making Connections

1. The Scriptures give two examples of those who grew in favor with man: _____ and _____.

2. Growing in favor with man is much deeper than an attempt to be liked by _____.

3. We need to teach our rockets how to live _____ the world without being a _____ of the world.

4. Godly _____ honors the Father and draws people to Him.

5. _____ is where rockets learn and practice people skills.

 ## Troubleshooting

1. What is the difference between the worldly view of popularity and being in favor with men?

2. If God had given us a "to do" list, what are some items that would be on that list?

3. List some of the areas where we need to model good people skills.

4. How can godly character combined with good people skills lead people to Jesus?

5. What three areas need to be considered as we wire our rockets to deal wisely with people?

6. How can harsh responses to mistakes be communication killers?

7. How can mistakes be handled so they become learning opportunities?

8. How can a sense of ownership lay a foundation for good stewardship?

9. Why is it important to use physical boundaries to lay a foundation for emotional boundaries?

10. When and under what circumstances should children be required to make physical contact with another person?

11. How can we teach our children to respect boundaries set by others?

12. Give some examples of ways to help children set boundaries.

9

Test Flights:
Going Out in Public

In the past chapters, we have looked at specific ways to wire our rockets. We used as our guide the verse that describes the growth and development of Jesus: "And Jesus kept increasing in wisdom and stature, and in favor with God and men" (Luke 2:52). Engineers know that new wiring must be tested before it can be trusted for regular use. Let's explore some ways of testing the wiring we have installed.

The Christian home is a launch pad where most of the wiring is done. Test flights are trips away from the launch pad where the things we have been learning are put to the test. Engineers can prepare themselves for test flights by remembering one very important fact of life. One of the main benefits to having children is they tend to improve a person's humility. Therefore, if a problem occurs during the test flight, a wise engineer can gather up what is left of his dignity, remind himself that this problem is good for his humility, and figure out how to solve it.

We all know that the thinking of society is like a pendulum. At one extreme is the attitude that "children should be seen and not heard." At the other extreme is the attitude that children should be welcome anywhere and that everything should revolve around the comfort of the child. The better way of thinking is much nearer the middle.

The short-term goal of test flights is to teach our rockets how to conduct themselves in any situation so that they and the people they meet will be blessed by the encounter.

The long-term goal of test flights is to prepare our children for the launch date. Test flights allow the engineers and the rockets to see how well the wiring will function in different situations. They help rockets learn to function away from the familiarity of the launch pad. Test flights also prepare rockets for the time when they will need to make godly decisions on their own. If we have done the wiring correctly, our rockets will know they are God's children, and they will behave in most situations in a manner that honors their Father in heaven.

Getting to the point where our children consistently function in a way that honors their heavenly Father takes several years. There will be successful test flights and there will probably be some disasters. Any time you take your child into a new situation or entertain guests in your home, you are conducting a test flight. You are using the situation to test the security of the wiring in your rocket. Think of it as a learning experience for you and your rocket. If you discover faulty wiring, you can go back to the launch pad and straighten out the wiring in order to have a more successful experience the next time.

As with the other areas we have explored, we will compare the Devil's Diagram to the Master's Schematics. When it comes to test flights, the Devil's Diagram has many variations on a theme. That's why people have such divergent views about how children should behave in public.

Here are some examples of worldly wisdom that determine how people will view our children.

 ## Devil's Diagram

» Children should be allowed to do whatever they want to do.

» They're just children. Ignore the obnoxious behavior and it will go away with time.

» Children are annoying. They should not be allowed to attend activities with adults.

» Children say the cutest things when they are angry.

» As long as children are having a good time, don't worry about their behavior.

» Children are not capable of behaving well until they are much older.

» I try to make sure my children are always happy.

Master's Schematics

» "Only conduct yourselves in a manner worthy of the gospel of Christ" (Philippians 1:27).

» " 'And I will be a father to you, and you shall be sons and daughters to Me,' says the Lord Almighty" (2 Corinthians 6:18).

» "It is by his deeds that a lad distinguishes himself if his conduct is pure and right" (Proverbs 20:11).

» "Correct your son, and he will give you comfort; he will also delight your soul" (Proverbs 29:17).

The Need for Test Flights

As a church family and as a society, there has been more of a trend to do things that are "adult only." If you will notice, there has been a direct correlation between a more permissive way of training children and the trend to have activities that are adult only. Most people do not enjoy the company of ill-mannered children. When we have activities for all ages and the children behave poorly, the situation grates on adult nerves and reduces the enjoyment of the activity. Parents who spend all their time trying to ride herd on their kids feel mistreated because they don't get to visit.

We're going to address some of those things as we discuss test flights and see if we can improve the ways our kids handle being away from the launch pad. One of the most important parts of parenting is training our children to follow our instructions, accept our discipline, and learn that they can control their behavior and feel good about it.

Home Preparation for a Test Flight

Before you attempt a test flight, make sure your rockets are consistently obeying you at home. No children obey perfectly, but if you are engaged with them in daily power struggles, you know they are not ready to leave the launch pad. You still have some wiring to do.

If you are having trouble with your children accepting your discipline, you are in good company. God had the same problem with His children at times. In Zephaniah 3:2, speaking of Jerusalem, God says, "She heeded no voice; she accepted no instruction. She did not trust in the Lord; she did not draw near to her God." God had to deal with that rebellious spirit in His children before He could say at the end of the book:

> "Shout for joy, O daughter of Zion! Shout in triumph, O Israel! Rejoice and exult with all your heart, O daughter of Jerusalem! The Lord has taken away His judgments against you, He has cleared away your enemies. The King of Israel, the Lord, is in your midst; you will fear disaster no more" (Zephaniah 3:14–15).

There can be no companionship, fun, and close fellowship until there is respectful obedience. That's why children prefer parents, teachers, and coaches who are good disciplinarians.

Sassy Savannah

It had been a long day at the Smith's. The six-month-old twins were teething and had required a lot of attention. Ginny, their mom, was glad to have them in bed for the night. Four-year-old Savannah had been moody and disagreeable most of the day. At last, Savannah was watching her favorite video, and Ginny had a few minutes to herself.

Ginny was doing the dishes and thinking about her husband who was deployed to the Middle East with his Army unit. She looked at the clock and realized that it was time for Savannah to start getting ready for bed. She called into the living room: "Savannah, go get your pajamas on and get your teeth brushed."

Savannah answered in a sassy and disagreeable tone of voice, "Don't bother me. I'm busy!"

Ginny dried her hands on a dishtowel as she walked briskly into the living room. She turned off the TV and said sternly, "Young lady, you know better than to speak to anyone like that. Mommy is going to give you a spanking so that next time you will remember to be more respectful."

After she spanked Savannah, Ginny sent her to get ready for bed. When Savannah had done her bedtime chores, she came into the kitchen and asked her mom to hold her. For the first time today, Savannah was pleasant and had a good attitude. Ginny noticed the difference but was a little surprised that Savannah was also aware of the change.

Savannah snuggled close to Ginny and asked, "Mommy, why am I so much nicer after I've been spanked?"

Ginny explained, "Sometimes we have to adjust your attitude so you can go back to being the sweet little girl that Mommy enjoys so much."

Savannah was too little to understand completely why discipline works that way but, after the rebellious spirit had been dealt with, there could be some cuddling and close fellowship.

Before we can conduct successful test flights, we have to make sure we have control of our children at home. If they won't obey us there, promptly and respectfully, the chances of their obeying in public are pretty slim. Once we have them under consistent control at home, we can start conducting test flights to learn how well the wiring functions away from the launch pad. Remember, modeling is the conduit through which these wires will run. We must make sure that in public and in private we are setting the right example for our children.

"I Don't Have to Mind You!"

One Sunday Lynette and her husband, Steve, were sitting up front in the adult Bible class. Steve felt a tap on his shoulder and looked up to see the teacher of the three-year-old class holding his daughter, Lindy, by the hand. The teacher whispered in Steve's ear, and he left with them. In the hallway, Miss Karen explained that Lindy was having trouble staying in her chair. When Miss Karen told Lindy to sit down, Lindy looked her in the eye and said, "I don't have to mind you! My mommy says you're not a good teacher!"

Steve said he would take care of it, and Miss Karen went back to class. As he carried Lindy outside, Steve talked to her about the disrespectful behavior. He gave her a spanking and took her back to class. He made her apologize to Miss Karen and promised her another spanking if she didn't behave in Bible class.

While Lindy took her afternoon nap, Steve and Lynette discussed the situation. They realized that they had probably set Lindy up for disobeying Miss Karen. On the way to church, Lindy had overheard Lynette telling Steve that Miss Karen wasn't a very good teacher. Lynette criticized her for being unorganized and ill-prepared at times.

After hearing her mom criticize the teacher, Lindy was not motivated to treat Miss Karen with consideration and respect. Lynette's spirit of criticism may very well have set Lindy up to have a problem with Miss Karen. Lindy heard and absorbed far more than her parents thought she could understand. That is one reason that modeling is so important. If Lynette had modeled the correct attitude toward the teacher, then Lindy would have been more likely to behave correctly.

Remember that as engineers we must model the rules, teach the rules, and enforce the rules. Modeling is the most important part of the job because our rockets will do what we do more often than they will do what we say.

Conducting Successful Test Flights

Assuming you have consistent control of your child at home, let's go over the types of test flights that need to be conducted and some ways to ensure their success. We want to rear positive, capable children who know how to handle lots of different situations with confidence.

Preflight Inspections

Proper preparation and a preflight inspection are necessary before any test flight. Explain to the child what will be happening and let the child know what behavior is appropriate in that situation. Let the child know the consequences for improper behavior.

Here is a sample checklist for the preflight inspection.

1. Where are we going?

2. What kind of clothes are we going to wear?

3. What will probably be happening while we are there?

4. What behavior is expected?

5. If I get bored, in what ways am I allowed to entertain myself?

6. How long will we be gone?

Proper preparation is necessary for a successful test flight. If a child can imagine himself in this new situation, his performance during the flight is more apt to be rewarding. Brainstorm any potential problems. For instance, if your child is potty training, talk about what to do if he needs to go potty during a test flight. If your child had a nosebleed earlier to-day and is worried about what will happen if he has one during the test flight, talk about how you will handle another nosebleed if you are not at home.

If you have had a particular discipline problem this week, talk about how a similar problem will be handled if it occurs away from the launch pad.

Preflight Inspection for a Business Call

Annette has to go see her insurance agent this morning. The babysitter cancelled at the last minute, so Annette will have to take her two preschool children with her to the appointment. Jonathan is two-and-a-half and William is only a year older. Before leaving the house, Annette conducts a preflight inspection.

Where are we going? "Boys, we are going to Mr. Johnson's office so Mommy can talk to him about our insurance."

What kind of clothes are we going to wear? "We need to quickly get you guys into some clean jeans and nice shirts. Miss Katy was going to come play with you while I went to this meeting, but she got sick and can't come. You will have to go with me."

What will probably be happening while we are there? "Mr. Johnson and I have some very important things to talk about."

What behavior is expected? "Mr. Johnson will sit at his desk, and I'll sit in one of his guest chairs. We will talk a long time. You will need to be very quiet and not interrupt unless it is very important."

If I get bored, in what ways am I allowed to entertain myself? "I have your travel bag packed with some sticker books and crayons.

When we get to the office, I'll help you find a good place to work on your things. I expect you to work quietly and without fighting so I can talk to Mr. Johnson.

"Jonathan, you've had a tough morning so far. The rule in our house is that when I say your name, you are to look at me and listen. You have to obey Mommy when I ask you to do something. I have had to spank you twice this morning because you did not obey me. I am putting my little paddle in my briefcase. I know where the bathroom is at Mr. Johnson's office. If you or William disobeys me while we are trying to do our business, I will stop long enough to take you to the bathroom and use my paddle. I expect both of my boys to be very well behaved this morning."

How long will we be gone? "This will be a long meeting. Mr. Johnson and I need about an hour to do our business. If you guys are really good while Mr. Johnson and I are working, we'll stop at the park on the way home so you can play for a while."

Preflight Inspection for Social Call

The family is going to a cookout at the home of Mr. and Mrs. Jones. Here's how the preflight inspection might go.

Where are we going? "In a little bit, we're going to the home of Mr. and Mrs. Jones."

What kind of clothes are we going to wear? "I'm going to wear this outfit, and you can pick which set of 'going out in public' clothes you'd like to wear."

What will probably be happening while we are there? "While we are at the Joneses', the adults will stand around and visit. The children will play. When it's time, we will eat supper there. Mrs. Jones told me we're having hamburgers and hot dogs."

What behavior is expected? "I expect my children to be on their very best behavior. The rules are just like our rules at home. If you need to interrupt, come put your hand on my arm and I'll know you need to tell me something. As soon as there is a break in the conversation, I'll ask you what you need to tell me.

"When we are in the house, we'll use our inside voices. Some of the other children may run inside the house, but I expect my children to walk inside the house. I understand that Mr. and Mrs. Jones have some very pretty things in their house. If you see something interesting and want to touch it, you need to ask Mr. or Mrs. Jones if it's something you can hold or if it's something to look at with your eyes. During meal time, we'll try to use our best manners and try to be neat."

If I get bored, in what ways am I allowed to entertain myself? "There are times that you may get a little bored. If the other children are playing outside, you can probably play outside. If the children are in the room where the adults are talking, you can play quietly with the other children or you can sit by my feet and color. If Mrs. Jones has a room where the children may play, you can play in there as long as you are playing nicely with the other children."

How long will we be gone? "We'll come home about bedtime. We probably won't read stories tonight. We'll probably put our pajamas on, brush our teeth, and go right to bed."

Preflight inspections will vary, depending on the situation. If you conduct preflight inspections before every test flight, the children will come to expect it and these inspections will prepare them to think things through in advance.

Ordinary Test Flights

We have talked about preflight inspections and how to prepare the kids for a test flight. Now we are going to address ways to prepare engineers for test flights. Even though we've been many places in our lives, we haven't been to all those places with children. Children are unpredictable. Expect the best of them and they will often live up to your expectations. Be smart enough to prepare for things that might not go the way you planned.

Kids have incredible radar systems. God probably installed those for the child's protection. The downside is that a child can pick up on how you are feeling. If you are a little insecure in a new situation, the child will know. If you are worried about making a good impression, the child will know.

Children do not have the same insecurities about social embarrassment that adults have. They don't care if you are embarrassed in front of people you are trying to impress. They are very curious about how you will respond when you are trying to make a good impression. They are not afraid to put you in an awkward situation. Embarrassing stunts are a very disconcerting part of a child's nature, but they are for the best. Engineers have to demonstrate that they can behave in a confident manner, even when they don't feel very confident. Children need to learn to act more confidently than they feel. They will learn that skill by watching engineers handle awkward situations.

Diagnosis and Strategy

Occasionally on a test flight, the rocket will not function properly. Engineers have to run a quick diagnostic to determine whether the rocket is having a technical difficulty or just testing the rules. The correct diagnosis determines the strategy for solving the problem.

Let's look at a couple of examples. We will use "Guess Who's Coming to Dinner" as our setting. In this church social setting, the host and hostess know how many adults and how many children will be coming for dinner. They know what time the guests are coming; they just don't know which guests from the church family are coming. The occasion provides great fun for hosts and surprise guests, and it's a wonderful place for test flights. In the following examples, our host family is the Thorntons. David and Susan's children, nine-year-old Thomas and seven-year-old Heather, are present for the evening.

Daniel's Mess

David and Susan knew that two guest children would be in their home. During one "Guess Who's Coming to Dinner" they served "kid friendly" food. Daniel, a first grader, came for dinner. Because of limited space, Susan had all the food on the kitchen counter. Guests served themselves and then had a seat in the living room/dining room area. Daniel was trying very hard to manage for himself. Just as he finished filling his plate, it started to wobble. His hot dog hit the floor, catsup side down. Chips scattered in a million directions.

Sarah had wanted so much for her son make a good impression. She froze when she saw the "disaster" and then started to fuss at Daniel while trying to clean up the mess.

When there is a problem with a rocket, engineers automatically run a quick diagnostic to assess the situation and try to correct it. In this case, Sarah's own embarrassment caused her quick diagnostic to fail her. Instead of coming up with a "technical difficulty" reading, it came up with a "testing the rules" reading. Therefore, she scolded. That was counterproductive. Children should not be scolded, criticized, or teased for having accidents.

Susan, the hostess, was more relaxed, and she came up with a more accurate diagnostic reading. She correctly realized that Daniel was doing his best. She calmly reassured him, telling him that everyone spills from time to time. She cheerfully helped him clean up the mess and start all over with adult help. Sarah was able to relax a bit when she had a chance to rethink her diagnostic. She also took the time to apologize to Daniel for scolding him.

Justin Overrules Mom

During another "Guess Who's Coming to Dinner" Susan knew that children would be in her home. She served hamburgers, hot dogs, and carrot sticks. She had cookies and ice cream for dessert. Four-year-old Justin didn't want to eat at supper time; he wanted to play. When the ice cream and cookies were being served, he wanted some. His mom, Nora, said, "You can have dessert as soon as you eat three bites of your hot dog and one carrot stick."

Justin complained and whined, but Nora stood firm. He ran into the kitchen and asked Susan for some cookies and ice cream. She asked, "What did your mom say?"

Justin said, "I don't know."

Susan said, "I know because I heard her. Your mom said for you to eat three bites of hot dog and one carrot stick. As soon as you do that, I'll be glad to fix cookies and ice cream for you."

Justin ran to Mom. He kept begging her for a bite of her ice cream and one of her cookies. Nora argued with him for a while, but Justin got louder and more annoying. Nora was embarrassed and gave in to keep from making a scene.

Nora had run a quick diagnostic and came up with "testing the rules." Her own sense of embarrassment caused her to handle the situation incorrectly. She gave in to her son to keep the situation from escalating. She knew how long he could whine and how loud his temper tantrums could be, so she took the course of least resistance.

When Susan came back to the living room, Justin grinned at her from Nora's lap. He was happily eating his mother's dessert. Susan knew what should have happened, but she kept her opinions to herself to keep from further embarrassing her guest.

If Nora had put her own embarrassment aside and handled the situation with confidence, the outcome would have been different. As it is, Justin learned that just as whining and temper tantrums work for him at home, they work even better in situations where Nora is trying to make a good impression. Justin was pretty sure Nora would cave in to social pressure, and he was right. Unless Nora does some serious rewiring, Justin has a powerful tool in his arsenal that will allow him to have his own way any time Nora is too embarrassed to take action.

Reworking the Wiring

To rework the wiring at home, Nora needs to set Justin up in such a way that he will be frustrated and turn on the whining. Then she can let him know that whining will no longer work for him and needs to stop immediately—if not sooner!

Here is one way that Nora can "set him up" at a time when she is in a good position to help rewire the "accepting instructions" and "obedience" portions of Justin's wiring:

Mom Modifies Justin's Wiring

Nora is baking cookies to take to the fellowship meal at church tomorrow. Even though supper will be ready in a few minutes,

Justin comes in and climbs up on the kitchen stool to see the cookies.

"Mom, can I have a cookie?"

"Not right now. The cookies are for the meal at church tomorrow. I've made enough so we can all have a couple for dessert after supper tonight. You'll have to wait."

"But I want a cookie now!" Justin says loudly with a definite whining tone.

Nora turns and looks Justin in the eye. With a stern tone of voice, she says, "Justin, what did I say?"

"I have to wait."

"What does that mean?"

"But I want a cookie," Justin whines.

"You are a very smart little boy. You heard what I said, and you know what that means. You have two choices. You can go play until supper is ready and have dessert with the rest of us after supper. Or you can ask me again and get a spanking. It's your choice."

Nora will likely have to assert herself a few times before Justin learns that pleading, whining, and arguing will not work for him. It will take some diligence on Nora's part because Justin, like most children, tends to use the whining and arguing ploy when Nora is too busy or too distracted to stop and take action. If the phone rings just as Nora finishes her conversation with Justin, she needs to keep a sharp eye on him. Chances are high that when Nora turns to answer the phone, Justin will grab a cookie and leave the area. In that case, Nora needs to tell the caller she will call back. Justin has just broken a couple of God's laws about obeying parents and not stealing. His rule-breaking is deliberate disobedience and needs to be handled accordingly.

Even if Nora is diligent at home, she will still have to prove herself a time or two during future test flights. Since Justin has already tested her under stressful circumstances and found her weak spots, she will have to prove she can and will do what is in his best interest. Successful rewiring of this part of Justin's rocket will make him far more appealing to others and reduce the stress level at home.

Head Off Trouble

Planning ahead always helps. Think about how your child responds to different situations. Try to head off trouble before it starts. Decide how you will handle different situations so you won't be caught off guard.

If you think your child is apt to disobey you deliberately when you are visiting, make sure your first test flights are conducted where you feel safe. If you wind up having to borrow a back bedroom for a refresher course in Obedience 101, you will be more at ease in the home of a dear friend than in the home of someone you are trying to impress.

Remember, you can always pack up and head home if the child is being difficult. Do not threaten and then cave in. Do not give in when you start to leave and the child's behavior suddenly improves. If you threatened to leave, leave quickly. Making idle threats destroys your credibility. Say what you mean and then follow through with calm confidence.

If the child was deliberately disobedient and is old enough to remember what he did, it's a good idea on the way out to the car to let him know he can expect a spanking as soon as you get home. It won't hurt to let him sit all the way home thinking about it. If the child is too little to remember very long, you can spank him as soon as you get into the car. Either way, make sure that packing up to go home is not a pleasant experience. Otherwise, the next time he is bored during a test flight, he will misbehave so you will pack up and take him home to his toys and fun stuff.

Preparing for Difficult Test Flights

Some test flights require special preparation. For example, if you know the doctor will draw blood from your child, talk to that child about how to handle the part that hurts. In one family, Mom always took care of the routine stuff, but Dad tried to make sure he was there for pre-op visits when blood was to be drawn. Like a lot of little children, Cindy wanted her daddy when something was going to hurt. Here's how the engineers prepared for a pre-op visit.

Little Cindy's Blood Test

On Friday morning, Sid and his wife, Elouise, took five-year-old Cindy to the hospital for her pre-op visit. She had had one case of strep throat after another and was scheduled for a tonsillectomy Tuesday morning. Sid took Tuesday off so he could be at the hospital. He also took Friday morning off to be available for the pre-op visit since he knew Cindy would have blood drawn from her arm for the first time.

Sid and Elouise filled out all the paperwork and paid the required deposit. While they were in the waiting area outside the lab, Sid said, "Cindy, in a little bit, you are going to have some blood work done. The lady in the hospital lab will need to get some blood out of your arm. When it's time to do that, I'm going to let you sit in my lap. I'll hold my hands like this, and you can squeeze my thumbs while the lady is getting blood out of your arm. If you squeeze hard enough, you can make my thumbs get darker. Let's practice and see if you can squeeze hard enough."

"How will the lady get the blood out?" Cindy asked.

"She'll put a tight band around your arm right here and use a needle to get the blood out. If you sit still and squeeze my thumbs while she's getting the blood out, it will be easier for you."

"I don't like needles!" Cindy whimpered.

"I know you don't like needles. No one does, but sometimes they are necessary. Even if you're feeling afraid, I expect you to sit still in my lap and let the lady do her job. If you squeeze my thumbs like we practiced and take slow, deep breaths, it won't hurt as much. If you can stay calm, it's interesting to watch the blood go out of your arm and into the little glass tubes. We'll stick together, and hopefully it won't take long at all."

Preventing Panics

Having a plan helps with the hard things in life. A child is less apt to panic if an action plan is in place. When something is going to hurt, save the preflight discussion until just before time to use the information. If Sid tells Cindy at 8:45 A.M. that she will have blood drawn at 11:00 A.M., she will have all morning to worry about it, which only increases the likelihood that Cindy will panic. Saving the preflight discussion until the last minute, on the other hand, reduces the stress level for all involved.

Trevor's Pre-School Shots

Jessica had to take her son Trevor to the doctor for the physical exam required before he could go to school. Jessica knew that Trevor would be getting a couple of booster shots. Trevor did very well with the injections because Jessica had done a good job preparing him for that situation. Any time Trevor had to get a shot, he and Jessica held hands. They would take a deep breath together and blow it out as hard and long as they could. Having something to do during the injection kept Trevor from tensing the muscle and made it a lot easier for the nurse to give the injection.

Some medical professionals prefer that parents leave the room while children get a shot or have a cavity filled. They have learned that some kids are much more difficult if Mom and Dad stay. The fear of the unknown and the hesitancy that children feel around non-family members make a child easier to control if Mom and Dad leave.

Each engineer will have to make that decision, but here is something to consider. A child should always know that if he wants to handle a situation on his own, the parents will applaud that decision and provide support, if needed. However, if an engineer has communicated, "I'm here if you need me" and then he backs off when the child is scared or insecure, he has damaged his child's ability to trust him.

Marilyn's Family Dentist Policy

Marilyn had always told her children, "I'm here if you need me." When going to a new dentist, Tiffany asked her mom to go back with her. The eight-year-old had had some bad experiences at a previous dentist's office, and she was always afraid when it was time to see the dentist. When Tiffany's name was called, she and her mother got up to go back to the exam room. The dental hygienist stepped between the little girl and her mom and said, "She'll be fine. You can wait out here."

"I know she'll be fine, but she has asked me to go with her and I told her I would."

"Our office policy does not allow parents to go back with their children."

"Our family policy does not allow us to abandon our children when they are feeling insecure and have asked for our support. You will have to decide whether you would like to modify your office policy or have us find another dentist who is willing to accommodate our family policy."

The dental hygienist backed down and Marilyn accompanied Tiffany. Marilyn talked to the dentist about the confrontation and explained the situation. The dentist was very willing to support the family policy. After several visits, when Tiffany knew the dentist and the staff and felt more at ease, she told her mom, "You don't have to go with me this time. I want to do it by myself now."

Calm and Steady

When supporting a child through a difficult situation, it is important for engineers to keep their own emotions under control. If the child sees tears in your eyes or fear in your face, his feelings will intensify. Any of us would change places with our children in a heartbeat to spare them pain, but one of the reasons God allows pain is so that we can learn to trust Him when the going gets tough. When supporting a child through a painful or scary procedure, keep your breathing slow and steady. Look away from the needle or blood if you don't handle that sort of thing well. Keep your voice calm and steady. A reassuring hand and a steady voice go a long way toward helping a child get through the tough stuff. Pray silently while you are supporting your child. Ask God to give you calmness and strength and to help your child face whatever must be endured.

Every child will have both physical and emotional pain in his life. If a child sees you as one who falls apart easily, he will not be inclined to come to you when life hurts because he will figure you can't handle it. If he sees you as strong and steady, he will come to you for support when needed.

He will learn that we can cry together as a family and pray together when life hurts.

Types of Test Flights

By the time a child is five, he should have experienced the following test flights. Most of them he will have repeated many times, and he will be able to handle them with confidence. These can be repeated many times during the school-age years. By the time the child is a teenager, he will have lots of experience and be quite adept at moving into new and unfamiliar surroundings. His people skills should be strong enough that he can look anyone in the eye and carry on a comfortable conversation.

Here are some types of test flights:

» Going to a good friend's house

» Having a good friend come to our house

» Going to the home of someone we don't know very well

» Having someone that we don't know very well come to our house

» Going to the home of someone whose company we don't necessarily enjoy

» Having someone come to our house whose company we don't necessarily enjoy

» Going somewhere we've never been

» Going to eat at a fast-food restaurant

» Going to eat at a nice restaurant

» Eating in someone else's home—a sit-down dinner

» Going to the store

» Going to an amusement park

» Going to the airport

» Going to the doctor's office

» Going to the dentist

» Going to a children's party

» Going to a movie

» Going to a museum

» Going to a circus

» Going to a state fair

» Going to a park to play with a group

» Going to a campground or other place with woods to explore

» Going to a lake or river

» Going to a hotel to spend the night

» Going to a craft show, train show, or other places where there are displays

» Going to visit someone who is sick

» Going to visit someone who just had a baby

» Going to help an elderly person

» Going to help during a work day at church

» Going to a potluck dinner at church

Conclusion

Test flights are a very important part of a child's training. They help a child learn to take the rules and principles being learned at home and apply them in the real world. As you reflect on the success of a particular test flight, look at the contrast between worldly wisdom and the wisdom of the Creator of our children. It is impossible to please all the people all the time, so don't even make people-pleasing a part of the plan. If the behavior during the test flight pleased our heavenly Father, the test flight was successful.

Successful test flights form the foundation for some of the happiest memories that will be treasured by your family through the years. Test flights also prepare the engineers and the rockets for a more reassuring separation when it comes time to launch the rockets. Both parties will know that many life skills have been programmed into the rocket, and the chances are much higher that the rocket will be a vital part of the Kingdom Fleet.

Drill for Skills

Making Connections

1. _____ _____ are trips away from the launch pad.

2. The _____ term goal of test flights is to teach our rockets how to conduct themselves in any situation.

3. The _____ term goal of test flights is to prepare our rockets for the launch date.

4. Behavior at home and during test flights should always honor our _____ in heaven.

5. Before attempting test flights, make sure your rockets are _____ _____ at home.

Troubleshooting

1. What is the purpose of test flights?

2. In what way do children improve the humility of parents?

3. Quote Proverbs 20:11.

4. How do daily power struggles at home indicate wiring difficulties?

5. List some strategies that can help eliminate power struggles.

6. Which minor prophet discusses the failure of God's people to accept His corrections?

7. Why is respectful obedience necessary before there can be close fellowship?

8. Engineers must _____ the rules, _____ the rules, and enforce the rules.

9. When running a diagnostic test, what things can interfere with an accurate reading?

10. Under what circumstances should the preflight inspections be delayed until the last minute?

Section

Working Through the Technical Difficulties

10

The Strong-Willed Child

As we get ready to explore the principles involved in wiring strong-willed children, we will be borrowing some concepts from Dr. James Dobson's book, *The Strong-Willed Child*. As with most of Dr. Dobson's books, this book is entertaining and incredibly helpful. If you have been blessed with a strong-willed child, you will be better equipped for the job at hand if you take time to read Dr. Dobson's book.

Engineers who have had experience with lots of children know that children come in a wide assortment of personality types and temperaments. There are a few very compliant, easy-to-wire children. They want to please their engineers. They rarely, if ever, have to be spanked because they penitently wilt under a stern look or at a word of reprimand.

On the other end of the continuum, there are the strong-willed children. Dr. Dobson describes them as the ones who enter the world smoking a big cigar and complaining about the temperature in the delivery room. These children are more challenging because they prefer to wire themselves; they keep trying to take control from the engineers.

Some children also fall in the middle of the continuum. These kids have a mixture of compliant characteristics and strong-willed characteristics. Most of what we have discussed so far in this book will work quite well with these children. In order to wire strong-willed rockets successfully, we will need to look at ways to modify the principles we have discussed in order to complete the wiring project.

Characteristics of Strong-Willed Children

Future Leaders

If your launch pad has been graced with the presence of a strong-willed rocket, do not despair. God has entrusted you with a future leader. With God's help, you can successfully wire this rocket to lead others toward righteousness and salvation. This rocket can be wired to be a tremendous encouragement to others who will share his flight path. In the Lord's church, many of the preachers, elders, deacons, and church workers were once strong-willed children. They probably have some hilarious stories to tell about the escapades that made their growing up years very lively. These leaders generally have tremendous respect for the parents who led them safely through the wiring difficulties.

Creative, Confident, In Charge

Strong-willed rockets are a challenge because they are idea people. They tend to be very creative. These rockets think they are experts on every subject and they prefer to be in control. They want to rule the world, and the best way to start is by commandeering the launch pad and ruling from that perch. These confident rockets rarely encounter situations they feel unequipped to handle. They often grow up to be extroverts who are comfortable in nearly any situation.

Many strong-willed children are misdiagnosed as having some variation of Attention Deficit Disorder or hyperactivity. Many of these kids are put on medication designed to make their behavior more manageable. In many instances, strong leadership, good discipline, and lots of love are far more effective in controlling behavior.

Engineers and Strong-Willed Children

Engineers who are assigned the task of wiring a strong-willed rocket need to be aware of some things. While these rockets tend to be very confident, it is easy to bruise their self-esteem because they "get in trouble" a lot. Wise engineers recognize that these children, more than most, need to hear the answers to the most important questions in a child's life, and they need to hear the answers every day: "Who loves me?" and "Who's in control around here?"

Engineers wiring these rockets often fall into a pattern of trying to use nagging and criticism to control a rocket's behavior. Besides being a poor parenting technique, nagging causes the rocket to feel like his folks are always mad at him. Who wants to live all day with a grouchy person who nags and fusses? Who wants to spend all day nagging and fussing and then realize at the end of the day how rotten everyone's mood has been today. When tempted to use an abundance of words to try to control a child's behavior, remember this wisdom from Proverbs: "When there are many words, transgression is unavoidable, but he who restrains his lips is wise" (Proverbs 10:19).

Strong-willed children who are given to strong-willed parents usually do fairly well. These parents remember their childhood power struggles. They remember which discipline techniques were effective and which ones didn't work so well. The engineers who have the most difficulty wiring a strong-willed little rocket are the ones with compliant temperaments. They don't like conflict. They want everyone to get along without a power struggle. Mild-mannered engineers fall into bed at night exhausted from doing battle all day with a rocket who thinks he knows it all.

 ## Devil's Diagram

» He's just a brat. He must have rotten parents.

» Just let her have her own way. She'll eventually outgrow this obnoxious stage.

» Ignore the bad behavior. Time will take care of it.

» Put this kid on Ritalin so we can stand to have him around.

» All kids go through these kinds of power struggles. It's good for her confidence to win.

 ## Master's Schematics

» "The fear of the Lord is the beginning of knowledge; fools despise wisdom and instruction" (Proverbs 1:7).

» "The rod and reproof give wisdom, but a child who gets his own way brings shame to his mother" (Proverbs 29:15).

» "My son, do not reject the discipline of the Lord, or loathe His reproof, for whom the Lord loves He reproves, even as a father, the son in whom he delights" (Proverbs 3:11–12).

» "But he who listens to me shall live securely, and shall be at ease from the dread of evil" (Proverbs 1:33).

Wiring a Strong-Willed Child

Earlier in the book, we described family life as being a game of "Follow the Leader." God designed it this way because the Christian life is the ultimate game of "Follow the Leader." Jesus is the leader and only by following Him faithfully will we get to live eternally with Him. In the home, there must be good leadership so that a rocket can someday move from following the lead of his parents to following the Lord's leadership.

Wiring a strong-willed child takes a lot of time and patience. During the preschool years, having a stay-at-home mom is very important. During the school years, Mom needs to be home when the strong-willed child is home. If Mom absolutely cannot be the one "on duty," she must make every effort to have a good Christian substitute. Strong, consistent, loving leadership is one of the components necessary if this rocket is to be wired successfully.

Structure and Order

Mom needs to be at the helm each day to make sure there is a solid, consistent routine. Strong-willed children need structure because it gives them a sense of order and lets them know that someone capable is in charge. Mom will also need to be a very calm, consistent disciplinarian. The rules and consequences need to be consistent so that the child can recognize good leadership. If a strong-willed child thinks you are not doing the job well, he will double his efforts to take over. You must prove to him that following your lead, listening to your instructions, and accepting your discipline are in his best interest.

Since men are usually trying to juggle the demands of career and family life, they often come home from work dead tired and stressed out. After he gets home from work, Dad may not want to be in charge of anything more complicated than the remote control. He might much prefer to put his feet up and find something on TV or settle in with the newspaper in order to take his mind off the stress of the workplace.

The desire to come home and crash can be very strong, but Dad must resist that temptation and come home to take his God-given position of leadership. Most often, when Dad fails to take the lead, it's because he's tired and doesn't want the hassle. If Mom is capable and has the situation well in hand, it's easy for Dad to abdicate responsibility. That kind of leadership is not worthy of a child's respect. Respect has to be earned, and parents of a strong-willed child have to be on duty whether or not they feel up to it.

Sharing the Load

When Dad comes home to take the lead, he needs to make sure he has a firm grip on his own emotions. Dealing with the children, and especially with discipline problems, requires a lot of self-control when a person is tired. It is better not to do the job at hand than to let anger and frustration overrule good judgment.

After Mom has been at the helm all day with the strong-willed child, she needs Dad to come in and assume his God-given role of leadership. He needs to take over as the prime disciplinarian and reinforce the concepts Mom has taught during the day. It is better for the marriage for Dad to take the lead when he is home. Even if Mom is a stay-at-home Mom, she is also on call for the family twenty-four hours a day for about twenty years. She can take a "mental health break" as she works on her evening chores if she knows that Dad is there to keep an eye on the kids.

> Children need Dad to take the lead. The only time available for Dad to confirm his love for the children is when he is home. If he is going to build a strong relationship with his children, Dad must be accessible.

Children need Dad to take the lead. The only time available for Dad to confirm his love for the children is when he is home. If he is going to build a strong relationship with his children, Dad must be accessible. That change of command each day is good for the children. If family rules are consistent and parents present a united front, the children will learn the strengths of each parent as the different leadership styles are modeled.

If a child is to learn respect for authority, that changing of command on a daily basis will help him when he needs to transfer respect to other authority figures. Only with strong leadership can the child learn to listen to the commands of his parents and obey.

Submit to God

In the discipline and training of this child, it is important to remember that we are looking at the word *discipline* as coming from the word *disciple*. We are wiring the next generation of the Lord's servants. It is necessary for them to accept the discipline of the parents before they can submit to the Lord's leadership and discipline.

The strong-willed child, more than any other, needs to know that "God is in charge of our family and we do what He says." Memory verses about obedience, honor, and respect for authority need to be in a strong-willed child's memory bank very early in life.

Principles of Discipline for a Strong-Willed Child

In the wiring of any rocket, the key to discipline is to communicate love daily. The strong-willed rocket must know that the rules and consequences have been designed for his physical, emotional, and spiritual safety. If he can't see the love in your actions, the discipline efforts will not be effective.

One way to communicate love is to verbalize daily the blessing that child is to your family. It's important to do this with all the children, but especially for the ones who "get in trouble" a lot. Let your child know that God has given him special leadership skills. Your job as a parent is to help him learn to use those skills in a way that honors the Father and is a blessing to others.

Be Consistent and Strong

You must have a good game plan in place for the wiring of a strong-willed child. Make friends with an older couple who have successfully reared at least one strong-willed child. They can be a very valuable resource when you are not sure how to handle a situation. To formulate a game plan, work with your mate to analyze the behaviors that are the most difficult for you to handle. Come up with a workable strategy. Pray for strength. You are going to need it. Your child will give you opportunities every day to practice being strong. Ask God to help you to be very consistent. A strong-willed child needs a calm, consistent, strong leader more than other children do.

Make sure the expectations are crystal clear. A strong-willed child needs to know the rules of the house. Because he is an idea person, he may get himself into some very interesting predicaments. Do not punish mistakes born of ignorance and inexperience. It is not fair to punish a child for getting in over his head or for doing something he didn't know was wrong. In those instances, learn to be a damage control coach. Help him learn to think his way out of a sticky situation.

Up on the Housetop

One Sunday afternoon, Hank and Cynthia were inside paying bills. Their daughters, three-year-old Ginger and five-year-old Eden, were outside playing in the fenced-in backyard. The girls came running in saying, "Daddy, Mommy, come see what we can do!" Hank and Cynthia left the bills and went outside to see the latest achievement. They watched as Eden and Ginger climbed the tall tree beside the house and stepped onto the steep roof of the house.

They couldn't punish the girls for doing such a dangerous thing because it had never occurred to them to make "don't climb the tree and up onto the roof" one of the family rules. Cynthia stood directly under the girls so she could catch them in case they fell. Hank said, "I want to see what it looks like from up there." The tree wouldn't hold his weight at the very top, but he got close enough to help the girls if they needed him while they climbed back down. Hank said, "Eden, I want you to show me the safest way to climb down from here." She did it almost effortlessly. When Eden was safely beside Cynthia, Hank said, "Ginger, I want you to show me what a good job you can do climbing down." Hank had to coach her a little as to where to put her hands and feet until she was close enough for him to hold on to her. They climbed down together.

When they were on the ground, Hank said, "I am very impressed with the way you did that. I didn't know you could climb so well. But that was a pretty dangerous thing to do. If you go up on the roof alone, you could fall and get hurt. We're going to make a new family rule. 'If you want to climb up on the roof, you have to wait until Daddy can go with you. You may climb the tree, but you may not go on the roof without me. If we go up there together, I can help you stay safe."

The next day, Cynthia was telling the widow next door about their adventure. To Cynthia's dismay, the neighbor said she had been watching in terror all week as the little girls had practiced. She didn't feel she knew Cynthia well enough to come and "tattle." Cynthia assured her that it would be much better for her to come and tell any time she saw the children doing something dangerous.

"You Are Special"

It is important to let a strong-willed child know that God has given him special characteristics. God has made him an "idea" person. He will have lots of good ideas. He will also have ideas that aren't so good. Teach him to ask before putting ideas into practice. The biblical principle for this one is: "The way of a fool is right in his own eyes, but a wise man is he who listens to counsel" (Proverbs 12:15). Only a fool proceeds without getting a second opinion, and on this launch pad, we are wiring for wisdom.

Sometimes engineers feel a bit intimidated by the intelligence of their strong-willed rockets. Engineers have to remember that even if the child scores higher on an IQ test than the engineers, he is far behind in experience. The strong-willed child needs to learn to come to an engineer for advice for two very important reasons:

1. The engineers have God-given roles of leadership in the family.

2. The engineers have been making mistakes and learning from them for years.

Because a strong-willed child is an idea person, he will have a wide assortment of ideas. Engineers will have to make him discard the ideas that are dangerous spiritually, physically, or emotionally. Because many ideas will have to be discarded, it is important to encourage the ones that can be tried. He won't always succeed with his ideas, but the things learned along the way can be extremely valuable. Besides, if you encourage as many of his ideas as possible, it will be easier for him to accept your leadership when you have to put a damper on some of his wilder notions.

Trina's Moon Trip Postponed

Evelyn was a gentle lady, the mother of strong-willed, seven-year-old Trina. So Evelyn was not surprised when Trina suddenly asked, "Mom, can I build a rocket to fly to the moon?"

Evelyn said, "Of course you can. Let's go out to the garage so you can show me what you plan to use for this project."

"I want to use this pile of boards," Trina said.

"No, we can't get into those. Daddy bought those so he can fix the railing on the back porch. Look over here in Daddy's pile of scrap lumber. I'll bet you can find some good pieces of wood over here that will work for your project."

Trina selected some wood, and Evelyn helped her find a safe place in the backyard for her project. Then every few minutes Evelyn went out to check on her. She had learned from experience to check frequently when Trina was working on a project.

Trina came in and asked, "Mom, Daddy won't let me use his drill by myself. Can you come drill some holes for me?"

"Honey, I would use the old drill, but it's broken. Daddy's new drill is too big and too heavy for me to use safely. Daddy will be home in about thirty minutes. See if you can work on another part of the project and let Daddy drill the holes when he comes home."

Evelyn started supper and then went out to check on Trina. Trina was working on fuel for her rocket. She and Christopher, the fifth grade boy from next door, were using matches and hair spray cans to make flamethrowers or rocket boosters. By holding a lit match to the spray coming out of the can, they made some really neat flames. Going straight out, it looked like a flame thrower. Pointed up into the air, it looked like the scenes on TV of the rocket boosters firing during launch.

Evelyn was horrified. She confiscated the matches and hair spray. She told Christopher, "I am very upset with you. I expect you to make better decisions when you are at our house. You put yourself and Trina in danger. The two of you are not allowed to play together for the rest of the week. Go home and tell your folks why I sent you home. If they have any questions, have them call me. Next week, we can try again and see if you and Trina can play together safely."

After Christopher left, Evelyn took Trina inside and gave her a spanking for playing with matches. Even though they had never discussed matches in regards to the construction of flamethrowers, Trina knew that playing with matches was against the rules. Evelyn made Trina stay inside for the rest of the evening. She had to wait until the next evening to work with her dad on the rocket.

Handle the Power Struggles

Since strong-willed children are out to conquer the world. Handling the power struggles can be an exhausting part of the job for engineers. Since each child is different, part of behavior management will be done by trial and error. Pay attention to what works with your child and to what leaves both of you frustrated. Go with what works.

Keep the home atmosphere as positive as possible. Reward positive gestures with a sincere compliment, a hug, or a comment to another adult that the child can overhear. There will be a lot of struggles for control. Make sure he hears lots of good things about himself. Make sure he knows when he's using his good leadership abilities. Teach him that good leaders make decisions based on what is good for the group, not on what is best for themselves.

In the training and discipline of strong-willed children, engineers must keep their emotions under control. If an engineer has a "short fuse," the wiring project will be in danger. Engineers who work with strong-willed children need to have God's wisdom deeply implanted in order to help with anger management and to ensure that their discipline techniques will be effective.

> "But let everyone be quick to hear, slow to speak and slow to anger; for the anger of man does not achieve the righteousness of God" (James 1:19–20).

> "All discipline for the moment seems not to be joyful, but sorrowful; yet to those who have been trained by it, afterwards it yields the peaceful fruit of righteousness" (Hebrews 12:11).

Manage Anger

God clearly states in James 1:20 that man's anger does not bring about the righteous life that God desires. The goal of discipline as stated in Hebrews 12:11 is to produce righteousness. This is the reason discipline combined with anger is counterproductive. It is punishment instead of discipline. It usually causes a child to become angry and resentful instead of leading him to repentance.

Engineers discipline the children until the kids have developed self-discipline in a particular area. If a strong-willed child is to do a good job controlling his own emotions and behavior, the engineers must present a consistent model for that kind of control. We want all our rockets, including the strong-willed ones, to have lives of righteousness and peace.

Anger management is an important component of righteous living, and engineers must model that characteristic as they wire their rockets. It is helpful to remember what Paul taught.

> "Love is patient, love is kind, and is not jealous; love does not brag and is not arrogant, does not act unbecomingly; it does not seek its own, is not provoked, does not take into account a wrong suffered, does not rejoice in unrighteousness, but rejoices with the truth; bears all things, believes all things, hopes all things, endures all things" (1 Corinthians 13:4–7).

In handling the power struggles, it is important for a strong-willed child to know you love him far more than he can ever imagine. That love is modeled as you show him how to live out the characteristics of love on a daily basis. When correction is necessary, make sure the child knows you are taking discipline measures because you love him too much to let him get by with violating the family rules. Teach him that you want him to grow up to be the person God wants him to be. Help him realize that ultimately he is the only one who can control his behavior. You will do whatever it takes to help him want to control his behavior until he can prove he no longer needs your help in that area.

Clarify Expectations

With all children, but especially with strong-willed children, it is important for the boundaries to be defined before they are enforced. Because a strong-willed child is an idea person, he will do some really foolish things. Not all of his ideas are great, and he may not recognize a rotten idea until he has already into trouble over his head.

Be extremely clear about what you expect. Be consistent. The strong-willed child has to know that the rules are the same yesterday, today, and tomorrow. Otherwise, he will see you as a weak leader and try to take control. One of the best ways to help clarify expectations is to read "The 21 Rules of This House" by Gregg and Josh Harris. This helpful kit can be ordered from

Noble Publishing Associates
1300 NE 131st Circle
Vancouver, WA 98685
1-800-225-5259

These rules are invaluable—especially for strong-willed children. Go over them with your children. Have them rules posted so everyone knows the expectations. One of the rules is, "In this house, when we don't know what to do, we ask." This rule is helpful because, when a child gets in over his head with a wild idea, an engineer can hold him accountable for not asking.

When there is a behavior problem, it is imperative for engineers to run a quick diagnostic test to determine if this is a case of "testing the rules" or "technical difficulties" or "immaturity." In the flurry of activity that comes with wiring a strong-willed child, it is easy for fatigue, time pressure, or stress to cause the diagnostic reading to come up with the wrong message.

Mom Arrests a "Fireman"

Three-year-old Timothy was running through the house making fire engine noises. Mom had a splitting headache and had endured about all the noise she could tolerate. Suddenly, she heard a crash and went to investigate. Her favorite potted plant was in the floor, and Timothy was covered in dirt.

Mom ran a quick diagnostic. It came up with "testing the rules." Mom was angry because she had often reminded Timothy to be careful not to bump into her plants when he was playing fireman.

"Timothy, you need to take a break. Mommy needs to take a break. You sit right here in this clean spot on the floor, and I'll sit in my rocking chair. Let's both be very quiet for a little bit."

That was a wise move on Mom's part. Her first inclination was to spank Timothy for making her angry, for giving her a headache, and for making it necessary to repot her favorite plant. Taking a break kept Timothy from doing any more damage. It kept him safe and in a contained area. It gave Mom time for a quick talk with God to get a grip on her emotions before running a second diagnostic.

After a short silence, she asked Timothy, "How did you knock over Mommy's plant?"

"My fire hose got stuck."

"Can you show me what happened?"

Timothy's dad had given him an old vacuum cleaner hose to use when he was playing fireman. Timothy showed Mom how he came running around the corner on his way to the "fire." The hose got caught on the leg of the little stool where Mom's plant was sitting. He pulled really hard to move it, so the stool toppled over and the plant fell.

Mom realized her first diagnostic was wrong. Timothy should have been spanked if he had deliberately knocked over her plant. He should not have been spanked for an accident. He was too little to figure out that if the hose was stuck, he should have asked Mom to help. Mom's correct diagnostic came up "immaturity." Timothy was simply too young and inexperienced to figure out that if he pulled, the stool would fall. Mom explained to him why the accident happened. That helped Timothy learn from his mistake and gain some experience for future reference. Mom made two new rules. She showed Timothy where the new boundary was. Timothy was not to run or play within about four feet of Mom's plants. She told him he would get in trouble if he broke the rule. She also told him that if his fire hose got stuck, he was to come get her to help him.

Mom had Timothy help her clean up the mess on the floor. He helped her repot the plant. When they were all done, they had to put Timothy in the tub and give him a quick scrub. When he was clean, Timothy had to help put the dirty clothes into the washing machine. Having him help clean up the mess, repot the plant, and take a bath helped him learn how to make restitution when his poor decisions cause problems for someone else. He also learned how one moment of not "thinking it through" can cause quite a problem.

Having him help clean up the mess, repot the plant, and take a bath helped him learn how to make restitution when his poor decisions cause problems for someone else.

Mom very wisely realized that her headache and fatigue, along with the stress of a busy little boy, had caused her diagnostic tools to malfunction. By taking a break with Timothy, she had a chance to regroup and make a good training choice instead of punishing for the wrong reasons.

Diagnose Defiance

Engineers have to be careful to distinguish between childish irresponsibility and defiance. It really isn't hard to tell the difference. Defiance comes in situations like the following:

Caitlin Defies Mom

It was almost time for bed. Caitlin, a strong-willed two-year-old, was playing with her toys in the living room. She'd had her bath and was in her pajamas. Mom was finishing the dishes and Dad was in the living room working at the computer. Mom called into the living room: "Caitlin, it's almost time for bed. I'm going to count to five, and then I want you to pick up your toys." Mom counted and Caitlin kept playing. Dad was watching Caitlin. He said quietly, "Caitlin, what did Mommy tell you to do?" Caitlin answered in an angry tone: "Mommy say pick up toys and I not gonna pick up toys!" As Daddy crossed the room to pick up Caitlin, he said, "You are not allowed to disobey Mommy, and you are not allowed to speak to anyone in that tone of voice. Daddy is going to spank you, and then you are going to pick up your toys."

Daddy followed through and Caitlin picked up her toys. In the face of that kind of defiance, spanking is the best way to bring the child to repentance and resolve the conflict. Before she went to bed, Daddy made sure he took time to cuddle a bit with Caitlin and reassure her of his love.

Jeremy Defies Grandpa

Grandma and Grandpa were taking the grandchildren out for lunch at a fast-food restaurant. Seems everyone else in town had the same idea because the place was packed. Grandpa and Jeremy were standing in line waiting to place an order. It was almost their turn when the three-year-old saw something interesting and went to investigate. Grandpa said, "Jeremy, come back over here with Grandpa." Jeremy turned around, stomped his foot, and said defiantly, "I won't!" Grandpa left his spot in line, picked Jeremy up, and went out to the van. On the way to the van, he spoke sternly to Jeremy: "You were very rude, disrespectful, and disobedient. Grandpa is going to give you a good spanking. When we go back inside, you are going to stand in line with Grandpa and behave yourself."

After the spanking, Grandpa let Jeremy calm down a little and then carried him back into the store. They got back in line; Jeremy behaved.

Get a Grip

Children, even strong-willed children, have to learn. They all make mistakes. That is why it is important for an engineer to be able to assess fairly quickly what caused the problem. If it was immaturity and inexperience, view it as a teachable moment. Back up, talk about what happened, and make plans to do better next time.

However, if the problem was due to defiance or deliberate disobedience, a spanking—hard enough to bring repentance—is the best solution. Strong-willed children will sometimes refuse to submit to the authority of an engineer, even after a well-deserved spanking. In this case, the appropriate response is usually another spanking. If you have to spank a second time, listen to the tone of his crying. If his crying has an angry tone, you may have to deliver a few more swats to get past the point of anger and to the point of repentance. If his crying is of the "I'm sorry" variety, stop. You have made your point. If you are afraid you may be crossing the line into abuse, stop immediately. Get a grip on your own emotions, and give your child time to calm down. Talk about the situation. If the child is ready to repent and submit to your authority, give him a hug and let him know the conflict is resolved. If he is still defiant, he may have to sit quietly in a corner until he is ready to behave, or he may have to go take a nap. If he is trying to fight you, you may have to sit and physically restrain him until he wears himself out. Hold him close and keep him positioned in such a way that he cannot hurt you or himself. After the rage has ended, talk it over quietly and let him know you expect him to do a better job controlling himself.

When in conflict with a strong-willed child, it is important to respond with calm, confident leadership. If you are frustrated, don't let it show. He will interpret your frustration as weakness, and his respect for you will diminish. This is one time to be a good actor or actress. Pretend you know what you're doing, even if you are trembling on the inside.

Restate and Reassure

After a conflict, always take time to restate the rules that were broken and reassure the child of your love. It does not do any good to punish a child unless he knows how he got himself into trouble. Always end the confrontation with a hug. Let him know that you are confident that he will grow up to do what is right.

With all children, but especially with strong-willed children, it is important to make sure expectations are reasonable and attainable. When working on a new rule or when learning a new skill, be sure to recognize and compliment progress. Do not hold a child accountable for something until you know he is capable of doing what you have asked.

Managing the power struggles with strong-willed children will be easier if there are clear rules about which areas of life each person in the family controls. Children need to have some things for which they are responsible; each child needs to have a sense of control over some facets of his life. Not only does this strategy minimize power struggles, but it also prepares a rocket for the future. Remember that engineers are trying to work themselves out of a job. Little by little, control has to be given over to the rocket as more of the wiring is completed. Otherwise, the family will be in serious trouble when the launch date arrives. A struggle often comes in knowing what things Mom and Dad are to control and what things the rocket can control.

It does not do any good to punish a child unless he knows how he got himself into trouble. Make sure expectations are reasonable and attainable.

A chart on his bedroom wall and another on the refrigerator may help to deal with power struggles. Since children are concrete learners, things they can see and touch are helpful. When in conflict over control of a specific thing or activity, go with the child to the chart and check the pre-established boundaries. If the chart was formulated during a family meeting where the child had an opportunity for some input, it will be especially effective. Make sure the chart has some extra blanks at the bottom so items can be added as needed. When in conflict over an area that has never been discussed, let the child have some input. However, the engineer in charge should make the final decision and add the information to the chart.

If the child can read, the chart can be written. (See sample chart below.) Otherwise, use pictures.

Our Family Responsibilities

Dad Controls	Mom Controls	John Controls
Which tools John can use for his projects.	What we have for meals.	Which play clothes I wear to play outside.
What time we leave for church.	Which of John's clothes are church clothes.	Which of my church clothes I wear to Bible class.
Whether we read our Bible story before supper or after.	Which of John's clothes are "going out in public" clothes.	Which of my "going out in public" clothes I wear when we go run errands.
The rules in this house.	What time John goes to bed.	Which two toys I get to sleep with tonight.
Deciding on good and bad consequences for the children.	Which books are good to read and which ones are not.	Whether we read one long story at bedtime or two short ones.
Where we go to eat when we go out for supper.	What TV shows we can watch and which ones we don't watch.	Whether I feed my puppy before breakfast or after.

Conclusion

As we conclude this discussion of strong-willed children, it is important to remember that this child is a future leader. Sometimes engineers fall into a trap of requiring more from the children who are compliant and less from those who are strong-willed. Don't let fatigue cause the enforcement tool to lock up. For instance, if Sally very willingly takes out the trash and feeds the dog, it's much easier to let her do it. However, that teaches strong-willed Bruce he can avoid doing his share of the chores by making it difficult for the engineers to enforce that rule. If the engineers are tired or in a hurry, it's much easier to let Sally do it. Eventually, Sally will learn to resent Bruce for not doing his share. Both children will be able to recognize that wimpy style of leadership, and the engineer's authority will be undermined.

Even when it is difficult to do so, chores should be rotated among the family members so that everyone in the family becomes proficient in the tasks that keep a household organized. Leaders need to be skilled in many areas and you must do whatever it takes to make sure your strong-willed rocket is up to speed on the skills he needs to know. Every child needs to be a contributing member of the household. In order for this future leader to be a good leader, make sure his childhood is an internship that prepares him for a life as a servant leader in the Kingdom Fleet.

Drill for Skills

 ## Making Connections

1. Strong-willed children want to take _____ from the engineers.

2. If properly wired, strong-willed children can grow up to be good _____.

3. Strong-willed children are a challenge because they are _____ people.

4. With good leadership in the home, a rocket can move from following the leadership of his parents to following the _____ leadership.

5. If a strong-willed child does not respect his leaders, he will double his effort to take _____ of the launch pad.

 ## Troubleshooting

1. What are some of the blessings that come with having a strong-willed child?

2. A strong-willed child, more than any other, needs to hear the answers to which two questions every day?

3. Why does the combination of strong leadership, good discipline, and lots of love work better than medication to manage behavior?

4. Why is a stay-at-home mom important to the wiring of this rocket?

5. Why do some men avoid assuming a position of leadership in the home?

6. What are some ways that Dad confirms his love for his children?

7. Why will discipline be ineffective if a child cannot see love in your actions?

8. Why does an engineer need to be a damage-control coach?

9. In what way is a strong-willed child protected by asking before following through on his ideas?

10. Why is good anger management important to effective discipline?

11

The Difficult Child and the Special-Needs Child

"I Did Put My 'Jamas On"

Regina was a sweet little girl with huge brown eyes, a bright smile, and long, curly, brown hair. She was usually kind to her older sister, Rosa. She was also obedient, but occasionally her behavior was quite confusing to her parents, Eli and Lois.

One Sunday afternoon, Miss Sheri, the teacher of the three-year-old class, came to Eli and Lois to discuss a puzzling situation. In class that day, Miss Sheri asked little Regina to go get the glue sticks. Regina cheerfully went to the supply cabinet and got the crayons. But when Miss Sheri asked Regina to come sit down, she went over and stood by the cabinet. Miss Sheri had to go get her and bring her back to the table. Miss Sheri was confused. Regina didn't have a defiant look on her face. She looked as if she was really trying to obey. Eli and Lois told Miss Sheri they were often confused with the same kinds of behavior at home.

Lois discussed Regina's case with their pediatrician. They decided to do some investigating, beginning with a hearing test. Regina enjoyed going to see the audiologist. She enjoyed wearing the headphones and playing the game with all those funny noises. Regina's hearing was well within the normal limits.

The next step was to do some observations at home. In the past, Regina had been spanked several times for ignoring what Lois and Eli told her to do. One Friday night, Lois told Regina to pick up her toys because it was nearly bedtime. Regina put on her pajamas, but she didn't pick up her toys. Lois said once again,

"Regina, come pick up your toys." Regina ignored Lois. "Regina, if you do not obey me, I will have to spank you." Regina ignored Lois.

Lois picked Regina up, sat down on a chair, and put Regina over her knee. Regina asked, "Mommy, why you going to 'pank me?"

Lois sat Regina up in her lap and said, "Regina, what did Mommy tell you to do?"

Regina replied, "You said put my 'jamas on and I did put my 'jamas on!"

"No, darling, Mommy said for you to pick up your toys."

Regina looked at the toys in the floor as if noticing them for the first time. She said, "Oh! Okay."

Lois was very glad she had not spanked Regina because it was now clear that even if Regina heard the words, she didn't get the meaning. Lois and Eli discussed the problem and made a new rule for themselves. Regina was never to be punished unless they first asked, "What did I say?" That strategy worked well. There were times when Regina would say defiantly, "You say 'pick up toys' and I not gonna pick up toys!" Those were times she definitely needed to be spanked. There were other times that the answer to "What did I say?" bore no resemblance to what was actually said.

Lois and Eli did a lot of observing during the rest of Regina's preschool years. They explained to babysitters and Bible class teachers that, for some reason, Regina had difficulty with instructions. They let the Assistant Engineers know that if it was a case of not understanding, they needed to try to assist and redirect. If it was a case of defiance or disobedience, it was to be handled as such.

One Sunday morning, Eli had to work. Lois was teaching the first-grade Bible class. Miss Sheri interrupted her. Regina had gotten angry with her teacher and told her to shut up! Lois left her first graders with a co-teacher and took Regina outside to administer a well-deserved spanking. She took Regina back to class and made her apologize to Miss Sheri.

Later Miss Sheri was apologetic for getting Regina into trouble. She felt sorry for the "poor little thing" who seemed to have such a hard time with some things. Lois reminded Miss Sheri that there is a huge gap between a learning problem and defiance. Learning problems would be dealt with patiently. Defiance and deliberate disobedience were character traits not to be tolerated. It wasn't in Regina's best interest to allow her to use a problem in one area as an excuse for bad behavior in another. Allowing bad behavior would compound the other difficulties that would be faced during this wiring project.

When Regina was nearing her fifth birthday, it was time to do some more testing. Fortunately for the family, Regina's grandma was a special education teacher. She lived in another state but agreed to do some diagnostic testing. The family went to Grandma's for a few days. They spent the first couple of days letting Regina get used to Grandma and Grandpa again, since it had been a while since they had been together. Then one day Grandma asked if Regina would like to play the penny game. Grandma explained that she was going to show Regina some pictures and ask her some questions. Every time Regina answered a question, whether or not she got it right, Grandma gave her a penny to put in the jar and keep.

Grandma and Regina played the penny game off and on all day. When Regina grew tired or became restless, Grandma sent her out to play with the other grandchildren. Grandma discovered that Regina had a learning disability that affected the way her brain processed incoming information. It was as if her brain scrambled every fifth word or so. To make the situation more interesting, Regina also had visual dyslexia. Words and pictures moved around on the page. If she made them backwards and wrote from right to left, Regina formed her letters perfectly, but if she tried to go left to right, she couldn't do it.

Lois and Eli decided to homeschool Regina because she needed one-on-one instruction. The next few years were a challenge, but with lots of help, Regina developed the compensation skills she would need to do well in life. She learned to work around the problems and maximize the things she did well. More important, she grew up to be a faithful child of God.

Parenting a Special-Needs Child

Regina would be classified as a special-needs child. Special-needs children come in a variety of shapes and sizes. Their needs are as individual as each child. That is why it is impossible to use this book as a tailor-made plan for your special-needs child. However, its principles can be modified to help engineers successfully wire the special-needs rockets entrusted to their care.

Remember, every child is a gift from God. God doesn't make junk. Even in the face of the most profound problems, there are blessings to enjoy. Every child of God is good at something. Make the most of the child's God-given talents, and don't fret about the other stuff. The most important rule for a special-needs child is this: "If it's going to keep you out of heaven, we have to master it. If it isn't going to keep you out of heaven, give it your best shot and move on." That principle can keep engineers from going stark-raving mad over a skill that seems impossible to learn.

Construction Barriers

There are some skills the child will try to master, usually because a teacher or engineer has decided that the skill has to be mastered at this time. The child may try hard to acquire the skill and still be unsuccessful. It's as if one of those concrete construction barriers has been set up right in the middle of where the child is trying to work. No amount of effort will move the barrier. No one really knows why barriers are popped into place and when they will just as mysteriously be removed.

When you encounter a barrier, don't let the whole family get stressed out over the situation. Give it a rest for a while and try again every couple of weeks. One day, when you least expect it, something will click and the child will be able to handle that skill. No amount of force or pressure will get that skill into a child's life any faster, so back off and try again later. She will "get it" when she "gets it."

Get professional help, as needed, to work around the problem areas. Learn to deal with problems without making your child feel like a problem or a burden. Remember, some of the things that distress engineers are the result of peer pressure. If every other third grader can rattle off the multiplication tables and your special-needs third grader can't, don't panic. Don't feel a sense of competition with your friends who have A-plus super stars in the third grade. Love your child. Work on the multiplication tables, but keep them in perspective. There is a marvelous little invention called a calculator. If the multiplication tables never "click," the child will learn to multiply with her fingers. Remember that when she stands before the Lord on the day of judgment, her salvation will not depend on saying the times tables all the way to twelve times twelve. Work on it. Help her give it her best shot and then move on. Make a copy of the multiplication table to keep inside her notebook so that she can refer to it when she can't remember.

Equip with Responsibility

Do not handicap your child by letting her be the "poor little thing" that we have to pamper.

Milking without Hands

George and Beverly were dairy farmers. They had seven children. Their fifth child, Louise, was born with little stubs where her arms should have been. No one knows why, and it really doesn't matter. Louise would have to deal with the reality, not with what we wish she had.

Every other child in the family, on his or her fifth birthday was given a cow to milk. Milking that cow was the child's responsibility, rain or shine. On Louise's fifth birthday, Daddy took her to the barn and showed her the cow that was to be her responsibility. Since she could dress herself and brush her hair and teeth by using her feet, Daddy knew she could learn to milk the cow.

Flossy was gentle—the easiest cow to milk. Daddy knew she was the best choice for Louise's difficult assignment. Louise had a hard time learning to balance on the milking stool while using her feet to milk the cow.

Louise did not know that every day her daddy stood where he could watch her try to milk the cow. He stood by silently so he could move in quickly if she was in danger. He knew that the skills he was forcing her to learn would be necessary for other things she would need to be able to do in life.

Louise never saw the tears in her daddy's eyes as she fell off the milking stool time after time. She never knew of the restraint it took for Daddy not to come in and help her. He didn't rescue her because he knew she had to learn to solve problems—to get the stool back into position and try again. She never knew that he saw her tears of frustration when she fell again and again.

When she finally conquered that stool, he "just happened" to come by to comment on how well she was doing. She was proud to show him what she could do.

Louise never knew, until she had mastered the ability to milk, that Daddy went back every day and finished milking Flossy. He finished the job for the health and comfort of the cow and to keep the milk supply strong.

Imagine the pain of a father watching his little girl struggle with a relatively easy chore, but knowing she had to struggle in order to learn to overcome obstacles. He couldn't afford to handicap her further by rescuing her when the going got tough.

Good engineers do not handicap their children by letting a problem be an excuse for bad behavior. Even the most handicapped children can learn godly characteristics. They can learn that even if you have pain, you don't have to be a pain. Special-needs children should learn to be obedient, polite, respectful, and considerate in spite of their difficulties. Godly characteristics should be the norm for behavior; they need to be wired into all our rockets. Rockets have to fly in storms as well as in sunshine, and the presence of godly characteristics will help determine the stability of the flight path.

The Difficult Child

Special-needs children are sometimes difficult children. Some difficult children do not have special needs, and some special-needs children are not difficult. Then there are the unique children who have a combination of special needs and difficult characteristics.

If we had to put it on a continuum, we would see that there are a few children who are very easygoing and incredibly easy to wire. These kids wake up happy. They sing a lot. It's hard to ruffle their feathers. They are a joy and delight to have in the family.

At the other end of the continuum are the truly difficult children. They are hard to please. Even as babies, they don't want to be cuddled.

They don't like the food you are offering. They don't sleep well. As toddlers, it gets worse. If clothes don't feel just right they panic and insist on taking them off. It's hard to buy shoes for them that don't feel yucky.

In the middle of the continuum, we have the "normal" kids who may have a few difficult characteristics, but for the most part are easy to manage. In this chapter we will work on ways to modify the principles we have learned in order to wire securely difficult children and special-needs children.

Source for Security

Every engineer should consider reading *The Difficult Child* by Stanley Turecki, M.D. If your child is truly a difficult child, Turecki's book will help preserve your sanity. If your child has some difficult characteristics, it will help you figure out what's going on so you and your child do not go through vicious cycles that raise the stress level in your home. Dr. Turecki is a medical doctor, a child psychiatrist, and the father of two normal children and one very difficult child. In his book, he shows how to evaluate your child. He gives strategies—not theory—that will work in the real world. He presents situations and proposes ideas for working through them. Check the 649.153 T section of your library or order it through a bookstore.

If you have a child with learning disabilities, ADHD, or a physical handicap, *The Difficult Child* will be valuable because many special-needs children have some difficult characteristics.

Many of the concepts presented in this chapter are adapted from Dr. Turecki's book.

The Ripple Effect

A difficult child creates a ripple effect within a family like a rock does when it is thrown into a pond. Mom is the first ripple since she is with the child most of the time. She is often frustrated, angry, and tired. Dad is the second ripple. He may feel guilty that he is not at home enough to do a lot of the wiring. When he is at home, he doesn't handle the difficult child the way Mom does, which results in conflict between the parents. To top it off, Mom is often tired from doing battle with the child. When she finally gets him settled for the night, she is ready to crash.

Dad is looking forward to having time alone with his wife. But Mom, tired and stressed to the max, may be appalled that he could even consider intimacy. She feels he is being selfish. Then she decides that she is being selfish because she knows she should contribute to keeping a healthy marriage, but for the life of her, she doesn't know where she will get the energy to be a good wife after being on the battlefield all day. The fatigue and stress that come with having a difficult child can put a lot of stress on a marriage.

Siblings are the third ripple. Because the difficult child is harder to handle, Mom and Dad may count on the easy-going siblings to do the majority of the household chores. They may let the difficult child get by with being lazy. Overlooking his laziness is much easier than the battle that will probably come with trying to get him to carry his share of the load. Siblings may begin to resent the difficult child, and all the children may lose respect for their parents because they see them as weak leaders.

Difficult children are not all the same any more than other children are the same, but they were born with a temperament that makes them more of a challenge to train.

Grandparents are probably the next ripple. They may assume that if the parents would quit engaging in power struggles and just give this kid a few good spankings, he would settle in and follow their leadership. Grandparents who are openly critical and give lots of unsolicited advice heighten the stress level in the family.

Teachers and fellow students who share space with this child are the final ripple. The frustrated teacher may assume that if the parents had better parenting skills, her life in the classroom would be easier. The fellow students may ignore or ridicule this child who doesn't seem to fit in. The parents may be expecting the teacher to have the expertise to handle this child. They may be expecting her to give him lots of one-on-one attention. The teacher is probably appalled by their expectations. Don't they know she has twenty-nine other children in her class? How can she be expected to give their child one-on-one attention? How dare they expect her to write down his assignments every day if he fails to do it for himself! These expectations add to the stress experienced by the family and teacher of the difficult child.

Break Destructive Vicious Cycles

Difficult children are not all the same any more than other children are the same, but they were born with a temperament that makes them more of a challenge to train. Parents of difficult children often feel angry, inadequate, or guilty. These feelings lead to ineffective discipline. When discipline is ineffective, the child becomes more difficult and the parents feel more angry, inadequate, and guilty. A family becomes locked in a vicious cycle that leaves children feeling like bad kids and adults feeling helpless. Our goal is to help break these destructive, vicious cycles. Another goal is to use the principles of discipline we have already discussed to help wire difficult children. Some modification will be necessary. Proper wiring will require diligence and consistency on the part of the engineers.

Difficult children can grow up to be positive, enthusiastic, and creative if they are well managed. There is hope. God wouldn't have given you this rocket to wire if He wasn't going to equip you for the task at hand. Trust Him and talk to Him daily about the struggles you are facing. Pray for wisdom and discernment, since wiring this rocket will require the engineers to make good daily decisions.

Nurture Yourself and Commit Full Time

Do what you can to make sure you get adequate rest and nutrition. A special-needs child—any difficult child—requires more physical, mental, and emotional energy from you than do other children. By taking good care of yourself, you are in a much better position to complete this wiring project successfully.

A special-needs child also requires constant supervision, so a stay-at-home parent is a must. These children need the constant routine that is best supplied by a loving parent who is committed to full-time training.

Before we can modify the principles for this project, it will be necessary to have a clear image of what it means to have a difficult child. To clarify our thinking, the following survey has been adapted from Dr. Turecki's book. Consider the most difficult child in the family and fill out the survey for that child.

Do You Have a Difficult Child?

(Adapted from the opening pages of *The Difficult Child*)
Rate each question using this scale.
0 = Not a problem
1 = Fair to Middlin' Problem
2 = Big Problem
3 = Very Big Problem

Level of Activity _____

This child is always moving. He fidgets. He tends to be impulsive. When he starts talking, it's hard to find his "off" button. He tends to be loud. He's easily excited and it's hard to get him to calm down. This child hates to be confined in a car seat, highchair, or even in a room with a baby gate.

Impulsivity _____

In a classroom, this is the child that calls out the answers before re-membering to raise a hand. This child may just "take off" without warning and leave his frazzled parents running to bring him back. This child may push and grab instead of using his words to get what he needs.

Distractibility _____

This child has trouble concentrating and paying attention, especially if he is not interested. It's hard for him to listen. He daydreams and forgets instructions. He can't concentrate if there is anything else go-ing on in the room.

High Intensity _____

Loud! Whether miserable, angry, or happy, this child is loud and force-ful.

Irregularity _____

This child is hard to predict. It's difficult to figure out a pattern about when the child will be hungry or tired because he doesn't have a pat-tern. This child doesn't sleep well. He is moody. He has good or bad days for no apparent reason.

Negative Persistence _____

Once this child gets started, he goes on and on. He will nag, whine, or argue if he wants something. It's hard to get him to "turn it off" once he gets started. He's stubborn. Once a behavior is started, he "locks in," and it's very hard to get him to "unlock." He may have long, in-tense tantrums.

Low Sensory Threshold _____

This child is very aware of how things look and feel. He may be picky about what he will wear. He's sensitive about how clothes feel. He may be unreasonably upset about being in a room with bright lights or music he doesn't like. Foods may be limited to the ones whose texture he can stand. He may be sound-sensitive and unable to handle the chaos of a busy environment.

Initial Withdrawal _____

He doesn't like new people and new situations, and he is usually a shy, reserved child. He responds to new situations by crying and clinging to a parent.

Poor Adaptability _____

This child has a difficult time with change. If he's busy with one activity, he may have an extremely difficult time moving to another activity. He has trouble with clothes and food that are not his favorite. He may "lock in" when he gets started with an activity and have a tantrum if he has to change activities.

Negative Mood _____

This child is very serious. He may be cranky without apparent reason. He does not have a friendly, sunny disposition.

What Your Rating Means

3-5 points	Some difficult features
6-12 points	Difficult Child
13 or more points	Very Difficult Child

The "How" of Behavior

Temperament traits make up a child's personality. Temperament is not the "why" of behavior; it's the "how." An engineer may ask, "Why is he doing this to me?" In reality, he isn't doing anything to you. He's being himself. A better question to ask is, "How does he react when he doesn't get his way or when something displeases him?" Does he pout, cry, slam doors, or have a tantrum?

Once an engineer starts answering the "how" questions, he is in a better position to modify the principles of discipline to help a child make some important behavior adjustments. There are some temperament traits that are more difficult than others. Since we are wiring our rockets to be able to fly with the Kingdom Fleet, it is important to teach them how to compensate for temperament traits that are contrary to godly behavior.

Here is one way to look at it. If your six-year-old son were hurt in a terrible accident and his right arm had to be amputated, you would not cease all expectations for growth and responsibility. You would help him learn compensation skills so he could work around the difficulty and go on to be a faithful Christian and a confident, capable adult.

If he were right-handed and just learning to write, you would work with his teacher to help him learn to write with his left hand. You would work on coordination by teaching him to throw and catch a ball with his left hand. You would help him learn to tie his shoes with one hand. You would do whatever was necessary to help him get past the loss of his right arm and get on with life.

Just as the space shuttles have backup systems in case something fails, God has designed our rockets to be able to compensate for things that don't function the way we prefer.

You would do him no favors by feeling sorry for him, doing everything for him, and giving him his way. You would not smother him with special gifts to try to make up for what he has lost. Overcompensating is the formula for raising a cripple who will always depend on society for his support and to solve his problems.

Since wise engineers do not want to launch crippled rockets, we have to teach our rockets to work around the difficult areas. Just as the space shuttles have backup systems in case something fails, God has designed our rockets to be able to compensate for things that don't function the way we prefer. With God's help, rockets and engineers will come up with very creative solutions to problems. Engineers teach compensation skills so that our rockets will be wired to function in a way that honors our heavenly Father.

Compensation Skills

In order to teach compensation skills successfully, it is very important to assess the situation and determine which areas will need some work. It is equally important not to label your child.

Introducing Mandy

A child is in a room full of adults. When someone speaks to the child, the child hides behind a parent and refuses to speak. The parent promptly says, "This is Mandy. She's our shy child." Putting a negative label on a child is a poor parenting technique. Children usually live up to our expectations, and if we expect Mandy to be shy, she will be. A much better response would be, "This is Mandy. She is five years old and absolutely delightful. When she is a little more comfortable in this new situation, you may have a chance to visit with her. For right now, she's decided to stay with me, and that's fine because she's one of my favorite people."

Just as parents mess up when they label a child as "shy," it is also very important not to put a negative label on your difficult child. If you are in a social situation and your child is showing the difficult side of his nature, do not say, "This is Harry. He's my difficult child. I just don't know what I'm going to do with him. He is such a brat sometimes." A much better response is, "Please excuse us. We're experiencing some technical difficulties, and we need a little privacy to get back on track." Remove Harry from the situation, get things under control, and rejoin the group. If the matter cannot be politely resolved, excuse yourself and go home.

In order to work on compensation skills, we're going to take a couple of examples, figure out the traits that need attention, and give some behavior-management strategies.

Obedience Saves Krystal

Krystal is three years old. She has big green eyes, pretty red hair, and a sweet disposition. She wakes up singing in the morning. She's usually polite and obedient, but sometimes she gets frustrated. Her frustrations often develop into major temper tantrums. Sometimes one of her parents has to hold her tightly to keep her from hurting herself or anyone else until the panic and rage have subsided.

For instance, when Grandma gave her a pretty velvet dress—Krystal's favorite shade of green—Mom helped her put it on. Krystal started yelling, "Yucky! It feels yucky! Get it off!" She couldn't stand the feel of the velvet. She almost ripped the dress in her frantic attempts to get it off.

Every garment Krystal owns has the tag removed because she panics if a tag scratches and irritates her. She wears green and black every day. All other colors are yucky. She has three play outfits, one "going out in public" outfit, and one dress for church that she wears willingly. All her other clothes are too irritating and "yucky."

Krystal is usually obedient, but once she starts an activity, she will "lock in." If she is playing with her blocks and the time comes to put them away, she is likely to have a major tantrum. Even if Krystal is leaving the blocks to go have ice cream, her favorite treat, moving from one activity to another often triggers a tantrum.

In group situations, Krystal is easily distracted. If the room is quiet, she can listen to the teacher and follow instructions. If there is anything else happening, she will try to do her job, but she can't stay focused enough to do it.

Krystal was invited to a birthday party at a fast-food restaurant. The mother in charge was one of Krystal's favorite adults, so Mom left her there for an hour. When Mom came back, Krystal was in the corner of a booth, shaking and crying. When Krystal first became upset, the mom in charge had tried to hold her, but Krystal became more upset as she started toward her. When Mom picked her up, Krystal was trembling from head to toe. She said, "Make them mind, Mommy, make them mind. They won't be quiet." The noise and confusion of an activity most children liked was absolutely overwhelming; Krystal couldn't wait to escape.

Krystal loved Bible class when Mrs. Barbara was her teacher. Mrs. Barbara was very good with classroom management. The children knew the rules and obeyed Mrs. Barbara. On Sundays, Krystal could come home and tell every detail of the Bible story. On Wednesday night, Miss Kerry was the teacher. The children were tired from a busy day, and rowdy. Miss Kerry was sweet, but she did not have good classroom management skills. Krystal cried before class, and she came out shaking and crying because the kids had been rowdy. She could not tell any of the details from the Bible story.

Krystal was very impulsive. She had a hard time linking actions to consequences; she had no sense of danger. Mom and Dad had trained her to "look at me and listen" any time one of them said her name. One day Krystal and Mom were walking down the sidewalk in their neighborhood. Krystal was running ahead of Mom toward a busy intersection. Mom saw a big truck approaching and called out in a commanding tone, "Krystal!" Krystal was so good with the command to "look at me and listen" that she stopped dead in her tracks and turned toward her mom. That obedience, no doubt, saved her life.

Temperament Traits

Let's take a look at which of the temperament traits are a problem for Krystal. We will also look at ways the engineers to whom she was entrusted worked around these difficulties and taught some compensation skills.

Distractibility

Krystal had a hard time staying on task, so Mom made charts displaying Krystal's chores. She used pictures and made checklists for the kitchen, the bathroom, the bedroom, and the car. Krystal marked each chore on the laminated chart as she finished it. When she had marked all the chores in a particular room, she notified a parent. That parent then double-checked the "to do" list. If Krystal skipped an item, the parent would say, "I think you skipped one of your chores. Can you look at the chart and tell me which one you skipped?" If Krystal could find the skipped chore, she was instructed to get it done. If she could not find it, the parent showed her where it was.

Along with the distractibility came a lack of organization and trouble remembering. Mom put picture labels on Krystal's dresser drawers to help her remember where to put her clothes.

Mom and Dad also worked on increasing her attention span. If Mom told her to "go put on your pajamas, put your clothes in the hamper, and pick out a book for me to read," Krystal might do one or two of those tasks, but she rarely did them all. Mom and Dad did not treat these incidents as deliberate disobedience. They made it a point to give fewer instructions. After Krystal's bath Mom would say, "Please go put on your pajamas." When Krystal successfully completed that assignment, Mom would say, "Now put your clothes in the hamper, please." When Krystal did that, Mom would say, "Go pick out a book for us to read and bring it to me."

> **Mom could have taken a second and put Krystal's clothes in the hamper. She could have grabbed a book to read for a bedtime story. However, Mom's goal was not to train herself.**

It would have been much easier for Mom to go get the pajamas and dress Krystal. Mom could have taken a second and put Krystal's clothes in the hamper. She could have grabbed a book to read for a bedtime story. However, Mom's goal was not to train herself. She already knew how to do all those things. The goal was to work on Krystal's wiring and help her learn to do the things for which she was responsible.

When Krystal learned to do one assignment without getting distracted along the way, Mom and Dad started giving her two assignments. They gradually increased that number to four. After that, they relied on "to do" lists to help her stay on task.

When Krystal was ready to start to school, Mom and Dad decided to homeschool her. They put her in a preschool for a week, just to see how she would do. The teacher said that if she was sitting right across from Krystal, Krystal could do her work. If the teacher went away, or if someone nearby was talking, Krystal couldn't pay attention. She really tried to do her job, but she couldn't focus.

When it was time to start home school, Mom and Dad fixed a special study place for Krystal. After Mom had gone over a particular lesson,

Krystal did her lesson in that special place. The special place was away from the distraction of the telephone and from the area where Mom was working on a lesson with Krystal's brother. With no distractions, Krystal could do her work all by herself.

Negative Persistence

Krystal had some problems with negative persistence. Once a tantrum began, turning it off was difficult. Mom and Dad explained to Krystal that God wants us to control ourselves. They explained that it wasn't nice to have tantrums.

Mom and Dad learned by observation what kinds of situations were likely to trigger a tantrum. Over time, they taught Krystal to recognize those situations. They then taught her she would get a spanking if she had a tantrum. So if they were at home, Krystal was allowed to go to her parents' room for some "cooling off" time before she became frustrated enough to start a tantrum.

In public, Mom and Dad were very vigilant for signs of pre-tantrum frustrations. If a tantrum seemed imminent, one parent would remove her from the situation to a private place. Often that private place was the car, with the parent standing outside. In hot weather, the parent would sit silently in the driver's seat while the engine idled and the air conditioner cooled the car. Krystal would sit in the back seat and regain her self-control. Mom and Dad kept books in the car so they could read and relax while Krystal calmed herself. Because Krystal had so many difficulties, she had a low frustration tolerance. Knowing she could "go and hide" when overloaded helped her develop self-control.

Low Sensory Threshold

Krystal had a lot of trouble with this one. Mom modified her environment as much as possible. Krystal helped pick out a soft blue color for the walls and carpets. Her room had few decorations—nothing with bright colors. Too much stuff was confusing and distracting.

Mom let Krystal wear the few outfits that were not yucky. She carefully removed all the tags from Krystal's clothing. For several years Krystal wore only green and black.

After one birthday party, when Krystal spent the hour in a corner crying, she never went to another children's party. She couldn't handle the chaos. For family birthdays, the honoree chose an activity or a restaurant for the special occasion. By the time Krystal was five, she always chose a picnic and horseback riding.

Krystal had a hard time with her Wednesday night Bible class and a teacher who wasn't a good disciplinarian. At the end of the quarter, Mom offered to give the teacher a break and take the class. Because Mom was an experienced teacher and a good disciplinarian, that situation worked well. Mom kept the class until Krystal moved to the next age group.

Initial Withdrawal

This one was a bit of a problem. Krystal loved a few people dearly, but she had a hard time meeting new people. Being in a group at church was hard. She spent most of her time clinging to a parent. Mom and Dad taught her to compensate by inviting people into their home on a regular basis. Every Friday night, someone came for dinner: a widow, an elder and his wife, or a family with well-behaved children. Mom and Dad did not invite parents with ill-behaved children because they knew that if they did, Krystal would get overloaded and have a tantrum. They were trying to teach her that being with people can be very pleasant.

Learning to visit with others was difficult, so at some point in the conversation, Mom would offer some help. For example, during one visit Mom said, "Krystal, did you tell Mrs. Jones what we saw in the backyard?" Before the company arrived, Mom had suggested that Krystal might like to tell Mrs. Jones about the 'possum they had seen today. When Mom asked the question, Krystal knew the answer and could tell about her experience. Positive feedback from the guests made it easier to learn to carry on a conversation.

Poor Adaptability

Krystal had difficulty making a transition from one activity to another. If she was playing with her toys and needed to stop and do something else, she would have a tantrum. Mom and Dad learned to ease the transition and prevent the tantrum. If Krystal was playing, Dad would say, "Krystal, it's almost time to eat. I'm going to say the books in the Old Testament, and then it will be time to pick up the toys." By the time Dad got to Psalms, Krystal had started to pay attention to him, and she would say the rest of the books with him. When they were done, she was no longer "locked in" on her play, and she could make the transition to the next activity.

Transition to Bible class was sometimes tough. On the way to church the family reviewed memory verses and sang. They talked about how much fun it is to go to Bible class. At the classroom door Krystal cried and clung to Mom, even though she loved her Bible class. Once again, Mom and Dad had to ease the transition. Krystal was "locked in" on the fun she was having with her parents and couldn't "unlock" by herself to make the transition. Mom or Dad would take Krystal to class early and stay about five minutes. Krystal had time to work a couple of puzzles. During the second puzzle, the parent would get Krystal to tell the teacher about an interesting personal event. Getting Krystal to focus on the teacher helped her "unlock" from her parents. At the end of class, Krystal would be "locked in" on Bible class. The teacher helped make the transition back to the parents by helping Krystal gather her things and assisting her in telling Mom and Dad the story.

Over the years, that ability to "lock in" proved useful when Krystal was studying. Her first response was an irritated "what!" if someone interrupted her activity. Mom and Dad helped her learn to respond politely to interruptions.

Krystal grew up to be a lovely Christian lady. She has learned so many compensation skills that no one would ever know she was a difficult child. The struggles of her childhood have made her incredibly patient with others. She is also very insightful. Because she knows what it feels like to struggle, she quickly senses when someone she loves is struggling. She does what she can to diffuse the tension and make the situation more comfortable for the other person.

High Activity Level

Now we're going to move to another example and see how the engineers modified the principles we've learned to help their rocket be more securely wired.

Jonathan: Loud and Frustrating

Jonathan was seven years old. He was in the local public school—always in trouble. At church, during the fall quarter, three teachers walked out of Jonathan's class in frustration. They flatly refused to teach any class Jonathan was in.

Frustrated and not knowing for sure what to do, Jonathan's parents enlisted the help of Mrs. Smith, a school teacher from church. Mrs. Smith sat in on Jonathan's class one Sunday morning. Jonathan fidgeted in his chair and kept tapping on the table with a pencil until his teacher took it. He had to be reminded several times to raise his hand instead of blurting out the answers to all the questions.

Jonathan was also very loud. When he sang, he was loud. When he called out the answers, he was loud. When he was happy, he was loud. When he was angry, he was especially loud.

When the teacher served the "manna" and "quail" she had prepared for the children to sample, Jonathan didn't want any. Jonathan didn't want to do the handwork. As the class was ending, Jonathan decided he wanted some manna and quail. The teacher refused. He protested loudly that it wasn't fair, but he still did not get any.

His parents thought perhaps Jonathan was ADHD. His teacher at school had suggested that he be tested and given medication to control his behavior.

Since it was such a problem to keep a teacher in Jonathan's Sunday class, Mrs. Smith volunteered to take the class. She did several things that helped with the situation, and she passed those things along for Jonathan's parents to try at home.

Jonathan was always busy. He was very smart and since his brain was almost always busy, his body felt the urge to keep up by being in motion most of the time. Mrs. Smith tackled the problem in two ways. She talked with Jonathan privately to determine his likes and dislikes. He told her he was bored with the same stories all the time. He wanted some new stories. Mrs. Smith promised she would work on some stories he had never heard. She let him know she was counting on him to be a good listener during story time.

Mrs. Smith also made an individual report card for Jonathan. She explained about being considerate of other people. She explained that it was good manners for him to do his handwork with everyone else so the teacher didn't have extra work to do. She explained that if a treat was served, he did not have to eat any of it. However, if he changed his mind after everyone else had finished, he would have to do without. Every Sunday morning, Jonathan and Mrs. Smith sat down immediately after class to evaluate his behavior and record it on the report card. Jonathan had to help grade himself. After Jonathan and Mrs. Smith had gone over his report card, he gave it to his parents. His report card looked like this:

Behavior	Grade
Today, I tried not to call out the answers.	_____
Today, I remembered to raise my hand.	_____
Today, I stayed in my chair and tried to be still.	_____
Today, I tried to use my inside voice.	_____
Today, I tried to consider the needs of others.	_____
Today, I did my work at the right time.	_____

Mom and Dad reinforced this plan by saving Jonathan's report cards. They made a chart on the refrigerator to track his progress. Every month, if he had improved in one or more areas, he got to have an outing with the parent of his choice.

By making Jonathan aware of his behavior and having him help monitor it, he started to improve. Mrs. Smith was also able to assure the parents that Jonathan was not ADHD. When she was telling a new story, Jonathan maintained eye contact with her and sat completely still until the story was finished. An ADHD child cannot sit through a fifteen-minute story.

High Intensity

Jonathan was very loud and very forceful. Mrs. Smith and Mom and Dad came up with a strategy to retrain Jonathan. He was allowed to be loud when he was playing outside. When he was inside, he was to use his "inside voice." This strategy took constant supervision on the part of Mrs. Smith and Mom and Dad, but with consistent consequences, Jonathan learned to "tone it down."

They also talked to him about using his inside voice. If he was too loud, an adult would touch his shoulder as a reminder to "park it" for five minutes. At first, he had to park his posterior in a chair and sit quietly many times a day. By being consistent and making him aware of his behavior, he gradually improved. The first Sunday morning that Jonathan went all the way

through class without being loud, Mrs. Smith gave him a special treat. The first time he went all day without having to "park it," Mom and Dad celebrated by serving his favorite dinner and then taking him bowling.

When Mom and Dad visited Jonathan's classroom at school they found out why Jonathan was bored. Then the school and parents began working together on behavior management.

When Mom and Dad visited Jonathan's classroom at school, they found out why Jonathan was bored. He already knew most of the things in the curriculum. The teacher was having to teach so that the slower children could keep up. Jonathan's parents decided to enroll him in a private school that had a more challenging curriculum. They advised the new principal of Jonathan's difficulties and the methods they were using at home to correct his behavior. The principal matched Jonathan to a teacher who was trained to deal with difficult children. Then the school and parents began working together on behavior management so that the rules and consequences would be the same wherever Jonathan happened to be.

Mom and Dad allowed Jonathan to participate in after-school sports so long as he maintained appropriate conduct. The intensive physical exercise provided a safe outlet for his extra energy.

Irregularity

Jonathan was an irregular child. As a baby, he cried a lot. He didn't like to be cuddled. He was overly picky about his food. As he grew, those conditions intensified. Jonathan was rarely hungry at mealtime. He was rarely tired at bedtime.

Finally, Mom and Dad conferred with Jonathan's doctor. They quit making "going to sleep" an issue. They made sure Jonathan got lots of exercise so he would actually feel tired at bedtime. He had to take a bath at 8:00 o'clock, as his brothers and sisters did. He had to be in bed at 8:30, as his brothers and sisters did. He had to get up at 6:30, as the rest of the family did. His parents quit telling him fifteen times a night to turn off his light and go to sleep. They required him to stay in bed and be quiet, but they recognized that they could not make him sleep. Eventually, Jonathan's body grew accustomed to the new routine; he started to go to sleep shortly after 9:00.

Mealtime was no longer an issue. Jonathan had to sit at the table with the family and be polite, but he did not have to eat. If he grew hungry after leaving the table, he had to wait until the next meal to eat—no snacking between meals, only water. Eventually, Jonathan's body adjusted to the routine and he started eating with the family.

Conclusion

Even the most difficult children have to learn how to manage their difficult traits and live in harmony with the family. In many areas, it's a matter of acknowledging the difficulty and then learning to deal with it.

Remember, even difficult children are gifts from God. They can be wired to fly successfully with the Kingdom Fleet. Proper wiring will take much time, wisdom, and patience. It will require diligence and constant supervision. A parent must be at home at all times when such children are home. Many difficult children do much better if they are homeschooled. The stay-at-home parent is committed to the wiring project. If the child is homeschooled, the stay-at-home parent has a lot more control over the routine; there won't be the daily "comparing of notes" between all the Assistant Engineers involved with this child. For the difficult child, it is much better to have one engineer treating childcare as a full time job. In the next chapter, we'll take a look at homeschooling and how it can benefit the family.

Drill for Skills

Making Connections

1. There is a huge gap between a _____ problem and defiance.

2. A great deal of wisdom and _____ will be needed when dealing with a difficult child or a special-needs child.

3. Like every other child, a special-needs child is a _____ from God.

4. It isn't good to let a problem in one area become an excuse for _____ behavior.

5. Get _____ help as needed, in order to work around problem areas.

 Troubleshooting

1. Discuss the value of good observation when dealing with a difficult child or a special-needs child.

2. How can a lax attitude toward disobedience complicate the wiring of a difficult or special-needs child?

3. Discuss the ways parents modify the principles of discipline to deal with a special-needs child.

4. What is the most important rule for a special-needs child?

5. What is the best way to handle a learning barrier with a special-needs child?

6. Why is it a bad idea to use pressure to try to force learning?

7. Discuss the importance of compensation skills.

8. How does pampering further handicap a special-needs child?

9. Discuss the ripple effect a difficult child can cause in a family.

12

Trouble in School

Trouble in school can come in many forms. The common thread is that it can make life on the launch pad pretty miserable for engineers and rockets. One of the most important things an engineer can do about trouble in school is to do the preventive maintenance.

If the engineers have correctly installed the wiring during the first five years, they have already done a lot to prevent trouble in school. A child who is obedient, respectful, and considerate is better prepared for learning. If he has been taught to accept the discipline of his parents and submit to their leadership, he is prepared to respect and obey his teachers.

If the engineers have provided him with a consistent routine and have taken him for many test flights, he will be ready to learn the things he will be taught at different stages. One of the most important parts of preventive maintenance is to limit TV and video viewing. These activities do little to stimulate thinking skills. A child has to learn to think in order to do his best in school. Learning is not always exciting or entertaining. If a rocket has been wired to expect all things to entertain him, he will have a hard time learning things that don't excite or entertain him.

Plan for School

A child will do better in school if he has been allowed to use his imagination and develop some creativity. Instead of expensive toys, give your child boxes, paper, glue, markers, and anything else that will stimulate creativity. Allow lots of time for creative play. Let him create his own entertainment and learn to amuse himself with the things that happen to be part of his environment. Encourage him to spend as much time as possible playing outside.

Make sure every child in the family has some one-on-one time with each engineer every day. Read to all the children in the family, sometimes as a group, and sometimes individually. Make a trip to the library once a week and check out different kinds of books. If your library has story time for little ones, it may be well worth your time to attend. Many good libraries have wonderful activities for preschool children and their parents.

During the preschool years, don't push a child to learn. The daily contact with a stay-at-home parent will teach him many lessons. As a child notices something new, talk about it.

Caroline's Rhymes

One day Nellie was reading a Dr. Seuss book to her three-year-old. Caroline said in an excited voice, "Mommy! *Cat* and *hat* match!" "That's right, Caroline. They do match. There is another word we have for words that match. We say that those words rhyme. Can you think of some more words that rhyme with *cat* and *hat?*"

Off and on all day, Caroline thought of words that rhyme. While Nellie and Caroline did the household chores, Nellie found ways to build on the child's interest in rhyming words. When they made the bed, they thought of words that rhyme with *bed.* When they washed the dishes, they tried to find words that rhyme with *dish.* By the time Daddy got home, Caroline had lots of neat rhyming words to share with him.

Many parents use baby talk when communicating with their children. That delays good language development.

Baby Talk?

When Mommy is talking to fifteen-month-old Tommy, she uses his vernacular: "Tonny 'unt a cacker?" Mommy thinks that by copying his speech, she is connecting with him in a loving way. Actually, she is setting him up to need speech therapy in school. A child has to hear the correct sound of words in order to copy them. Talk in a gentle tone of voice, but use normal adult vocabulary. That's a marvelous way to build listening comprehension.

> When a child notices a new word and adds it to his vocabulary, pay attention. Without saying anything more about it, use that word a few times in appropriate sentences so he can confirm the meaning from the context.

Stuttering

Some children, often around two years old, begin to stutter. Don't panic. This isn't usually the same as true adult stuttering. This type of stuttering happens when a young child's head is full of words and he can't get them out in the order and at the speed he wishes. Be patient; he will sort it out. Helping him will make him feel as if he's doing it wrong. Excitable moments will add to his problem, but time and patience will take care of it.

Parents can create a stuttering problem by trying to change which hand the child prefers. If the child is consistently picking up things with his left hand, it is unwise to insist that he use his right hand. Trying to change the dominate side is one cause of true stuttering. Being left-handed is not a curse. It's really not even a huge inconvenience. Being left-handed won't cost him his salvation, so let him use the hand natural for him.

Essentials

Good nutrition and sufficient sleep are essential parts of preventive maintenance. In addition to providing them well-balanced meals, make sure preschool children go to bed by 8:00 and grade school and junior high school students are in bed by 9:00 each evening. Sleep-deprived people don't learn very well. Far too many engineers let the schedule become so cluttered that having a consistent bedtime schedule is impossible. Model responsibility by controlling the schedule so the children are not rushed, frazzled, and sleep deprived. Quiet evening routines are much more conducive to good sleep than a hectic, hurried lifestyle. On Sunday nights and Wednesday nights, many parents of little ones find it helpful to bring pajamas with them to Bible class. After Bible class or worship, let the little ones "go potty" and put on their pajamas. They can fall asleep on the way home and be ready to be tucked into bed.

With a lot of adult attention, lots of books to read, and lots of time to play and create, most children will be prepared when it comes time to go to school. But here is a word of caution about boys. Educators have known for a long time that little boys develop more slowly than little girls do. Most little boys are not ready for kindergarten before they are six. Even if they are very bright, emotionally and physically they will enjoy school more and do better if they stay home an extra year.

It's not a bad idea to keep children home until their sixth birthday. When a child goes to kindergarten a year late, he will be older and more mature than most in his class. He will also be older and more mature than his peers when he is ready to graduate from high school. Maturity can be a tremendous asset during those years when peer pressure is such a challenge.

Choices in Education

Americans are blessed with more options for educating children than almost any other people in the world. Let's look at the three most common educational choices and evaluate the pros and cons of each. Then we will look at some of the different kinds of trouble in school and propose some possible solutions.

Homeschooling

While homeschooling is not the correct choice for all families, it has been a tremendous blessing for many. Having school at home requires a stay-at-home parent, usually the mother. It requires organization and self-discipline. A parent who has been trained as a teacher has an advantage, but that certainly is not a necessity. Homeschooling is often the best decision for a special-needs child or a difficult child. Children can be extremely cruel to one another, and for a child who is different, the comments and taunts of his peers can do great damage. If he's at home with his mother all day, she can have a lot of control over which people have contact with him. That control can do a lot to protect his spirit.

We've already discussed the need for a consistent routine for preschool children. Following a consistent schedule is also important for the first eight years of homeschooling. The steady routine is the means by which a student learns self-discipline and time management.

High school students should be permitted to have part-time jobs and set their own schedules for school work. The teacher still grades papers, issues report cards, and keeps the transcript up to date. Turning time management over to the student during the high school years is wonderful preparation for college. College professors don't follow their students around nagging them about their work. They give them an assignment and a due date. On the due date, they collect the completed assignments. A wise homeschool teacher can prepare her students for that part of college life by transferring responsibility to the student during the freshman year of high school.

Here is how homeschooling worked for one family.

At-Home Teacher and Classroom

Homeschooling introduced many changes into the Johnson family. Mary Ann, the mom, had always been busy with church work, as well as her work at home. She had to delegate much of the church work to others when she began to concentrate on giving her children a quality education. Since her children were her mission field, she knew that devoting a few years to training them *was* church work. Congregations are only as strong as the families that make up the church family.

Mary Ann let her friends and family know that school was from 8:30 A.M. to 3:30 P.M., Monday through Friday. She asked them to respect those school hours and to call only in an emergency. If someone called with a non-emergency, Mary Ann would say, "I'm sorry but I can't visit now. We're in the middle of math class. I'll have to call you back after school." Her friends soon learned to respect school time.

Mary Ann also gave up Tuesday morning ladies' Bible class for about six years. Taking two hours out of one morning a week was too disruptive. Her youngest child wasn't mature enough to work on her own in a nearby classroom while Mom was in class. It just worked out better for Mary Ann to forego ladies' class until all the children were able to work independently.

The family had always been pretty organized, so doing the school work didn't require a huge shift in organization. Mom ordered the curriculum early. She spent most of August going through the teacher's manuals, focusing on study areas that required extra preparation. She was ready to start school on the first Tuesday after Labor Day.

Family school holidays were not the same as those of the county schools. Family holidays were planned to coincide with Grandma and Grandpa's visits. Even then, time wasn't wasted. Mary Ann entertained the grandparents and children by taking them to interesting historical sites. Grandpa almost always brought his guitar, and the children learned some music fundamentals while enjoying time with Grandpa.

Mary Ann was usually successful in scheduling visits of other guests during the summer.

One of the most important things Mary Ann did to ensure that her children got a good education was to treat her work as a teacher seriously. There can be a lot of flexibility with home school, but it has to be handled wisely. Mary Ann was diligent and didn't let an "I really don't want to do this today" attitude undermine the effectiveness of her school. She treated it just as seriously as if she were getting paid to get up every morning and drive across town to teach a classroom full of children.

Mary Ann also changed her decorating scheme. The decorative items that adorned the living and dining rooms were put into storage and replaced with maps, charts, and appropriate visual aids. A timeline stretched along one wall, and historical figures were added as their biographies were studied. When guests came, Mary Ann explained that the new decorating scheme was called "Early American Home School."

Every morning Mary Ann got up at 5:00 to have her quiet time with God and to do her exercises. At 6:00 she was getting showered and dressed for the day. At 6:30 the family got up. Each of the four children had an alarm clock. Each one was responsible for getting up, making his bed, and being dressed for the day at 7:00 when breakfast was served. They all sat down to eat with Daddy before he left for work.

After breakfast, it was time for chores. The chores were rotated among the family members, so everyone learned to do all of the household chores. School began promptly at 8:30 with the

Pledge of Allegiance and the singing of a patriotic song. A Bible class and a prayer followed.

Mary Ann divided the subjects being studied into 20- to 45-minute blocks of time. She rang the school bell at the end of each period so that those working independently in other areas of the house knew to come back to the dining room table. Recess was from 10:15 to 10:30 every morning. The neighborhood children came to play but Mary Ann sent them home when recess was over. Lunch was at noon. After lunch, everyone rested for an hour. At 1:30, school resumed. The neighborhood children learned that at 3:30, Mary Ann's children could come back out to play.

Homeschooling Advantages

There are several advantages to homeschooling. On standardized tests, homeschool students usually score a lot higher than students in public schools. Because the students are with an engineer all day, they gain real life experience. They observe and participate as the engineer deals with everything from an overflowing washing machine to being of assistance when there is a death in the church family. Because they are participants in real life, homeschoolers develop maturity and independent thinking skills. They become more resistant to peer pressure.

Homeschool students can also go to school in their play clothes. No one is there to make fun of them for not having the latest fashion fad. Homeschool scheduling usually provides time for the children to get all of their "homework" done during home school hours, so the evenings are free for family time. In homeschool, there are plenty of opportunities to supplement the curriculum. The teacher and students can go into more detail when studying something of great interest. They can be satisfied with the basics when studying something of less interest. The teacher can modify the lesson to fit the needs of the individual.

Another plus is having Dad get involved with special projects. For instance, Mary Ann saved the science unit on electricity for Dad. As far as Mary Ann was concerned, if the lights came on when she flipped the switch, that was all she needed to know. She has never been interested in the "why" of how things work.

Dad is an electrician and is fascinated with how and why things work. He spent about four nights one week studying electricity with the children. While Mary Ann washed the supper dishes, Dad and the kids built an electric motor on the dining room table. Each of the children took a turn soldering wires. Not only did they learn much from first-hand experience, but they enjoyed that special time with their dad.

Every well-run school needs a principal. In the Johnson's home school, Dad was the school principal. From time to time, a child would challenge Mary Ann's authority. Mary Ann always handled those challenges, but she also made the child tell the "principal" what had happened at school and why he got into trouble. If it was a first offense, the principal delivered a stern warning about future behavior. If it was a repeat offense, the principal had a paddle in his desk that was applied to the "seat of the problem" in order to convince the offender that the teacher's authority was to be respected.

Homeschooling Disadvantages

There are a few negatives about homeschooling. If the wiring in your rockets is not securely anchored by time to begin school, home school will be more challenging. If Johnny won't clean his room when Mom tells him to, it's not very likely he will do his school work when she tells him to. On the other hand, if Johnny has some pretty sloppy wiring installed, home school may be the perfect chance to rework some of the wiring.

Home school can be very expensive, depending on which curriculum is being used. Careful research needs to be done before selecting curriculum. If you select a curriculum that has "Bible" as one of the subjects, check it out carefully. There is a lot of false doctrine in some of those programs. Some teachers use everything but the Bible portion of the curriculum. They assure doctrinal soundness by designing their own Bible curriculum.

Help Groups, Laws, Diplomas, Rewards

Many parents benefit from the experience of others by joining a homeschool group. Should you decide to homeschool your children, be sure to register with the local school board and follow their procedures for beginning a home school. In some ways, one might think, "It's not any of their business what I do at my house with my children." Even though registration is a nuisance, it is important to model for our rockets the steps required in obeying the laws of the land. "Let every person be in subjection to the governing authorities. For there is no authority except from God, and those which exist are established by God" (Romans 13:1).

By law, parents must notify the state of their intent to homeschool. Whether or not you happen to agree with that law, it is important to obey the laws of the land in order to be obedient to God. It is important to let your children know that unless it conflicts with God's laws, you will obey the laws of the land.

A lot of folks worry about a homeschooled child not getting a high school diploma. Most of our Christian colleges admit home-schooled freshmen without hesitation. Often, all they require is a signed transcript. It is very important to do report cards and transcripts for each student so that you have documentation to prove the work was done. Because homeschooled students are "knocking the socks off" other students in areas like standardized testing and the National Spelling Bee, many state universities actively recruit them.

Because homeschooled students are "knocking the socks off" other students in areas like standardized testing and the National Spelling Bee, many state universities actively recruit them.

Home school requires a huge sacrifice of time and effort on the part of the teacher who usually doesn't get a pay check. However, the joy of watching children grow up well adjusted, well educated, and with godly character is a wonderful reward. The chances are much greater that a child will become a faithful follower of God if he is allowed to spend all day every day under the loving influence of godly parents. The maturity, discipline, independent thinking, and time-management skills learned in a well-run home school will be a tremendous asset for the rest of his life.

Public School

We hear a lot from the media about the problems in public schools. The government attempts to correct the bad situation by throwing money at the problems, part of which is used to study them and recommend changes. The effect has been that methods and curriculum change often, but the core problems remain.

Core Problems

We hear a lot about gangs, drugs, and violence in schools. We hear a lot about the lack of discipline. Many of the problems we are seeing are the result of children being reared in daycare centers instead of by concerned parents. One reason for the lack of discipline is a society that thrives on lawsuits. Many years ago, if a child disobeyed in class, the teacher was allowed to use the paddle in her desk. If a serious discipline problem occurred, the teacher could send the disobedient student to the principal's office. No one wanted to go to the principal's office. The offender was likely to be reprimanded, paddled, and told to wait in the office for his parents. Upon reaching home, the offender usually got another lecture and spanking, followed by a stern warning about obeying the teacher.

Because Dad stood up for the authority of the teacher, his daughter was a very cooperative student the rest of the year. When engineers refuse to support the authority of the teachers, they contribute to school problems.

Several years ago, a young teacher, Miss Edwards, paddled a fourth-grade girl for deliberate disobedience. After the paddling, Miss Edwards sent her to wash her face and regain her composure. When the girl came out of the bathroom she said, "My bottom's red and I'm going to tell my daddy and he'll sue you for everything you've got!"

Miss Edwards replied, "Well, I've got fifty cents, and if he wants it he can have it." Although calm on the outside, Miss Edwards was terrified. The threat of a lawsuit is very scary. That night at open house, a very large man came in escorting this girl. He said sternly, "Are you Miss Edwards?"

"I am," she replied.

The man said, "My daughter has something to say to you."

"Miss Edwards," the little girl said, "I'm sorry I talked ugly to you and I'm sorry I didn't obey, and I'm going to be really good for the rest of the year."

Dad said, "I don't know if her bottom was red when you got finished or not, but it was when I got finished, because I was looking at it and I made sure it was red."

Because Dad stood up for the authority of the teacher, his daughter was a very cooperative student the rest of the year. When engineers refuse to support the authority of the teachers, they contribute to school problems. A rocket will not respect a teacher if the engineer does not model respect for the teacher.

Get Involved

Since corporal punishment has been outlawed in most school districts, students have little to risk if they choose to be defiant. "Whatcha gonna do about it?" has become the predominant attitude on the part of many rebellious students. They know that other than detention and suspension, there isn't a lot the authorities can do to get them to conform to the standards expected in school. Many of these children know that if their parents are notified about the misbehavior, there will be no penalties. As long as the parents can have an eight-hour break from dealing with these children, that's all that matters.

Many towns still have excellent public schools from which to choose. If you are in the process of checking out the local schools, get to know a teacher at church. Very likely, that teacher will be able to point you in the right direction. It's a good idea to visit the schools being considered. Meet the principals and the office staff. Request permission to sit in on a class. Remember that these Assistant Engineers will be wiring your child every day. Choose carefully and then monitor the situation. These people will have your child for the most productive hours of his day and will have tremendous influence on him. Make sure you can trust the wiring they will install.

If you choose to send your child to public school, be a very involved parent. It may be best to limit involvement with the PTA because it stays so busy on so many projects. It's easy for an engineer to give a lot of time to benefit the "group" at the cost of time she should be devoting to the family. Volunteer to be the room mother or a teacher assistant so you can keep tabs on what's happening at school and be directly involved with your child.

What to Expect

In years past, classes at public schools were divided into groups. There was an accelerated group, an average group, and a slower group. Teachers could teach to the needs of their group. In recent years, there has been more mainstreaming. Even special-education children who need a lot of time and attention are in regular classes for much of the day. It is a tremendous challenge for a teacher to handle a classroom of thirty children with diverse needs. The teacher will have a few children in the class who come from two-parent, stable families. The children from these homes will have been through many test flights and will be far ahead of their peers in terms of positive experience. They will have been read to on a daily basis, and they will be considerably ahead in knowledge.

There will be several children from single-parent homes. These kids have spent most of their time in daycare centers. When they are home, the parent in charge is so busy doing household chores, paying the bills, and such like that the children get very little one-on-one attention. These children probably have the TV schedule memorized. They probably also spend a lot of time playing video games. Single parents often rely on electronic babysitters so they can do the things they have to do. The single parent will probably do the best she can, but she's working three full-time jobs trying to be Dad, Mom, and the breadwinner. Not even a super mom can be all things to all people at all times. Some of these children of single parents spend a lot of time on their own.

Single-Mom Problems

Cynthia's husband deserted the family when the baby was a year old. Not that it was such a loss. He was a drunk and a drug addict. He abused Cynthia and the kids. He has been a guest of the state on several occasions. He called Cynthia every time he was arrested until she finally decided not to bail him out anymore. The family is better off without him.

Cynthia works in a hospital. She is qualified only for jobs that require shift work. Her oldest son is eleven. Her daughter is eight, and the youngest is six. Day shift isn't too bad. Cynthia gets the kids up before she leaves for work. They prepare their own cereal breakfasts and get themselves off to school. Unless there is an emergency, Cynthia gets off at 3:00 P.M., arriving home shortly after the children.

The afternoon and the "graveyard" shifts are different stories. When she works afternoons, she has to be at the hospital at 2:30 and gets home at 11:30, providing there are no emergencies. The children come home to an empty house. They are supposed to do their homework. They fix sandwiches or have cereal for supper.

They are supposed to take baths and be in bed by 8:00. Sometimes they do what they are supposed to do; sometimes they stay up late playing video games or watching TV.

When Cynthia works the graveyard shift, she can sleep while the children are in school and supervise them after school. She has to be at work at 10:30 P.M. and doesn't get home until after the children have left for school.

Cynthia and her children live in a run-down apartment in a bad part of town. They have no family in town, and because her bum of a husband left her near the point of bankruptcy when he walked out, Cynthia cannot afford a babysitter. She is terrified to leave her children alone and she just prays they don't get hurt while they're home alone. She's also afraid someone will break into the apartment and hurt them. She's afraid her ex-husband will break in trying to find money for drugs. Her biggest fear is that the apartment will catch fire and the kids won't get out.

Cynthia also fears that the children will start roughhousing and one of them will get hurt badly enough for social services to intervene and try to take custody of her children. She has warned the children never to tell the teacher or anyone at school that they live alone most of the time. She has warned the children to be very careful when she is gone. She's afraid someone will learn that they are alone, social services will be called, and she'll lose her children to a broken-down foster-care system.

Assortment of Children

Children like Cynthia's pose special problems for teachers. Because they aren't getting adequate nutrition, their brains are not prepared to process information quickly. Because they often stay up late, they are tired in school. Tired children don't learn very well. Sometimes the children are clean and neat. Sometimes the teachers can tell it has been a while since the children have bathed or brushed their teeth.

A few children in a typical classroom are from dysfunctional homes. They have no self-discipline because there has never been an adult with the time and commitment to teach and train them. Some of these children were born to mothers who smoked, drank, or used drugs during the pregnancy. Academically, they are handicapped because some of their brain cells could not develop to their full potential. They are culturally deprived because the parents never made the commitment to parenting. The parents never took the time to make sure these children had the stable foundation or the rich and varied experiences that contribute to preparedness for learning.

There will be some children whose parents are divorced. These children "live out of a suitcase" as they are shuttled from parent to parent during the week. When they are not in school, they spend a lot of time in daycare or on their own. Their parents often try to provide "things" to make up for the lack of time and attention.

With this assortment of children, many teachers complain that they spend more of their time teaching social skills and civilized behavior. The academics often get pushed to the background in the face of more pressing problems.

Teacher Challenges

Since the public school teacher often has to teach in such a way that the slowest children don't get too far behind, the brighter children are often bored. The brighter children may become discipline problems if they aren't given a healthy way to channel their extra energy. Brighter children may not do as well in public school if there is nothing to challenge and stimulate them.

Remember that the Assistant Engineers who spend a lot of time with your child will help with the wiring. Remember that it is very important to control what influences your child. Some of these children from dysfunctional families will probably introduce your little rocket to some undesirable language and behavior. If you allow your rocket to be in this situation, you will have to do a lot of wiring checks and be prepared to do some rewiring.

Some Christian parents send their children to public school so their well-wired little rockets can be a good influence on others. Wherever our rockets are, they are to behave in a way that honors the Father and the values of the family. However, we would not send soldiers into battle until they had been through boot camp. Then we would pair them with a more experienced soldier when they go into battle. It is unwise to send a partially wired rocket into an unsecured area alone. It puts demands on him that he has neither the circuitry, the maturity, nor the experience to handle. His wiring needs to be very secure before he experiences daily test flights into what can be dangerous territory.

Some very good public schools are still available, mostly in the more affluent neighborhoods of big cities. There are also some exceptional schools in some of the smaller communities. A good public school can provide an excellent education. With a good teacher of high moral character, the rocket can do well. Anything less can be disastrous; it can put a great deal of stress on the occupants of the launch pad.

Private Schools

Many parents who don't like the public school choices in their area aren't in a position to homeschool, so they send their children to private schools. If that is the choice you are making, look for a school that teaches Bible, but does not teach a particular religion. Since all your household rules are based on God's laws, a school that teaches Bible in its religion classes will not conflict with what is being taught at home.

Private education has many advantages. Because of a higher population of children from more stable families in private schools, discipline is easier to maintain. The curriculum is usually challenging and designed to prepare students for college. Teachers' salaries are usually below normal, but many Christians are willing to sacrifice in order to teach in better schools. These teachers are usually dedicated and efficient.

In private schools, there is often a division between the "haves" and the "have nots." Status is important and many of these kids use possessions to measure status. Therefore, a child who has every available gizmo and gadget may set the norm for what possessions are required to be part of the "in" crowd. Unless uniforms are required, the "haves" may set the fashion standard and make outcasts of the "have nots." For a family struggling to give its children a good education, the battle between the "haves" and the "have nots" may be painful.

Expense, Attention, Commitment

A private school may be just as expensive as a college. Two incomes are required for most families to afford private school. If that is the choice you are making, try to arrange work schedules so that one parent can greet the children when they come home from school. This rule applies even in the case of older children. Teen years are turbulent and the temptations real, so it's important to have a parent available to talk with the child immediately after school. In the "how did your day go today" kind of discussions, a parent with good listening skills can do a lot to ease an adolescent through troubling times.

Even as teens, children have needs when they have them. A calm parent will be in a better position to hear about the day and help with problems or celebrate successes. An attentive parent can tell by the way a child comes into the house what kind of day he has had. If the rule is, "Call me at work when you get home from school," the atmosphere is different. For most who work outside the home, spending time on personal calls is discouraged. Even if personal calls are allowed, the telephone cannot transmit facial expressions and body language, and visual clues are very important to good communication. Also, it's hard to give undivided attention while at work. With the office phone ringing, or customers coming and going, or the parent covering the mouthpiece to give or receive instructions, the teen knows he is in second place.

Our rockets need to know at all stages of the wiring process that "I'm here if you need me." It's important for engineers to live up to that commitment. When both parents hit the door at day's end, dead tired and in a hurry to get dinner on the table, the atmosphere isn't conducive to the discussions rockets need to have with engineers. Consider very carefully whether or not the dual income is worth its costs in family time and stability.

Problems in School

Academic Difficulties

Academic problems come in many forms. Some kids handle every subject in school easily. Others excel in some subjects and struggle with others.

Remember the rule we used for special-needs children, because it applies to most problems: "If this is going to keep you out of heaven, we have to master it. If it is not going to keep you out of heaven, give it your best effort and move on."

Passes Math but Flunks Honesty 101

Ann was a bright, happy child. During her first four years of school, she had been at the top of her class in reading and in history. But for some reason, math just didn't make sense to her. At every parent-teacher conference, the main focus was on trying to boost Ann's math skills. Now that she was a fifth-grader, she was really behind, and the teacher was feeling the pressure to make sure she was ready for junior high.

Dad loved math, so he had always assumed responsibility for helping the children with their math homework. Dad sometimes became frustrated because, after careful instruction, Ann just didn't get it. Many homework sessions ended with Ann in tears and Dad fuming.

Mom and Dad finally decided Ann should be responsible for doing her own work. Her teacher allowed her to stay after school to work on her math. She made some progress, but not much. The teacher and Mom and Dad finally decided to work on basic skills and skip the stuff the book said Ann had to know. The goal was that by the end of high school, she would be able to add, subtract, multiply, and divide. She would be able to work with fractions. She would be able to write a check and balance a checkbook with the help of a calculator. When making a purchase, Ann would be able to know whether or not she received correct change.

Ann went through school making D's in math and A's and B's in other classes. Mom and Dad carefully checked all report cards. They made sure Ann was being polite and respectful in math class. They made sure she attempted to do her homework, even if she didn't solve all the problems correctly. They wisely decided that grades would not be an issue. If Ann did her best, that was all they required.

Ann's small-town school still graded student conduct. Ann's parents demanded that all their children made A's in conduct, regardless of their academic grades. One day, Ann came home with her fifth-grade report card. She had a B in conduct for chorus. Dad asked about it. Ann lied and said her teacher didn't give A's in conduct. Dad called the teacher. The teacher had given several A's in conduct. Ann got a B because she had been talking and goofing off in class.

Dad took Ann to the bedroom and conducted a refresher course in Honesty 101. He let her know that she had been spanked for lying to him and for her disobedience in class. She had to write an apology to her teacher. Dad read and initialed it and had her take it to school. For the rest of her school career, Ann brought home some pretty low grades in math, but she always made A's in conduct.

Different Learning Styles

Sometimes a different learning style can be the cause of academic difficulties. We are all aware that we have five senses. We can hear, see, smell, taste, and touch. Many people learn best by seeing. Others learn best by hearing. Many learn best by using a combination of seeing and hearing. Most classrooms are designed to teach children by letting them hear information and by showing them examples and visual aids. That works great for the majority.

But what if you have a rocket that doesn't learn best by hearing or seeing? Even without special training, observant engineers can tell a lot about the learning style of their rockets.

Learning By Touch and Feel

Daniel was a sweet seven-year-old boy. He was obedient, polite, and kind to others. But Daniel was already off to a poor start in school. It wasn't for lack of effort. It wasn't for lack of intelligence. It was because he had a different learning style.

When Mom took her children to the store, she always said, "Hands in your pockets. If we aren't buying it, we don't touch it because it doesn't belong to us." Daniel had an incredibly hard time with that rule. He couldn't get information about things just by looking. He had to touch them.

Daniel's first-grade teacher figured out what was happening. Daniel couldn't say the names of the letters. When the children were working on "what sound does this letter make," Daniel couldn't do it. The principal scheduled an aide to work in the classroom with Daniel. The aide used flash cards. Daniel traced a letter with his finger. Then he "drew" the letter in the air. The aide gave him a carpet scrap. Daniel used his finger to "draw" letters on the carpet scrap. Letting Daniel "touch and feel" the information helped him tremendously.

The teacher and the aide came up with ways for Daniel to "touch and feel" things in all subjects. Daniel wasn't being difficult. He just had a different learning style. When the teacher and aide started teaching to his learning style, Daniel began to do better in school.

The teacher helped Daniel's parents find ways to reinforce the lessons at home so that Daniel could catch up and be successful in school.

Just as some children learn best by touching, others have to connect movement to learning.

"Be Still!"

Beverly was sometimes a difficult third-grader. Her teacher was inexperienced, having just graduated from college. Beverly was a real challenge. When the teacher was talking, Beverly kept her head down and doodled on her notebook paper. Beverly rarely made eye contact with her teacher.

The teacher would sometimes put Beverly on the spot by asking her a question about something that had just been said. Beverly usually knew the answer. That Beverly could answer questions without being attentive greatly perplexed the teacher.

One day the teacher had all she could take of being ignored. She made Beverly clear her desk, sit up straight, and listen. Beverly did as she was told, but she couldn't sit still. She rocked in her chair and swung her foot while the teacher was talking. Finally the teacher shouted at her in exasperation, "Beverly! Be still!" A frustrated Beverly sat crying quietly while the teacher finished the lesson.

The teacher then gave a quiz over the material just covered. Beverly missed every question. The teacher, thinking Beverly was being stubborn, sent her to the office. Fortunately, the principal was a former special-education teacher. He soon discovered that Beverly learned best when she was moving. He also recognized that having her in a class with an inexperienced teacher wasn't a good idea. He assigned her to a teacher with twenty years' experience. That teacher was able to help Beverly get the most out of class.

The teacher and principal helped Beverly's parents learn how to use movement to help Beverly with memorization. Beverly had a hard time sitting and memorizing spelling words. However, if she and her mom did jumping jacks while spelling words, Beverly could remember them. Her teacher allowed Beverly to tap her foot to the rhythm of jumping jacks when she took her spelling test.

When learning math facts, Mom, Dad, and Beverly tossed a beachball. Mom threw to Dad and said "3." Dad caught it and said "plus 6." He threw it to Beverly who said "equals 9." Movement helped Beverly improve her grades, and she became a much happier student.

Problems Getting Along with Others

A problem getting along with others can have many causes. If your rocket is being wired to fly with the Kingdom Fleet, he will be different from other children, and children can be cruel to those who are different.

Perhaps the best strategy is to remind your little rocket that Jesus was not liked by everyone. Teach your child how to adhere to a better standard of behavior without pointing out the poor behavior of others. One of the most important guidelines for Christian behavior is this:

> "But sanctify Christ as Lord in your hearts, always being ready to make a defense to everyone who asks you to give an account for the hope that is in you, yet with gentleness and reverence" (1 Peter 3:15).

Because of immature people-skills, rockets don't always handle people-problems well. They know we are supposed to do what God wants us to do. They sometimes take it upon themselves to try to control the behavior of others. That isn't a good plan. Very few things are as obnoxious as a bossy grade-school child who spends her time telling others: "That's not nice. God doesn't want us to act like that. You'll go to hell if you do that."

Instead, teach your child to go quietly about her business. She is not responsible for the way others behave and she has no authority over them. Her job is to obey the teacher and to be kind to the children who don't have many friends. We can't force others to listen to the message, and being pushy repels people. It is far better to live a quiet life and, when people ask about the ways we are different, have a kind and accurate response prepared to share with them.

Respond, Don't Just React

If there is a school dance, or some other activity that would not be appropriate for people who profess godliness, teach your child not to make a big deal about it. Instruct him to tell the teacher quietly that this activity is not something he participates in, and ask to be given an alternate activity or to be quietly excused.

So many school and sports activities are scheduled at a time when God's children are attending worship or Bible class. Many sports tournaments are scheduled to go all day on Sunday. People of the world are busy the rest of the week, so they take the one day set aside for worship to enjoy the things that bring them pleasure. Since they have no interest in God, they don't mind using His time for themselves. Putting one's personal pleasure before honoring God is a form of idolatry. Giving someone else the time, the energy, the money, or the interest that should have been devoted to God is spiritual adultery.

> **Putting one's personal pleasure before honoring God is a form of idolatry. Giving someone else the interest that should have been devoted to God is spiritual adultery.**

Teach your children that God comes first. If that means they come to Wednesday night Bible class in their cleats and uniforms, so be it. If the coach makes a big deal about the practice time missed, it's time to make a choice. Do we take a stand for what is right and forfeit the temporary pleasures of sports, or do we submit to worldly pressure and give God our left-over time? Many Christians have decided that Wednesday Bible class and

Sunday evening worship are optional, if there is something else scheduled.

Prioritize

The question is not, "Will I go to hell if I skip church?" The principle
to wire into the rocket is that God has first place in our lives. When money
comes into our possession, we take out the portion belonging to God before we spend any on ourselves. When planning how to use our time, God
comes first. Earlier in the book we talked about the clothing we choose
and how it either confirms or confuses the message we are trying to con-
vey to the lost. Our friends and neighbors know how much we value our
relationship with God by the way we prioritize the events of our lives. By
our priorities we will communicate to those around us that God has first
place in all areas of our lives, or we will teach that we worship and serve
God at our convenience, giving Him our discards and leftovers.

When God's people are coming together to be in His presence, we
should want to be there. "For the eyes of the Lord move to and fro throughout the earth that He may strongly support those whose heart is completely His" (2 Chronicles 16:9). We can gain quite a bit of strength from
the Lord by daily contact with Him. However, when we assemble to offer
Him our worship and praise, we are blessed and strengthened by being in
His presence with others of like mind.

If serving God is our top priority, we demonstrate that by giving him
the first fruits of our time, as well as the first fruits of our money. (See
Exodus 23:14–19.) It would also be helpful to read Malachi 3:6–18 as a
family and talk about the principles taught there. Even though we are not
under Old Testament law, God hasn't changed His character. We are always to give Him our best, not our leftovers, whether time, money, or energy. If those around us are to learn that our relationship with God is the
most important part of our lives, we must not reprioritize our schedules to
accommodate our pleasures and give Him the time that doesn't matter to
us. When making decisions, engineers and rockets must learn to choose
between things that give momentary pleasure on earth and things that
give eternal blessings in the presence of God.

Teacher-Student Conflicts

Personality conflicts happen. Even a properly wired rocket will sometimes have problems with certain teachers. Worldly people don't handle
personality conflicts in the same way God's children are to handle them.

If it seems that a teacher doesn't like a child, schedule a parent-teacher conference and try to resolve the problem. Be kind and be respectful, but keep your child's best interest in mind.

Sometimes a teacher doesn't like a child but won't admit it.

Mary and the Wise Guidance Counselor

Mary made good grades in most of her junior high classes, but she always dreaded English. Mary was sure her teacher, Mrs. Simpson, didn't like her. Mrs. Simpson was openly critical of Mary, and Mary got D's and F's on a lot of her work.

One day Mary reached the end of her patience. She walked out of class to go to the counselor's office. As she left the classroom, she literally bumped into the counselor, Mrs. Dean, in the doorway. Mrs. Dean had a note from the principal to excuse Mary from English. Mrs. Dean took Mary to the office and asked her how English class was going. Mary started crying as she talked about her frustrations. She felt that nothing she did would satisfy Mrs. Simpson.

Mrs. Dean told Mary that she had become aware of the personality conflict and felt Mary would do better in Mrs. Sanderson's class. Mrs. Dean didn't know it, but Mrs. Sanderson had been Mary's teacher at church, and Mary loved her.

Mrs. Dean had become aware of the problem with Mary and Mrs. Simpson when she overheard a conversation in the teacher's lounge. She heard Mrs. Simpson talking about how much she hated Mary. Mrs. Dean checked the schedule and classroom size of the other English teachers. Mrs. Sanderson had room for another student during the same period as Mary's current English class.

After school, Mrs. Dean informed Mrs. Simpson that Mary was being transferred. She also informed Mrs. Sanderson, who let Mary know how delighted she was to have her in class. Mary made A's and B's in English the rest of the year. Having a teacher with whom she was compatible made all the difference.

Discipline Problems in School

Make a point to get to know your child's teacher. Consider having the teacher over for dinner at the beginning of the school year. The goal is to establish a comfortable relationship so that conflicts are easier to resolve, which is especially important if you have a difficult or strong-willed child. Engineers and teachers must present a united front when wiring these rockets. If the adults aren't united, it is easy for rockets to try to manipulate the situation by playing the adults against each other.

Master of Manipulation

Fifth-grader Jessica absolutely hated English. It was boring. When her parents asked, "Have you done your homework?" Jessica told them she didn't have any homework. When the teacher asked her why she hadn't done her English homework Jessica replied, "My mom said I didn't have to do it since we were really busy last night." Unless the engineers and the teacher get together and compare notes, Jessica will continue to play the adults against each other in order to avoid a distasteful task.

Jessica's teacher had met some really irresponsible parents during her career, but she refused to give up on Jessica. She sent notes home asking Jessica's parents to call and schedule a conference. The parents never called, so she assumed they weren't interested. It wasn't until mid-term reports came that Jessica's parents realized she was failing English. They called the school to schedule a conference.

The engineers angrily asked the teacher why she had failed to advise them of the problem. The teacher explained that she had sent several notes home and hadn't gotten a response. Once the engineers and teacher voiced their frustrations, they were able to have an open, honest discussion. The problem was not with the adults. Jessica had been dishonest in not delivering the notes to her parents. She had repeatedly lied to her parents and to her teacher. After identifying the problems, the adults came up with a strategy to get Jessica back on track.

During the meeting with the teacher, the parents were given the page numbers of all the work Jessica should have done to this point. The teacher stated that every Monday she wrote the week's assignments on the board for the children to copy into their assignment notebooks. Dad said that he would stop by the school on the way home from work on Mondays and copy down the assignments. The plan was to have Jessica be responsible for writing down her assignments, but if Dad had a copy, Jessica couldn't get by with lying to him about whether or not she had homework. Mom and Dad assured the teacher that Jessica would be doing Saturday school for quite some time, until she made up all the work she had missed.

When Mom and Dad got home, they confronted Jessica with her manipulative, dishonest behavior. Dad let her know that every evening he was going to check her assignment notebook to make sure she was keeping track of her assignments. He was also going to check her homework. Dad let her know that until the missed work had been completed, she would be doing English every Saturday. Then he gave her a spanking for being dishonest and manipulative and had her write an apology to her teacher that he read and initialed.

For several weeks, Jessica spent every Saturday in her room working on English. An engineer set the timer for forty-five minutes. Every forty-five minutes, Jessica was given a fifteen-minute break so she could get a drink, go to the bathroom, and take care of other personal business. Each time Jessica was on break, the engineer on duty checked her work to make sure she had not been playing or staring out the window. An engineer was available if she needed help, but it was Jessica's responsibility to stay on task and get her work done. Jessica had to spend six "periods" each Saturday doing make-up work. She was allowed no TV or computer time on Saturdays until all the make-up work was done.

Since Saturday was usually reserved for family time, the parents alternated taking the other children for fun outings while one parent stayed and supervised Jessica's "Saturday school." Jessica's restitution was hard on the whole family. Schedules had to be shifted, and whichever engineer had Saturday-school duty had to be in the house monitoring the situation. That engineer missed out on the fun outings with the other children. Enforcing the rules is sometimes inconvenient. It's a good thing that Jessica had engineers who loved her enough to make her learn the high cost of trying to shirk responsibility.

Expect and Inspect

Make time in your schedule to do surprise inspections of your children's school activities. Drop by the school office and ask to stand outside the classroom where you can observe without being seen. If your child never knows when you will show up, she might improve her behavior.

Ralph's "Hoochie Coochie" Dance

Mrs. Ellerson had sent home a couple of notes with Ralph, one of her fifth-grade students. Ralph had a delightful sense of humor but poor timing. He used his humor at inappropriate times and disrupted the class. Ralph loved physical humor. His favorite, and a favorite of his audience, was his "hoochie coochie" dance. When Ralph was particularly pleased with himself, he would jump up on his chair and do his little dance to celebrate.

With the first note, Mom and Dad gave Ralph a stern lecture. With the second note, Ralph was grounded for a week. Mrs. Ellerson advised Mom that Ralph's behavior had not improved.

Mom and Mrs. Ellerson worked together to find out about what time would be most likely for Ralph to do his "hoochie coochie" dance. Mrs. Ellerson and Mom made a date to "set him up." Mom was watching the back of the class from the hallway. Ralph won a spelling bee and jumped up on his chair to celebrate. Before he could get his dance started, Mom came in and removed him from the chair. Mom said, in front of the class, "Mrs. Ellerson, I'm taking Ralph outside to work on his behavior. We'll be back when Ralph is ready to behave according to your class rules. If you need us, we'll be right outside your window." Naturally, Ralph's classmates watched out the window to see what Ralph's punishment would be.

Mom took Ralph outside and gave him a trash bag. She sat in her lawn chair with a drink and a book while Ralph pulled weeds and picked up trash. After Ralph had worked an hour in the hot sun, Mom asked if he was ready to behave. He told her he was ready to go back into a nice, cool classroom and behave. Mom let him get a drink and go to the bathroom before she escorted him back to class. Ralph had to spend an extra hour after school making up the work he had missed while working in the yard.

By knowing the teacher and showing respect for her authority, Mom helped Ralph learn to behave in class. There is a time to be funny and a time to be serious. Mom and Dad helped Ralph learn the difference. They set up a private report card and made several copies. At the end of every school day, Ralph was to take his report card to Mrs. Ellerson. He was graded on how well he controlled himself in class and whether or not he used his timing wisely. Since the system was easy—either "pass" or "fail"—it didn't require much of Mrs. Ellerson's time to grade the report card.

Every day when he got home, Ralph had to present his report card to his Mom. If he passed, he could choose thirty minutes of extra play time or thirty minutes extra computer time. If he failed, he had to spend thirty minutes washing walls, scrubbing baseboards, or cleaning the bathrooms. Since he was rewarded for monitoring his behavior and using his self-control and penalized for failing to use his self-control, he quickly learned to conform to Mrs. Ellerson's class rules.

One-Parent Discipline

Working with the school to handle discipline problems is easier with a two-parent family. With a single parent, it's much harder because Mom can't so easily drop in at school. If there is a problem at school, she can't always take off from work and handle the problem. That sets up a natural "penalty-free zone" and, as we've discussed previously, that is a very dangerous thing.

A Switch for Eduardo

Maria was a single mom. Her husband was killed in an accident when she was seven months pregnant with her third son, Mario. The oldest boy, Juan, was now in the sixth grade. The middle boy, Eduardo, was in the first grade. Four-year-old Mario attended a neighborhood preschool while Maria worked in the laundry at a nearby nursing home. Juan picked up Mario and Eduardo on the way home from school and stayed with his younger brothers until Maria got off work about 7:00 P.M.

One morning, Maria got a call at work. Eduardo had been suspended. He had been working at the craft table when he and another boy got into an argument over who got to use the glitter first. In a fit of anger, Eduardo stabbed his classmate in the arm with a pair of scissors. The injury wasn't serious, since Eduardo had been using safety scissors. Still, the school penalty for that form of aggression was a three-day suspension. It was Wednesday morning, so Eduardo was suspended for the rest of the week. Maria had used all her sick days and vacation days when Mario was in the hospital, but she asked her supervisor for the rest of the day off. Permission was granted—without pay. She went to school and got her son.

Maria took Eduardo home and delivered a stern lecture followed by a hard spanking. She let Eduardo know that fits of rage would not be tolerated. She made him write an apology to the student he had hurt. Eduardo spent the rest of the day either studying or doing chores that his momma assigned. That afternoon Maria considered her options. She had no family in town. She certainly could not leave Eduardo home alone. She couldn't keep Juan out of school to stay with him. She couldn't take the time off without pay and risk losing her job. What to do?

Fortunately, Maria had a good church family. She contacted Mrs. Jenson, Eduardo's Sunday school teacher. She was a full-time homemaker and had often kept the boys when Maria was in a tight spot. They agreed that Mrs. Jenson would keep Eduardo on Thursday and Friday.

When Maria dropped Eduardo off at 7:00 A.M. Thursday, she came prepared. She had Eduardo's school work organized: "Mrs.

Jensen, I really appreciate your keeping Eduardo for me. He loves you so much and loves to come to your house. Eduardo knows this is not to be two days of fun and games. He has gotten himself into very serious trouble.

"I expect Eduardo to work hard during his two days with you. I have all of his school work right here. His assignments are clearly marked. Eduardo is to be sitting at the table working on school, or he is to be providing free labor for you. He is not to go outside to play. He is not allowed to watch TV or videos. He is not allowed to play on the computer. If he gets tired, he can take an afternoon nap."

Before Maria kissed her son goodbye, she put a switch on the table. She said, "Eduardo, I'm leaving this switch with Mrs. Jenson. If you give her any trouble at all, I expect her to give you a good spanking. She and I both love you too much to let you get by with being disobedient."

Mrs. Jenson was kind but very firm with Eduardo. He had to study a school subject for forty minutes and then wash walls for fifteen minutes. With that schedule, Eduardo had a very full twelve hours with Mrs. Jenson. She fed him good meals and allowed him to take a nap after lunch. He was working hard enough that he needed the rest. By the end of two days, Mrs. Jenson's walls were nice and clean from the chair rails to the baseboards.

On Friday afternoon, Eduardo whined, "Mrs. Jenson, I'm tired. I've worked hard all day and I don't want to do any more homework. I'm tired of washing walls. Can't I watch TV—pleeeze?"

"Eduardo, you heard what your momma said," Mrs. Jenson explained. "I've raised three boys, and I'm much too smart to listen to whining and complaining. You are much too good a boy to do anything other than what your momma said for you to do. You have a choice to make. You may either do what you are supposed to do, or I will use the switch, just like your momma said. I'm telling you now that if I go get the switch, it will be used. You need to think about that and decide if you are going to obey or if you are going to continue whining and complaining."

Eduardo made a wise decision and improved his attitude. He knew enough about Mrs. Jenson to know that she always kept her promises.

Conclusion

Trouble in school comes in many forms, and we certainly haven't covered them all. Hopefully, the things we've covered will be a springboard for your own thoughts as you work through any difficulties that may be encountered. The time spent in school can really enrich a child's life, but it can be a heavy burden if school time is plagued with problems.

Conscientious engineers will make sure that the type of school that has been chosen for the rocket is a "good fit." They will make sure that the rocket is taking care of his responsibilities and doing his best in all areas of life.

Wise engineers reward effort, not success. They recognize that each rocket is equipped with a unique set of talents. We can't all be superstars in every area. If a rocket is doing his best, it should be acknowledged and appreciated.

Engineers should be acutely aware of the curriculum being used. There will likely be a lot of evolution taught and a good deal of "take care of Mother Earth" concepts. Wise engineers stay on top of what the rockets are learning so they can turn controversial subjects into opportunities to open God's word and see what He has to say on the subject.

Learning is like eating fish. You have to know which part to swallow and which to spit out. "Swallow" only those things that are in agreement with God's word.

Drill for Skills

Making Connections

1. Trouble in school can make life miserable for engineers and _____
   _____.

2. _____ maintenance can do a lot to avoid trouble in school.

3. Limiting _____ and video games can help prevent trouble in school.

4. Encourage _____ play rather than buying a lot of expensive toys.

5. Children need nutritious meals and a _____ bedtime and sleep schedule.

 # Troubleshooting

1. Discuss the pros and cons of home school.

2. Discuss the pros and cons of public school.

3. Discuss the pros and cons of private school.

4. What is the most important rule for a child who is having academic difficulty?

5. Discuss the different learning styles.

6. What is the learning style of each of your rockets?

7. Discuss some of the problems children can have with other children.

8. How can one manage conflicts between school activities and worship assemblies?

9. What is the scriptural foundation for the way we prioritize when there is a conflict between worship assemblies and extracurricular activities?

10. How do we help our rockets learn that God comes first in all things?

11. Discuss ways to handle personality conflicts with teachers.

12. What are some common discipline problems in school? Discuss problem prevention and ways to work with the school to solve problems.

Section

Preparing for the Launch Date

13

Ready for Blastoff

Preparing for the launch date should be on an engineer's mind every day. We stated earlier that a rocket's launch date should be as firmly in an engineer's mind as the date of birth. The launch date is a very special event on the launch pad and requires careful preparation. It takes eighteen to twenty years to complete the preparations for a successful launch. In this chapter, we will look at the most important parts of preparing for a successful launch.

Preparing the Engineers

When we think of a rocket's being launched, we think of the things a rocket will need in order to do well in flight. We sometimes forget the "behind the scenes" people—the engineers. Engineers must do a very good job with their part of the program or the rocket will not be prepared for a successful launch and a stable flight.

Preparing for the launch date requires a special mindset. A successful launch is much more likely when the engineers have the proper attitude. Engineers have to recognize that the whole goal of parenting is to launch rockets that will be physically, mentally, emotionally, and spiritually prepared to fly with the Kingdom Fleet. Successful engineers realize that a successful launch is much more apt to happen when they relinquish control little by little as the rocket is being wired. If the engineers hand over all the controls at the last minute, the circuits are likely to overload, with disastrous consequences.

One of the most common mistakes an engineer can make is to keep too much control in order to feel needed or to protect the rocket. Just as Hannah released Samuel so he could prepare for the Lord's service, an engineer is to be emotionally and spiritually stable enough to relinquish control a little at a time in order for the rocket to prepare for service. If control is transferred from the engineer to the rocket in tiny stages over a long period of time, then the final controls can be handed over at the last minute and the rocket can be safely launched.

We have already considered the different roles the Chief Engineers play in the wiring of the rocket. Now as we consider the launch date, we will look at the differences in the way the two Chief Engineers approach it and how they react to the actual launch.

Mom Prepares for the Launch Date

Moms typically have a much harder time with the launch than dads do. God, in His infinite wisdom, gave males and females different emotional characteristics. The differences in the emotional wiring are useful in successful marriage relationships and in successful wiring projects. Mom is usually sensitive; she picks up on emotional subtleties that Dad misses. She can help him do a better job relating to his children because of that ability. The downside is that women are generally more emotional, which can be hard on everyone as a launch date approaches.

There is a wide variation among mothers. Some are very tenderhearted and cry over commercials shown during the holidays. Others rarely cry. They have learned to keep a tight rein on their emotions and maintain a certain level of objectivity. Then there are the moms who approach the launch date at the same time their hormones are on the warpath. Launch dates are really tough on these gals.

For a tenderhearted mom, the launch date can be especially painful because she knows how much she's going to miss this child. She knows she has to let go, and letting go is going to take every ounce of her strength. She cries a lot, perhaps every day for a year after the rocket has been launched. She goes through a real grieving process.

At-Home Moms

The launch date brings a myriad of emotions, especially for moms who have been at home for eighteen years giving full time to the wiring project. There is a very strong emotional bond between mothers and their children. God planned it that way. That strong maternal instinct is what allows a mother to face any challenge in order to protect her young. Since mothers generally get to spend more time with their children than fathers do, they get to enjoy all the fun and funny things that happen each day. They enjoy their children and derive a great deal of pleasure from their company.

Preparing for the launch is emotionally difficult. Mom knows she will miss the day-to-day interaction. She will miss being able to step in and nurture when there is a problem. Mom's life will be forever changed when she launches her rockets. Even though there will be return visits to the launch pad from time to time, life will never be like it is right now. Daily chats will be reduced to emails and phone calls. Because of the hectic schedule of most newly launched rockets, communication opportunities will not be as frequent as Mom would prefer.

When the last rocket is launched, a mom may feel all the stresses that come with a career change. If she has devoted eighteen to twenty years to mothering, making a career change will be tough. Whether she is staying at home or taking a job outside the home in order to help pay for college, the changes brought to the launch pad can be alarmingly stressful. A job change is stressful at any time. Changing careers at the same time as launching a rocket is doubly stressful.

Pre-Parting Depression

Many moms suffer from PPD. Most of us are familiar with postpartum depression that can occur after the birth of a baby. But this PPD is pre-parting depression, a form of anticipatory grief that moms go through when they begin to come to grips with the rapidly approaching launch date. It's the emotion that makes Mom stand in the middle of the discount store with tears rolling down her face because she sees something that reminds her of the rocket she's launching. She knows her relationship with this rocket will never be just like it is now.

PPD is also hard on Dad because his wife seems to be on an emotional roller coaster. Dad can't figure out where the "off" switch is for the roller coaster, so he has no way of rescuing his wife from a wild and bumpy ride.

On the emotional roller coaster there are high points. There is the sense of pride that Mom feels over successfully completing her part of the wiring project. There is wonder as she watches her rocket testing the engines and preparing for flight. There is amazement at the intelligence of her offspring. Did any of that come from her?

There are low points on the emotional roller coaster. There is fear over the "what ifs" that can plague a mother's mind. "What if he crashes?" "What if he gets sick and

I'm not there?" "What if he runs out of money?" "What if he makes a really bad decision and I'm not there to bail him out?" The common thread is, "How will he solve his problems if I'm not there to help him?" "How will he escape painful consequences if I'm not there to warn him of danger?" There is also the fear of "Did I do too good a job?" and "Has he outgrown his need for me?"

Many moms have a fix-it mentality that comes from years of kissing "boo boos," cleaning up messes, helping untangle sticky situations, and brainstorming solutions to the problems of childhood. For many moms, being able to "fix it" is a major part of the job. Launching a rocket brings a sense of frustration because once this rocket is launched, Mom can't get out her tool kit and fix things for him. She has to let him find his own solutions, and she may not agree with the ways he chooses to solve problems.

When Mom is suffering from a bad case of PPD, it makes the approaching launch date harder on the rocket. If Mom cries every time she looks at him, he may feel guilty for the pain he is causing. He may wrestle with whether or not to stay home until she can let go. The urge to leave is strong. He needs to go. He has things to accomplish in life, and the milestones won't happen if he stays on the launch pad. He is torn between the desire to leave and the guilt he feels every time he sees Mom with swollen eyes.

Prepare for Launching

There are some things Mom can do to prepare herself for the launch date. Launching a rocket is similar to giving birth. Just as proper education helps prepare for the birth of the baby, proper understanding of the launching process can help lessen the pain for all involved.

When a woman is pregnant, there is joy and anticipation at the wonderful things the future holds. There is joy at the movement of the baby within and the wonder of being God's partner in the creation of new life. The nesting instinct is strong as the time approaches. Even though there is discomfort, there is also a sense of urgency as Mom prepares to care for this baby.

The first contractions aren't too bad. Mom thinks, "I've had cramps a lot worse than this. I can do this." As labor progresses, the pain becomes more intense and more frequent. Mom begins to understand why the process leading up to birth is called labor. Working with the contractions and enduring the pain for several hours are exhausting. Then comes the moment of transition. It's the toughest part of labor. It's the part when Mom wishes desperately that she could change her mind and call the whole thing off. Childbirth is just too hard!

Launching a rocket is similar to labor. Understanding the process and having some coping skills will help. There will come a moment of transition when your entire being will cry out to call the whole thing off, because letting go is just too hard. If you know that painful time is coming, you can mentally prepare for it and lessen the severity of the pain.

What If?

Most moms are skilled at the "what if" game. They can think about the "what if this happens" scenarios with little effort. In preparation for the transition point of the launch date, it is often helpful to learn a new game. Learn to put things in perspective by playing the "this is tough but compared to what" game. In this new game that Mom needs to play, combining the "what if's" with the "compared to what" can be a big pain reliever during transition.

It Could Be Worse

Donita was having a hard time launching her first rocket. She had always had an unusually close relationship with Amelia. Now it was time for her daughter to leave, and she had chosen a college half way across the country. Money was tight and Amelia couldn't fly home very often. Donita and her husband were letting Amelia take one of the family cars to school. It would take three hard days of driving to get to school, so Mom knew she would see Amelia only at Christmas and during summer vacation. During other school breaks, Amelia would have to go home with friends.

Playing the "this is tough but compared to what" helped Donita get through the transition period. She looked around at acquaintances her age and saw what they were facing:

"Mom, I'm pregnant."

"I'm moving in with my boyfriend."

"I've been arrested. Can you come bail me out?"

"The judge says it's a drug rehab center or jail time."

"I tried to kill myself, and now they've got me in the psych ward for a while."

"I'm not going to college. I'm not going to work. Work is boring."

"There was an accident. I was speeding and I hit a kid on a bicycle. He's dead."

Looking at all the different things that she could be facing at this stage of her life made Donita most grateful. Amelia was a faithful Christian who was ready and able to go to college. She was going to a Christian college with a good reputation. Emails and telephone calls would make it easier to stay in touch. Counting her blessings made it easier for Donita to face the transition time.

Connie's Comparison

Connie did many things well; pregnancy wasn't one of them. She loved children so much, but her first child came after two miscarriages. Connie had a difficult time with the pregnancy and almost lost her baby a couple of times.

When Connie was pregnant with her second child, the complications began early. Connie's doctor had her come in once a week during the first few weeks so he could keep an eye on things. Each week, it seemed there were more difficulties, and Connie was progressively more uncomfortable. Each week there were problems that made the doctor suspect that carrying this baby would not be good for Connie. Because of the medication that she had to take during the pregnancy, the baby's health was at risk. Near the end of the first trimester, the doctor told Connie that the chances were very high that this baby would be retarded and multi-handicapped. The doctor urged her to give careful consideration to terminating the pregnancy.

Connie didn't have to give it careful consideration. She told the doctor: "God has blessed our family with one beautiful, brilliant child. If the child I'm carrying now has two heads and no arms or legs, it will still be a gift from God that we will cherish. If this child dies, it will be God's decision, not mine. We're not doing any sonograms or an amniocenteses. God's been making babies for years without our help, and He's perfectly capable of making this one."

The doctor did what he could to keep Connie and the baby healthy throughout the pregnancy. When Todd was born and Connie held him for the first time, she looked into his big eyes and knew there was intelligence behind them. Over the years they had to work around some learning disabilities. It hadn't been a problem. Todd was a wonderful blessing to the family. The joys of wiring this rocket had far outweighed some of the technical difficulties that had to be conquered.

A few years later, Connie was facing Todd's launch date. Launching her oldest son had been hard, but Travis had been ready to go. She knew it was best for him. Travis was a faithful Christian, a wonderful young man, and a joy to have in the family. Connie knew she had given him all the life skills she could and it was time to release him. She did what a Mom does. She stepped back and let him go because it was best for him. She put aside her pain and let him fly his own rocket. Having Todd still at home made Travis's launch a little easier.

Launching her last son was more difficult for a number of reasons. Because of his struggles in school, mom and son had become extremely close as they worked through the learning problems together. Once Travis left home, Todd spent more time hanging around his parents and visiting with them. Connie had learned to cherish those daily talks. She adored having this lovable and quick-witted son underfoot most of the time. She knew their days together were numbered, and she tried to make the most of the ones that they had. Now it was time to let him go. Connie was facing an empty nest. The "what if's," paired with the "compared to what" game helped her put things in perspective.

She thought back to that difficult pregnancy, the weeks of bed rest, and the times she nearly lost him anyway. She thought back to the doctor's predictions. How wrong he had been! But what if he had been right? What if this son had been retarded and handicapped? Connie wasn't getting any younger. Todd was a big fella like his dad. At six-four and 230 pounds, there was no way Connie could lift him.

What if he had been handicapped and she was no longer able to lift him, change his diapers, or move him from the bed to a wheelchair? What if she got too old to take care of him and had to put him in an institution? Would they have loved him and kept him clean like she did? Would Todd have been happy or would he have spent his days crying and trying to find his mommy and daddy?

When Connie compared the pain of taking care of a helpless young man to the pain of launching a wonderfully capable son, it was easier to let him go. The future was bright and Todd's wiring was secure. She knew he could maintain a stable flight path without her assistance.

Children on Loan

When a mother sees her children as being "on loan" from God, the launching process is easier. Mothers need to realize that children aren't possessions to be kept. God loans us His special creations and lets us enjoy them as we do our part of the wiring. When our job is finished, the terms of the loan expire. We are to launch our rockets and release them to God, fully trusting in His ability to do what is best for them. He loves them even more than we do. He shares them with us by letting us enjoy their adult lives. He lets them return to the launch pad from time to time for visits. He lets them reproduce, and we get to enjoy being with little ones again.

When a mother releases a rocket, she has two choices. She can release it to God and trust Him, or she can worry. When a mother worries, she is modeling a lack of faith in God's abilities. Worry is giving a situation to God and then grabbing it back with a "you're not doing it right; I'll do it myself!" attitude.

A better solution to the angst that accompanies a launching is to become even more faithful in prayer. Every time a concern arises, talk to God. Every time you miss your child, talk to God and ask Him to watch over and bless your child. Start each day with a prayer for each of your children. Trust the Father, who loves them more than you do, to take good care of them. As long as they are with Him, whether in this life or the next, they are His and He will keep them safe.

Dad Prepares for the Launch Date

Dad's reactions to the launch will be less noticeable than Mom's, but he will still have some struggles. Many men find that watching their wives struggle through the launch is more painful than the actual launch. Dad's reaction to the launch is based in a large part on the relationship with the rocket. Many men find it easier to launch a son because a young man is expected to be tough. Whatever comes his way, a young man is to be strong enough to handle. It's often harder for Dad to launch a daughter he has loved and protected for years. He may wonder if he did a good job and if she can fend for herself.

Dad won't have the changing role that Mom has, especially if she has been a stay-at-home for years. However, if Mom is struggling with her changing roles, Dad is apt to feel the tension. Dad will probably feel a lot of financial pressure as the rockets are launched.

Avoid Extremes

Some engineers approach the launch with an attitude of cutting the support lines completely. If a rocket wants a college education, he has to pay for it. If he needs anything, he has to figure out how to get it for himself. At the other extreme are the engineers who do absolutely everything for their rockets. They hang on and try to maintain full control over the rocket. Both of these extremes can be harmful for a rocket.

A better and more loving approach is to celebrate and encourage the new-found freedom and responsibility while providing a safety backup system. It is a good idea for a rocket to pay for at least part of the college experience. When a college education is provided with no effort, it isn't appreciated as much as when a student has to work in order to stay in college.

Most young people are not in a financial position to provide for themselves when they leave the launch pad. Dad may feel a lot of financial pressure if he is the primary provider for the family. It's a good idea to keep the newly launched rocket on Dad's health insurance plan until college graduation or marriage. Health care is expensive and an uninsured young person can get into real trouble without it.

Everyone's goal should be to "make it on my own," but engineers need to check occasionally on the rocket's financial situation. The lines of communication need to be such that a rocket can let the engineers know when he needs some financial assistance in order to make it to next payday. As long as the rocket is behaving responsibly, providing help, especially with unexpected expenses, is a wonderful way to communicate love and support.

Dad will also be the primary resource for quite some time. When a rocket is confronted with car trouble, insurance questions, tax questions, and the like, he will find it helpful to get Dad's opinion before proceeding. Even if Dad tried to prepare the rocket for these things before the launch, chances are that a refresher course will be needed as the rocket gets his first real experience with them.

Engineers as Lifetime Models

In our discussion of the wiring process, we addressed the importance of modeling. Modeling is important because a rocket will follow the example of the engineers. During and after the launch, modeling is still very important. Mom has to recognize that even in the midst of her pain, she hasn't finished the modeling process. She must model a selfless maturity during the launching process. Then when this rocket has to launch offspring of his own, he will have a good model to follow.

Dad will have to continue to model good family leadership. Daughters will marry someone like Dad. Sons will follow Dad's model in the way they treat their wives and children. As the family grows through various stages, Dad will always be a valuable source of wisdom when leadership questions arise.

Engineers have to realize that the wiring is completed, but the modeling will continue for years. Engineers have to model the releasing process required, if children are to become adults. The college years or the first four years away from the launch pad are critical. During these years a rocket will do some serious questioning of the principles he has learned. He will run diagnostics on his wiring system to see if the wiring will serve him well in this new environment. It is during these years that a newly launched rocket will establish lifelong friendships with people the engineers may never meet.

Evaluations and Emotions

Part of the launching process is to discuss this questioning and evaluating process before a rocket is launched. Encourage rockets to form good, close relationships with folks at church. It is a good thing when rockets "adopt" parents and grandparents from among the folks that comprise his new church family. As he goes through the questioning phase that accompanies a launch, these new contacts may be a valuable source of maturity and wisdom for him. They may offer a fresh perspective that will be helpful.

During the launching process, a rocket not only leaves the launch pad physically, but he also leaves it emotionally. Engineers can feel abandoned and unappreciated during this phase of the launch. It helps to realize that this growing "away" from the launch pad is not abandonment. The rocket is setting up some stabilizing forces that will be of tremendous help as he establishes a new launch pad. After he has established the new stabilizing forces, he will realize the value of the wiring installed by the engineers and will have a new appreciation for their work.

> **During the launching process, a rocket not only leaves the launch pad physically, but he also leaves it emotionally. Engineers can feel abandoned and unappreciated during this phase.**

If a rocket is going to follow the instructions of Matthew 19:5 to "leave his father and mother" in preparation for marriage, he has to go through this process. Wise engineers send loving communications during this time but with "no strings attached." Keeping the love lines open during this time will be helpful when the rocket needs to reconnect for brief periods. When the testing time is over, the rocket will be able to reciprocate that loving communication, and the pattern will be set for a lifetime of honoring and loving.

Always a Model

Engineers must recognize that the days of training and controlling are over. The relationship has changed. If the wiring days were handled wisely, the years of the new relationship can be times of special joy and blessings. Trust your rocket. Even if you think he is making a mistake, refrain from giving unsolicited advice, because such advice usually does more harm than good. Pray for him fervently, daily. Remember that you had to learn many things the hard way. It is very hard to watch a rocket go through the "School of Hard Knocks," but some things can be learned only from that particular university. Love him enough to let him take risks. Let him know you trust his judgment. Let him know you are confident that he will be successful.

Engineers have to model releasing a rocket to marriage. If engineers have given the rocket a healthy marriage model to emulate, he will usually choose a mate carefully. If the wiring was installed correctly, he will not marry someone who is not a Christian; he will choose someone who will help him go to heaven. He will choose someone who will be a wonderful engineer for his children. Engineers have to model loving acceptance of the spouse a rocket has chosen. Rockets will have a much better chance of a happy home life if the engineers love and accept the new son-in-law or daughter-in-law.

Once a person accepts the role of engineer, he will spend the rest of his life as a model. Even after rockets have been launched, they will watch the way engineers face the storms of life. Does an engineer's relationship with God sustain him in a crisis? How does an engineer face the technical difficulties that come with the aging process? Does he become a pain when he's facing physical pain and illness?

Finally, engineers model how to prepare for death. They model how to live each day prepared to go when the time comes. They model confidence in their heavenly Father's promises as their time on earth fades away. Good engineers honor their commitment and model godliness all the way home.

Preparing the Rocket for Launch Date

Preparing the rocket for the launch date starts from the very beginning of the wiring process. Engineers usually follow one of two models for accomplishing a task: they are either procrastinators, or they are always prepared. A look back at the college years can be a good indicator. The "always prepared" group headed for the library the first day a term paper was assigned. They worked on it a little each day because they knew that with their luck, they would get the flu the week the paper was due. Because they worked on it every day, the paper was ready to hand in a week before the due date.

The procrastinators really intended to get started on the project. However, other things kept coming up, and they wound up burning the midnight oil for several nights trying to get it done. At the last minute, they rushed in and put the paper into the professor's hand. They really wished they had done a quick proofread, but there was no time.

What's the difference? Did the procrastinators really run out of time? Everyone has the same amount of time. Everyone has emergencies to handle. Urgent things often pop up at the most inopportune moments and try to steal our time. The "always prepared" group knows the unexpected will occur, so they allow time for it. They don't fill every available minute and leave themselves no time to handle a crisis.

When preparing for a launch date, procrastinators need to make a conscious decision to move into the camp of the "always prepared." That may require paring the schedule and eliminating some enjoyable activities. It most certainly will require controlling time and priorities. During the wiring years, parenting is a full-time job that requires constant attention to details.

> **Because we will all stand before the judgment seat of God and give an account of how we spent our time, it is very important to make sure we were among the "always prepared" during the years spent wiring the rockets entrusted to us.**

Old engineers have often been heard to say: "Enjoy them while you've got them because the time goes so quickly." Time does some interesting things as an engineer ages. During the early years of the wiring project, eighteen years seems like a long time. As the launch date approaches, however, an engineer can understand what the old engineer meant. The time flew by and an engineer might be hard-pressed to give an account of how the time was spent.

Because we will all stand before the judgment seat of God and give an account of how we spent our time, it is very important to make sure we were among the "always prepared" during the years spent wiring the rockets entrusted to us.

The Final Checklist

NASA goes through a final checklist and verifies each system before launching a rocket. The final countdown begins when each system is confirmed and functioning within normal limits. In this section, we're going to look at some necessary life skills that should be wired into the rocket. The ages listed for acquiring these skills are approximations, since every rocket is different and matures at its own rate. However, if you notice a huge discrepancy, consider it a warning light indicating an area needing attention. For instance, if the checklist says a fourteen-month-old should "come here" when a parent calls and your first grader runs the other way when called, you know that you need to redo some obedience wiring.

Birth to One Year

The rocket learns to love and trust the engineers. The rocket learns that his needs will be met, but he might not always get what he wants. For instance, Mom may put him in the playpen and expect him to stay there for a few minutes, even if he had rather be held all the time. She may offer him meat on his spoon, even if he had rather have another helping of fruit.

He learns to love books and songs. He needs lots of eye contact with his engineers. He needs to hear them singing to him and reading to him. He needs to be in Bible class every Sunday morning and Wednesday night. It is during this year that he learns "God loves me. He made me. He takes care of me."

During the last six months of this year, a rocket is introduced to the idea of boundaries. He learns he cannot go certain places in the house. He cannot pull up on the potty and throw his toy in the water. Discipline is easy at this age. Have at least one baby-proofed room in the house and scatter fascinating things around to encourage exploration. When he grabs a "no no," have an interesting toy available to trade with him. Be prepared to catch the forbidden object when he drops it. Babies are very easily distracted.

For the few times that he keeps going back to a dangerous item, a firm no will usually hurt his feelings and cause him to heed your command to leave it alone. If not, a light swat on his diapered bottom will communicate the idea that he must obey you.

During this stage, a rocket learns which engineers are his very own. He learns that his engineers will always be there when he needs them. The love and trust developed during the first year are critical to healthy development in every area.

Twelve to Eighteen Months

Every age is fun, but this one has its own set of delights. The little one is learning to explore. Not only can he crawl, but he's also learning to walk and run. It's a dangerous time. An engineer has to be alert and on duty every minute the child is awake. The little explorer must never be left alone because he has no sense of danger and an accident can happen in a heartbeat. He will master climbing, but getting down is harder. It's important to have an engineer close enough to offer assistance. He is insatiably curious. He wants to see and be involved in everything you do. He is an accident waiting to happen. He wants to see what you put in that pot on the stove. If he can reach the handle, he will pull it down so he can see, never dreaming that the contents can cause a serious burn. He wants to see what you have in your cup, so set it up higher than the counter top, too high for him to reach.

The little one is learning to talk. He will start stringing words together and using short sentences. It's a wonderful learning time. Books and songs are fascinating. He will learn to sing simple songs with you. He wants to watch your face. He wants to help you. Unless it involves heat or chemicals, let him be your little helper. It's a wonderful time to start teaching him to be a good worker. Keeping him by your side as you go about your activities will teach him many concepts. He will grow in his love for you as you express how much you enjoy having him nearby.

Many engineers make the mistake of doing everything for their rockets because it's just easier. Mom has learned to do things quickly and efficiently. Rockets don't have speed or efficiency until they have acquired some experience, and they don't acquire experience when an engineer does everything for them.

In terms of discipline, this is an important time. A rocket needs to learn by the age of fourteen months to "look at me and listen" every time an engineer says his name. He also needs to learn to "come here" every time he is called. Because he is learning to play, he will go through a stage of running away when told to "come here." Many engineers make a mistake by chasing their little one and making "running away" a game. It is important to separate playtime from obedience time. It's all right to say, "Can you catch me?" and run from your child during playtime. But when an engineer says "come here" and the rocket runs the other way, giggling, it's time for training. Say, "Oh, no. That is not nice. Mommy said come here." If the child continues to run, pick her up and speak to her sternly. Bring her back to where you were standing. The second time it happens, give a stern warning and if she doesn't obey, give her a mild spanking. Be consistent until she comes every time you tell her to "come here."

"Come here" and "look at me and listen" are key commands that must be mastered during the first eighteen months.

Eighteen Months to Thirty-Six Months

Although delightful, this time in the life of the family can also be physically exhausting. Do not let yourself be heard talking about the "terrible two's." The only terrible two-year-olds are the ones who are unfortunate enough to have engineers who lack diligence. Parenting is hard work. It requires constant supervision. The time between eighteen months and three years is prime training time.

> **Do not let yourself be heard talking about the "terrible two's." Be diligent and consistent.**

Very likely the "conquering times" come now in the life of a rocket. It's the time when an engineer will have to prove he intends to retain control of the launch pad. A rocket may have to be spanked several times a day for a couple of days. Be diligent and consistent because the conquering times are usually followed by long periods of cheerful obedience and loving behavior. If the parents are diligent during the testing periods and use the right tools for consistent discipline, by the third year this little rocket will be a joy and delight.

This is also prime Bible teaching time. Have lots of Bible story books around. Have your big Bible out all the time, and let the child see you reading it. Tell him lots of short and simple Bible stories. Emphasize God's care for Noah, Abraham, Daniel, or whichever character is involved in the story. Emphasize that "God loves me and will always take good care of me." Work on prayers and short memory verses. Make sure your child is in Bible class every Sunday morning and Wednesday night.

Start the transfer of responsibility. Let him do as much of his own dressing and undressing as he can manage. He needs to pick up his toys and put them away. Cheerfully help him, as needed. Involve him in your chores and express appreciation for the ways he tries to be a good helper.

Three to Six Years

Engineers will need to be building on the skills taught during the last time period. The rocket should learn more details about lots of Bible stories. He should learn simple memory verses. Kindness, obedience, respect for authority, good manners, and consideration of others are qualities that need to be refined during these three years. Children of this age love to help, and it's a wonderful time to teach them how to do nice things for others.

Transfer more responsibility by having him be responsible for taking his Bible to class and bringing it home. Give him the money for contribution before you leave the house. It is his responsibility to take care of it until time for the offering.

He should dress and undress himself. Put pictures on his dresser drawers and have him put away his own clothes. Teach him to make his own bed and straighten his room. He can empty wastebaskets and set the table. He can also help clear the table, help feed the pets, and help with simple kitchen chores. Cheerfully assist as needed. Teach that "we are a good team and we help each other."

Six to Nine Years

Make sure every child in the family is learning to do each of the chores needed to maintain a household. Work alongside the children with a good attitude so they will learn the joy of being responsible.

It is time to transfer a little more responsibility. School work is primarily the child's responsibility, with assistance as needed. Keeping his room clean and taking good care of his things should be completely his responsibility. Children of this age can start simple cooking projects with an engineer carefully supervising the use of sharp knives and hot stoves. By the end of the ninth year, a rocket should be able to plan and prepare a simple meal.

A child should have his own alarm clock and be responsible for getting up and dressed in time for school and in time for Bible class on Sunday morning. A rocket should learn to manage his time so that all his homework is done before time to leave for Bible class on Wednesday night.

Nine to Twelve Years

All the concepts previously learned are still in place. As his body gets bigger, it is time to transfer more responsibility. If a rocket is always going to be fairly small, start using stools and step ladders so that more kitchen skills can be learned.

By this age, a rocket should be able to put away the food and clean the kitchen. He should be able to do a good job cleaning his room and the bathroom. He should be completely responsible for the care of his pets.

A rocket of this age should be able to use most of the hand tools in Dad's tool box. With Dad's careful supervision, he can begin to learn to use power tools. A child should be able to assist with simple repairs and painting projects.

A child of this age should be perfectly able to do the laundry, including ironing, folding, and putting things away. He should be able to clean and organize a linen closet and the area under the kitchen sink.

Twelve to Fifteen Years

All of the previous skills should be in place. Spiritually, this rocket should be a daily Bible reader. He should know how to use a concordance, Bible dictionary, and Bible encyclopedia, and he should have access to them. He should be able to open his Bible and show someone how to become a Christian. He should have a solid prayer life. He should know enough Bible geography to be able to find important locations on a Bible map and know what happened in those places. He should be a full participant in church work-days, vacation Bible schools, and regular worship assemblies. He should be completely responsible for his school schedule and for completing his assignments.

He should have regular chores that are his responsibility. By the time he's fifteen, he should be considering a part-time job. From his earnings, he should budget for contribution, savings, and spending.

Sixteen to Eighteen Years

The launch time is nearer, and more responsibility needs to be transferred. Each rocket in this age group should have the opportunity to run the household for a couple of weeks. He should be able to plan and prepare meals for the entire family. The rocket should be given the grocery money for this pay period and be in charge of using that money responsibly to provide for the needs of the family. The rocket should be able to do the shopping, the meal preparation, and the cleanup. The rocket should be responsible for delegating the work load and making sure the household is well run.

This plan works great if Mom has surgery and has to stay in bed for a couple of weeks. If surgery isn't scheduled, Mom needs to go out of town or have a project that demands her attention so that she is not available to take over if something goes wrong. When a rocket sets up a home of his own, he must be able to manage it. Most rockets do very well with this particular test flight and it does wonders for the morale to know the engineers have full confidence in their abilities to run the household.

Rockets should not date before the age of sixteen. The rule should be that in this house, we only date faithful Christians. Rockets need to marry someone who flies well with the Kingdom Fleet. The most important decision a person can make is the decision to be a faithful follower of Jesus. The second most important decision is the choice of a mate for life. Since the mate chosen will be helping train the next generation of the Lord's servants, it is absolutely necessary for that person to be a faithful Christian, thus the rule about dating only Christians.

It's time to make plans for life after the launch. Rockets should be encouraged to choose a Christian college. Although they are going to school to get an education, the bulk of their dating experiences will occur during the college years. If most of the people on campus are Christians, it is far more likely that a faithful Christian mate will be selected during these years.

Conclusion

As the launch date approaches, many engineers are overcome by a sense of panic. The rocket is busy with that last year of high school and planning to go off to college. The engineers suddenly realize that this rocket has no wiring installed for survival skills. This rocket has never done a load of laundry, folded and put away clothes, changed a tire, changed oil in a vehicle, mowed a lawn, washed dishes, shopped for the family, prepared a complete meal, made a bed, painted a room, or made a budget. That sense of panic causes some engineers to hold onto the rocket to prevent or delay a launch. It's too late. Much of the rebellion experienced by college students is caused by engineers who will not relinquish control.

That's why it's vitally important for every engineer to be in the camp of the "always prepared." If responsibility is transferred gradually over a series of years, the survival skills will be firmly in place, and the rocket will be properly prepared for the launch date.

Launch your rocket. Wipe the tears from your eyes and roll up your sleeves. Life isn't over. There is Kingdom work to do, and now your hands are free to serve in a new way. The skills you acquired during the wiring project will make you a valuable asset to the Lord's work. You are still important to your rocket but in a different way. Be his cheerleader. Celebrate his successes. Keep on modeling, because your rocket will be watching and learning from you. Show him how to manage the launch and how to take his place as a member of the Kingdom Fleet.

Drill for Skills

 ### Making Connections

1. Preparation for the launch date should be on an engineer's mind _____ day.

2. It takes _____ to _____ years to prepare for a successful launch.

3. A launch is more apt to be successful when engineers have the proper _____.

4. Engineers relinquish control a _____ at a time.

5. Many moms suffer from PPD, _____ _____ depression.

 ### Troubleshooting

1. In what way is Mom's life forever changed after launching a rocket?

2. How does PPD affect life on the launch pad?

3. What are some coping skills Mom can use to help face the pain of launching a rocket?

4. In what way are our children "on loan" from God?

5. What type of struggles does Dad face at launch time?

6. How can engineers provide a safety backup for a newly launched rocket?

7. In what way is Dad the primary resource after the launch?

8. Why are the first four years after the launch so critical?

9. Why should families have rules about dating Christians only?

10. Why should engineers refrain from giving unsolicited advice after the launch?

11. Why should engineers make the effort to join the camp of the "always prepared"?

12. Discuss the idea of "growing away" from home.